PELICAN BOOKS

THE PSYCHOLOGY
OF INTERPERSONAL BEHAVIOUR

Michael Argyle, D.Sc., D. Litt., Hon. D.Sc. Psych., is Reader in Social Psychology at Oxford University and a Fellow of Wolfson College. He was born in 1925, went to Nottingham High School and Emmanuel College, Cambridge, and was a navigator in the RAF. He has been teaching social psychology at Oxford since 1952. He has been engaged in research in various aspects of social psychology and is particularly interested in the experimental study of social interaction and its application to wider social problems. In recent years he has been greatly helped by his very active research group. During sabbatical terms and long vacations, he has been a Fellow at the Center for Advanced Study in the Behavioral Sciences, Stanford, and has been visiting professor at the Universities of Michigan, British Columbia, Ghana and Delaware; the State University of New York at Buffalo; the University of Leuven; the Hebrew University, Jerusalem; the Universities of Adelaide and New South Wales; York University, Ontario; and the Universities of Nevada and Kansas.

Michael Argyle is the author of *The Scientific Study of Social Behaviour*, *Psychology and Social Problems*, *Social Interaction*, *The Social Psychology of Work*, *Bodily Communication*, *Gaze and Mutual Gaze* (with Mark Cook), *The Social Psychology of Religion* (with B. Beit-Hallahmi), *Social Skills and Mental Health* (with P. Trower and B. Bryant), *Social Situations* (with A. Furnham and J.A. Graham) and *The Anatomy of Relationships* (with Monika Henderson), and has written numerous articles in British, American and European journals. He helped to found the *British Journal of Social and Clinical Psychology* and was Social Psychology Editor (1961–7). He is the editor of the Pergamon Press *International Studies in Experimental Social Psychology*. He was Chairman of the Social Psychology Section of the British Psychological Society (1964–7 and 1972–4).

He is married and has four children; his hobbies are travel, interpersonal behaviour, Scottish country dancing, Utopian speculation, theological disputation and playing the goat.

MICHAEL ARGYLE

THE PSYCHOLOGY
OF INTERPERSONAL
BEHAVIOUR

FOURTH EDITION

PENGUIN BOOKS

PENGUIN BOOKS

Published by the Penguin Group
27 Wrights Lane, London W8 5TZ, England
Viking Penguin Inc., 40 West 23rd Street, New York, New York 10010, USA
Penguin Books Australia Ltd, Ringwood, Victoria, Australia
Penguin Books Canada Ltd, 2801 John Street, Markham, Ontario, Canada L3R 1B4
Penguin Books (NZ) Ltd, 182–190 Wairau Road, Auckland 10, New Zealand

Penguin Books Ltd, Registered Offices: Harmondsworth, Middlesex, England

First published 1967
Reprinted 1967, 1968, 1970, 1971 (twice)
Second edition 1972
Reprinted 1973, 1974, 1975, 1976, 1977
Third edition 1978
Reprinted 1979, 1981, 1982
Fourth edition 1983
Reprinted 1984, 1985 (twice), 1986, 1988

Printed and bound in Great Britain by
Cox & Wyman Ltd, Reading

Set in Baskerville by
Rowland Phototypesetting Ltd
Bury St Edmunds, Suffolk

CONTENTS

LIST OF FIGURES AND TABLES

TABLES

EXTRACT FROM THE PREFACE TO
THE FIRST EDITION

MAN is a social animal: he collaborates with others to pursue his goals and satisfy his needs. It is well known that relations with others can be the source of the deepest satisfactions and of the blackest misery. Moralists, novelists and others have written about these things, but the detailed analysis of social interactions and relationships has been lacking. Recent research by social psychologists has made these phenomena very much clearer. In particular there have been important advances in the experimental analysis of social encounters at the level of such things as eye-movements, the timing of speech, and non-verbal communication.

This research has a number of possible applications. The work of many people consists of dealing with people, rather than with things — teachers, psychologists, air hostesses, managers, and many others: research has been done into the social techniques which are most effective, and into how such skills can be taught. Many people are lonely and unhappy, some are mentally ill, because they are unable to establish and sustain social relationships with others. Many everyday encounters are unpleasant, embarrassing, or fruitless, because of inept social behaviour. Conflicts between different social classes and different cultural groups are partly due to the difficulties of interaction. Many of those difficulties and frustrations could be eliminated by a wider understanding, and better training in the skills of social interaction.

PREFACE TO THE FOURTH EDITION

There have been important new developments in research into many of the topics covered by this book, and it has been extensively revised to incorporate them. I have included, but not emphasized unduly, some of the findings of the social psychology research group at Oxford, and the thirty doctoral theses which it has produced so far. Some of the more substantial additions and revisions are on:

sex and aggression;
verbal communication and conversational analysis;
non-verbal communication: facial expression and gaze;
cognitive processes in perception;
personality–situation interaction and the analysis of situations;
long-term relationships;
cross-cultural differences and inter-cultural interaction;
identity crisis and self-presentation;
social behaviour of patients and the effects of stressful life-events;
professional skills of doctors, nurses and managers;
new developments in social skills training.

I am particularly indebted to the following for their collaboration and ideas – Rosalie Burnett, David Clarke, Peter Collett, Joe Forgas, Adrian Furnham, Jerry Ginsberg, Jean Ann Graham, Rom Harré, Jos Jaspars, Peter Marsh, David Pendleton, Peter Robinson, Ben Slugoski and Peter Trower; to Ann McKendry, secretary extraordinaire, for typing yet again; and to the SSRC for research support.

Department of Experimental Psychology   MICHAEL ARGYLE
South Parks Road
Oxford   February 1982

CHAPTER I

SOCIAL MOTIVATION

MOST people spend a great deal of their time engaging in some kind of social interaction. They live together, work together, and spend spare time with their friends. Why do they do this? Why don't we all behave like hermits, living and working alone? In fact for most individuals solitary confinement, or other forms of isolation for more than short periods, are very unpleasant indeed. Loss of 'face' in the Far East is a cause of suicide, and rejection by friends in our own society is a common source of distress. People seem to seek a number of goals in social situations – to be approved of and to make friends, to dominate or to depend on others, to be admired, to be helped or given social support, to provide help to others and so on.

Different people seek different things in social situations. In the present state of knowledge it looks as if social behaviour is the product of at least seven different drives. A 'drive' can be defined as a persistent tendency to seek certain goals. As well as directing people towards goals, a drive is a source of energy; when the drive is operating there is a general increase of vigour. Much the same is true of biological drives, such as the need for food: when a person is hungry he will seek food with increased effort. Furthermore the drive can be subdivided into a number of more specific ones for salt, sugar, and so on: animals deprived of one of these substances will select a diet which makes good the deficit. It is necessary to postulate these various forms of motivation to account for variations in the behaviour of the *same* person on different occasions, e.g. when hungry and not, and to describe differences between *different* people in the goals they pursue, and the energy with which they do it.

There is as yet no final agreement on how social motivation should be divided up. What will be done here is to offer a provisional list of motivational sources of interpersonal behaviour. These are sufficient to account for the phenomena described in this book, and each has been extensively studied by psychologists and others.

Later in this chapter, some account will be given of how these drives function, and of their origins in childhood experience or innate tendencies. Here, then, is the provisional list, together with a note of the goals which are sought in each case (except for biological needs) – either responses from, or types of relationships with, other people:

1   *Biological needs* – eating, drinking and bodily comfort;

2   *Dependency* – help, support, protection and guidance, at first from parents, later from people in positions of power or authority;

3   *Affiliation* – warm and friendly responses from, and social acceptance by, peers, shown by physical proximity, smiles and gaze;

4   *Dominance* – acceptance by others, and groups of others, as the task-leader, being allowed to talk most of the time, take the decisions, and be deferred to by the group;

5   *Sex* – physical proximity, bodily contact, etc., eye-contact, warm, friendly and intimate social interaction, usually with attractive peers of the opposite sex;

6   *Aggression* – to harm other people physically, verbally or in other ways;

7   *Self-esteem and ego-identity* – for other people to make approving responses and to accept the self-image as valid;

8   *Other motivations which affect social behaviour* – needs for achievement, money, interests and values.

This list is provisional, but moderately well established: drives 1–6 have all been studied in animals, and their biological and evolutionary basis is understood; they have also been studied in humans, and we know how they are affected by childhood experiences, how they are aroused and how they affect social behaviour.

The biological functions of social behaviour in animals During the last few years studies have been carried out on apes and monkeys in the wild; these studies have shown clearly how their social behaviour is important for the biological survival of these animals. A set of partly innate social drives has emerged during the course of evolution; these drives produce a pattern of partly instinctive social behaviour that enables groups of apes and monkeys to eat and drink, defend themselves against enemies, reproduce themselves, care for and train their young.

1 Apes and monkeys need access to water, and to suitable vegetables and fruits to eat. They occupy a territory which contains these resources, and may defend it against rivals. The patterns of social behaviour described below vary considerably between species. They also vary between groups of the *same* species, depending on the ecology, e.g. the availability of food and nesting sites; such 'cultural' patterns are perpetuated by socialization (Crook, 1970).

2 Most species live in groups, with a fairly stable dominance hierarchy which is established by aggressive displays between adult males. Certain adult males provide leadership in defending the territory and keeping internal order.

3 There is a definite family structure, which can vary from one species to another. Opposite sex pairs mate in order to continue the species, while adult males look after their females for a time and act as generalized fathers to the infants in the group.

4 Mothers feed and look after their young, and provide socialization experiences which complete the partly 'open' instinctive systems. They have maternal patterns of behaviour which are aroused by the sight of young; the young have dependent patterns of behaviour which are aroused by the sight, feel and sound of the mother.

5 Aggressive behaviour is used to defend group and territory; it may also occur between males of the same group who are competing for dominance or for access to the same female. However, such aggression is usually limited to ferocious displays in which the most terrifying animal wins – it would not be in the interests of the group for much real fighting to take place.

6 Young apes and monkeys engage in play, adults in grooming; these are two examples of affiliative behaviour which probably have the functions of restraining aggression inside the group and making cooperation easier.

Social behaviour in lower animals is almost entirely instinctive: the entire pattern of social behaviour is innate and has emerged during evolution because of its biological survival value. The apes and monkeys are different in that their instinctive systems are more open, and remain to be completed during socialization experiences. There are also components of culture, perpetuated in particular groups of animals; these include washing food in sea water, in one group of Japanese macaques, and swimming in another.

The behaviour of apes and monkeys is quite illuminating for understanding human social behaviour – they are certainly more helpful than rats. However, there are some very important differences between men and monkeys: we use language, and our behaviour is more affected by plans and social rules. In men innate factors are less important, and there is a longer period of socialization. Human groups build up a far more elaborate culture, which is passed on to later generations, so that we live in an environment which is not only physically constructed by us, but has been given meanings by us – as in the case of clothes, cars, and everything else around us. Much of this is made possible by language, which enables us to accumulate and pass on culture, and which also makes our social behaviour entirely different.

Biological and other drives The best-understood drives are those aroused by hunger and thirst. There seems to be a self-regulating system which keeps the levels of food and water in the body at an equilibrium level. For example, when there is a shortage of water, thirst is experienced and the drive is aroused, leading to behaviour which makes good the deficit and restores the equilibrium. (The self-regulation of eating or drinking can go wrong, as in cases of obesity.)

The social drives, which we are interested in, do not work like this. In the drives for affiliation and money, the contents of the bloodstream are not involved; whatever physiological basis they have must be in the brain. There is no deficit, so that satisfaction of the need does not lead to a cessation of activity. These drives still resemble hunger and thirst in that relevant internal states and external stimuli result in autonomic arousal and the direction of behaviour towards the goals in question.

Sex is an interesting intermediate case: in lower animals sexual arousal depends on the level of sex hormones in the blood stream – though there is no deficit here; in higher mammals and in man there is little connection between hormones and sexual arousal and activity; castration after puberty leads to no loss of sexual desire.

Arousal and satiation People are not hungry all the time, and the momentary strength of any drive depends on how far it has or been recently satiated. It is now known that the activation of any drive system involves a similar pattern of physiological arousal. This consists of electrical activity originating in the hypothalamus, and of activity in the sympathetic nervous system, producing higher blood pressure, a faster heart-beat and perspiration – though the physiological pattern varies between individuals.

It has long been known that there is an inverted U-shaped connection between arousal and effective performance, i.e. people perform best when arousal is neither too low nor too high. Extraverts and sociable and impulsive people have often been believed to be *less* aroused than introverts; however, it has been found that introverts are more aroused in the morning, extraverts in the evening. Caffeine affects arousal, and giving extraverts coffee in the evening impairs their performance since they are highly aroused already, but the same treatment improves the performance of introverts (Revelle *et al.*, 1980).

Arousal is stronger when the expected reward or 'incentive' is larger, when it is greatly desired, and when its probability of being attained appears to be greater. The effect of incentives varies with the drive strength, and may vary between different cultural groups. For instance, working-class children are aroused more by cash incentives, while middle-class children are more affected by hopes of 'success'.

We turn now to the conditions under which needs are satisfied. The hungry person is made less hungry by eating; the hunger drive builds up gradually with time until it is satisfied again. The drives behind social behaviour do not seem to work quite like this. A person who seeks money or fame does not cease to do so when he receives some gratification. Indeed the reverse is more likely: a person who seeks fame and never receives any is likely to give up and seek different goals instead. In other words, gratification seems to reinforce rather than satiate the goal-seeking tendency. There may still be some parallel to biological drives, in that there might be temporary satiation before further goals of the same type are sought.

Goals Motivation can be looked at in terms of the goals people are seeking. The pattern of people's lives, in which they move from one event or situation to another, can therefore be explained in terms of the goals they seek. Goals are associated with positive affects, with cognitions about how they can be attained and with patterns of behaviour. People enter situations because they anticipate that they will enable certain goals to be attained (p. 120). Personalities can be studied by sampling the goals pursued, discovering the categories into which they fall and investigating their hierarchical structure (Pervin, in press, and p. 127).

Emotions and motivations These are different aspects of the same states. The main emotions are happiness, fear, anger, disgust/contempt, sadness, surprise and interest; these are conscious experiences combined with a physiological condition, and also with facial expressions and other non-verbal signals. Fear and anger also appear on our list of drives – as states that motivate behaviour.

An ingenious series of experiments by Schachter and Singer (1962) showed how the same physiological state may be experienced differently, and how physiological and external stimuli may interact to produce a particular kind of emotional or motivational state. Some subjects were given an injection of adrenalin, while others had neutral injections of salt solution. Some of each group of subjects were placed in the company of a confederate of the experimenter, who generally behaved in a wild and crazy manner. Further groups of subjects were subjected to an insulting interview, in the company of a confederate of the experimenter, who became very angry with the interviewer. The main finding was that the adrenalin-injected subjects became very euphoric in the first situation, and aggressive in the second – more so than those injected with salt solution. Thus emotion depends partly on the operation of cognitive factors.

However, it is now thought that this theory over-emphasizes the role of cognition: there is evidence that different emotions have distinctive bodily reactions, and that children experience these before they have learnt how to label them. Other factors in emotion include awareness of one's own facial expression and of other aspects of one's spontaneous, involuntary behaviour, such as laughter, as well as learnt patterns of emotional response (Leventhal, 1980).

There is a close connection between emotions and facial expression. Studies by Ekman and others (1972) have demonstrated that the seven emotions listed above are shown by similar facial expressions in very different parts of the world, and Eibl-Eibesfeldt (1972) has found that some of them are used by blind infants. So they are probably innate, though there are cultural rules about when one is supposed to laugh or cry.

Darwin maintained that emotional expression was part of a behavioural response, for example, showing the teeth in anger. A number of psychologists have argued that we know what emotion to experience through awareness of our own reactions, especially our facial expressions (Izard, 1971). Several experiments have shown that if subjects are asked to assume a certain facial expression for a time, then they come to experience the corresponding emotion (see p. 100).

The measurement of motivation People vary in the energy with which they pursue the goals of sex, dominance, affiliation and so on. How can these individual differences be assessed? We need to distinguish between their normal or typical level of anxiety, anger, etc., and their state at a particular moment. Questionnaires have been constructed by Spielberger (1972) for *state anxiety* and *trait anxiety*, using rather different questions. Like other questionnaires there is the problem that they can get only at the conscious part of motivation, and errors are caused by people trying to give a favourable impression. Nevertheless, some questionnaire measures have been successfully validated against behaviour.

Conflict In the cases of sex, aggression and probably affiliation, there are restraining forces which often prevent the goal being attained. When the drive is aroused, there is also arousal of inner restraints, probably because of punishment in the past. These are cases of approach–avoidance conflict – where the same object is both desirable and undesirable. It is found that as the goal gets nearer, its desirability increases, but fear or other avoidance forces increase even more. The anxiety induced by the prospect of parachute jumping, for example, increases rapidly as the time approaches. A small child who wants to stroke a horse finds that her fear increases as she gets closer to the horse, and she vacillates at a short distance from it. Rats who are both fed and shocked at the end of a maze stop part of the way down it. Miller (1944) presented a theoretical analysis in terms of approach and avoidance 'gradients', where the avoidance gradient is steeper, and the crossing point shows where they balance (Figure 1).

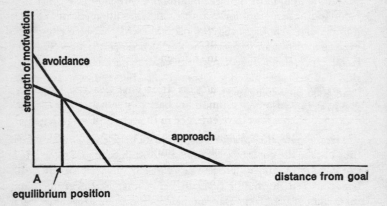

Figure 1. Analysis of approach–avoidance conflicts.

Other kinds of conflict between drives are very common. We found, for example, that nurses experience a conflict between their desire to look after patients and the desire to look after their own bodily well-being (pp. 122f).

The origins of drives Hunger and thirst are innate bodily needs, though the way that they are satisfied is partly learnt from the culture. Sex, aggression and affiliation also have an instinctive basis; in other words all human beings have an innate tendency to pursue these goals when aroused. However, particular environmental conditions may be necessary for the drive to develop.

Some social drives may be wholly learnt, as is the need for money. Drives may be acquired in childhood in a number of ways. A pattern of behaviour may become a drive because it consistently leads to other kinds of satisfaction: the origin of the need for money is probably that it leads to gratification of hunger and then becomes a goal which is sought for its own sake. Drives may be acquired through other learning processes, such as identification with parents: a child who takes a parent as a model is likely to acquire the parental pattern of motivation. There are great variations between cultures in the typical strength of these drives. Some cultures are very aggressive, some are greatly concerned about status and loss of face. These variations can sometimes be traced to the environmental setting – tribes which are constantly having to defend themselves against enemies need to have aggressive members, and so aggression is encouraged in children (Zigler and Child, 1969).

The origins of restraints and altruism It is now believed by many biologists that although animals are basically selfish, some aspects of altruistic behaviour have emerged in the course of evolution, and it is found that people enjoy being able to help, or prevent the distress of, others. Sociobiologists think this is because we want our genes to survive and so look after our immediate relations, who share a proportion of those genes – 50 per cent for children, brothers and sisters, 25 per cent for cousins and grandchildren, etc. A tendency towards generalized reciprocal altruism will also lead to survival, since those who exhibit this will benefit when they in turn are in need (Dawkins, 1976a). However, the main sources of restraints on selfish behaviour in man come from cultural learning. As well as biological evolution, there is also social evolution, whereby the elements of culture which help a society to survive are retained. Some of the most important aspects of culture are the moral values, and other norms of behaviour, which keep aggressive, sexual and selfish behaviour in check.

To a limited extent people are willing to help certain members of the public in public places. In one experiment it was arranged for a stooge to collapse on the New York underground. Strangers came forward to help more rapidly if (a) the stooge was white rather than black, (b) he was not drunk, and (c) there were not many people present (Piliavin *et al.*, 1969). Other studies show that helping behaviour is more likely to occur if another person has just been seen giving help in a similar situation.

THE ROOTS OF SOCIAL BEHAVIOUR

In this section we shall give a brief account of each of the motivational systems listed earlier. It must be emphasized that this is a provisional list which will probably have to be revised in the light of future research.

1 *Biological needs* Basic biological drives, such as the need for food, may lead to various kinds of interaction. They may result in drawing together the members of a primitive group in a cooperative task which none could accomplish alone. This happens with animals and leads to the formation of cooperative agricultural and pastoral groups in primitive communities. In modern societies work leads to the satisfaction of biological needs less directly. However, bodily needs for food, drink, warmth and comfort affect our behaviour a lot of the time, and are important sources of motivation which have been overlooked by social psychologists (Graham, Argyle and Furnham, 1980).

2 *Dependency* This is the first form of social motivation. Infants are physically dependent on their mother (or whoever is looking after them). There is an innate tendency to respond to pairs of eyes and to female voices; both are in range during feeding, and this is part of the rather complex process whereby the infant develops an early attachment to the mother.

It is not clear how similar human infant-mother bonding is to imprinting in animals. Infants can't walk, and perhaps following the mother with the eyes is the equivalent of following physically. There may also be learning by reward here: the important reward appears to be not so much food as the reduction of anxiety brought about by physical and visual contact with the mother. The critical period for the development of visual dependence on the mother is probably between six weeks and six months. The earliest forms of social behaviour are repeated rituals with mother, for example at bath-time and feeding-time, such as 'peek-a-boo', which involve interactive sequences of bodily contact, visual contact and vocalization (Bruner, 1975).

During the period of one to five years, children can bear greater physical distance from mother, and longer periods of separation. They may have to be trained to be more independent, if younger children appear on the scene. Dependent behaviour is stronger when the mother has been most responsive to the child's crying and there has been a lot of interaction between them (Schaffer and Emerson, 1964). It is found that dependency is greater in first-born and only children.

Dependency may be aroused in adults in situations which are new and frightening, and where others know the ropes. Dependence, or submission, is closely related to its opposite, dominance, in that some people may show both types of behaviour on different occasions. The so-called 'authoritarian personality' is submissive to people of greater power or status, and dominant to those of less. He can be found displaying these alternating styles of behaviour in organizations with many levels in the hierarchy, and where little authority is delegated to those in lower ranks. Authoritarians come from homes where parents have been very dominating and strict.

3 *Affiliation* Most people seek the company and approval of others, are unhappy if they are lonely or rejected and are very distressed by isolation. Need for affiliation, or 'social extraversion', is measured by questions with items like 'I join clubs because it is such a good way to make friends' (Mehrabian, 1970). In laboratory situations it is found that subjects strong in affiliation spend time establishing personal relationships with other people, rather than getting on with the appointed task. This dimension is closely related to 'social extraversion', in that both describe the people who are strongly motivated to interact with others. In particular they are keen to interact with other people of similar age, position, etc. to themselves. It probably leads to interaction with members of the opposite sex as well, and at present we are unable to disentangle its

effects from those of the sexual drive – with which it appears to be rather closely related.

Women seem to have stronger affiliative needs than men: they spend more time in the company of others, have more friends and form more intimate friendships (Dickens and Perlman, 1981).

How is affiliative motivation aroused? It has often been observed that fear makes people seek each other's company. Schachter (1959) found that college girls who had been made anxious by the prospect of receiving electric shocks from 'Dr Zilstein' chose to wait with other subjects rather than alone: this was especially the case for those who were made most anxious, and for first-born and only children. If affiliation is to be regarded as a drive in some way similar to hunger and thirst, it should be aroused by deprivation, in this case by isolation. A number of experiments have been conducted in which subjects have been isolated for periods up to four days. It has been found that periods of isolation as short as twenty minutes make children more responsive afterwards to social rewards. However, other experiments suggest that isolation does not arouse affiliative motivation unless it creates anxiety (Walters and Parke, 1964), and Schachter's experiment showed that anxiety alone can arouse it. Probably affiliative motivation is also aroused by anticipation – of parties and other social events. Affiliative behaviour may bring a number of benefits – reducing anxiety, providing a means of checking opinions against those of others, inhibiting aggression and making cooperation easier. However, affiliation appears to act as an autonomous drive, quite apart from such consequences.

Of course, we do not want to be intimate with everyone, and we also need privacy – it is possible to have too much of people (Altman, 1975).

There is probably an innate basis to affiliative motivation, but it is mainly acquired from early experiences in the family. It has long been believed that affiliative behaviour develops in some way out of dependency. There is quite a lot of evidence to support this theory – the Harlows' monkeys showed no later affiliative behaviour if they had been reared in isolation, and affectionless psychopaths often have a history of maternal deprivation. One way in which this might happen is via anxiety reduction. First-born and only children, when they are upset, are likely to be comforted by mother, and thus learn the affiliative response to anxiety which is described above.

4 *Dominance* This refers to a very important group of motivations, including needs for power – to control the behaviour or fate of others, and for status or recognition – to be admired and looked up to by others. We shall be mainly concerned with its effect in face-to-face situations, such as small groups. Dominant people want to talk a lot, have their ideas attended to, and to be influential in decisions. People strong in dominance take part in a struggle for position, the winner emerging as the 'task leader', i.e. the person responsible for decisions (see Chapter 8). The same is true in groups of monkeys: dominance here is usually established by threat displays or actual fighting, and the winner receives deference from the others, and most access to the females. The need for dominance can be assessed by questionnaires or projection tests, which will give a prediction about how hard a person will struggle for position (Winter, 1973). Whether or not he will be successful depends on social skills, which will be described later.

There may be innate, instinctive origins of dominant behaviour: dominance is thought to have developed during evolution since it has the biological function of providing leaders who can keep order in the group, and repel enemies. Males are more dominant than females in every human society, and among monkeys and other mammals (Wilson, 1975). It has been shown that injecting male monkeys or other male animals with male sex hormones produces more aggression and dominance.

Dominance is also affected by childhood experiences, such as identifying with a dominant parent. However, this appears to be a need which is only aroused at certain times and in relation to certain groups. Once a hierarchy has been established it is fairly stable, and struggling for position ceases. Dominance is also aroused during elections to office in groups, when the struggle for power becomes salient.

5 *Sex* This motivates important forms of social behaviour, such as approaching members of (usually) the opposite sex in order to engage in certain kinds of social interaction and bodily contact. In

the lower animals sexual motivation is instinctive; arousal is controlled by sex hormones and leads to the fulfilment of the biological purpose of reproduction. In man sex seems to have become a pleasurable end in itself, and is controlled by the cortex rather than by sex hormones. For present purposes sexual motivation can be looked at as a social approach drive similar to the need for affiliation, but which is usually directed towards members of the opposite sex. We shall not be concerned with the specific consummation to which sexual motivation is directed: in social situations it is similar to affiliation in leading to physical proximity, eye-contact, and other aspects of intimacy. Perhaps the most important difference is that rather greater degrees of arousal are generated, and this will occur when presentable members of the opposite sex come together, especially if they are within the fifteen to forty-five age-group.

Sexual arousal is produced by certain non-verbal cues – seeing physically attractive members of the opposite sex (p. 110), being touched in certain ways and certain places, and experiencing smells such as those from perfume. In addition, erotic pictures and films are very arousing – as measured by subjective reports or penis expansion; the most arousing are films of intercourse, genital petting, and oral sex (Baron and Byrne, 1981). Humans can also be aroused by a wide range of stimuli which have become associated with sex.

Although sexual behaviour depends on inbuilt physiological systems, it is also affected by childhood socialization and by attitudes and beliefs about sex, derived from the culture. Human beings apparently need a lot of instruction: elaborate cultural rules are built up governing sexual behaviour, and special social skills are needed to negotiate it.

Guilt and restraints may be acquired from parental discipline of early manifestations of sexuality, such as playing with the genitals; sexual behaviour in later life comes to be associated with anxiety. Homosexuality (among boys) is a product of an over-strong attachment to the mother and a peer-group without girls.

There are individual differences between the very inhibited, who fear and avoid sex, and those who seek it without any feeling of guilt, though the restraints are greatly weakened by alcohol. There are great variations between individuals and between cultures in attitudes towards sex – in whether, for example, pre-marital inter-course, extra-marital intercourse, homosexuality, etc. are considered desirable or not. (There has been a great increase in the accept-ability of pre-marital intercourse in the last thirty years.) There are many mistaken beliefs about sex, which no doubt also affect behaviour, e.g. that masturbation makes you go blind, that blacks have bigger penises then whites, etc. (Mosher, 1979).

Among monkeys and other animals sexual behaviour tends to be unrestrained; in civilized society it is possible only under very restricted conditions. Even the most primitive tribes have rules controlling intercourse and marriage – the structure of society depends on it. Sexual motivation is continually being aroused, though there are difficulties in the easy satisfaction of this need. This is partly due to external restraints – the potential partner is unwilling, or others would disapprove. It is also due to internal restraints in the personality. Sexual motivation thus affects social behaviour in many situations. This is another example of an approach–avoidance conflict, in which the equilibrium consists of various forms of sexual behaviour short of intercourse, and often without physical contact at all, such as conversation and eye-contact. A great deal of humour is based on sex; Freud was probably right in thinking that this provides an alternative outlet.

6 *Aggression* This is behaviour which is intended to harm, physi-cally or verbally, people (or animals) who want to avoid such treatment. It includes not only *angry* aggression but also *instru-mental* aggression – to gain another goal such as escape or approval.

Aggression in animals is biologically useful – in defending terri-tory and group, and in giving individuals priority over food and (for males) access to females. Aggression in animals occurs when they are frustrated, i.e. when goal-directed activity is blocked and expected rewards are not obtained. It happens in humans if the frustration is fairly severe, if it is perceived as arbitrary or illegiti-mate, and if there is no great danger of punishment or disapproval for aggressive behaviour. Animals fight when attacked (unless they run away); for humans, insults provoke more aggression than frustration. Insults and attacks are more likely to evoke an aggres-sive response in the presence of an audience – in order to preserve one's reputation, a form of self-presentation. Aggression is heightened by pain, heat, high levels of sexual excitement or other sources of physiological arousal. It is increased by large, but not by small, quantities of alcohol. When a person is in a bad mood he is more likely to respond aggressively to small annoyances.

Aggression is quite common – 28% of married couples reported hitting each other, 16% in one year (Strauss *et al.*, 1980). Boys and young men fight most, and aggression is a normal part of life in some parts of the world, e.g. Northern Ireland. Aggression appears to be an innate response to frustration and attack in animals and men, but is not a drive, since it does not occur in the absence of these stimuli and is not a need which must be satisfied.

A lot of apparently aggressive behaviour in animals and men is symbolic, not intended to do any real damage. Most of the 'violence' at football grounds is like this (Marsh *et al.*, 1978). Aggressive behaviour is restrained, controlled and often directed to harmless channels by social rules, without which life would be uncivilized and impossible.

Patterns of aggressive behaviour may be learnt in childhood, if, for example, a child is unloved and rejected, receives inconsistent and physical punishment, and has a parent who provides a model for aggressiveness, or who actually encourages violence. When boys were experimentally exposed to violent TV films over a period of time, they were observed to be more aggressive during normal activities than boys who had seen non-violent films (Leyens *et al.*, 1975). Some of the most violent offenders, however, have been found to be *over*-controlled – they have very strong restraints against provocation, until they suddenly crack (Megargee, 1966). While women normally show much less physical aggression than men, it has been found that when no one can either observe their behaviour or retaliate, female subjects give as many electric shocks as males to an aggressive opponent (Richardson *et al.*, 1979).

Aggression is prevented in animals if one or other antagonist gives appeasement signals – looks away, adopts a submissive posture, etc. It has been found in experiments that human subjects will give lower electric shocks to a victim if they can see his signs of pain, because they experience the same suffering themselves, by empathy. Aggression often results in punishment, so that for most people there is a strong avoidance component in the first place, partly internalized as part of the conscience, partly due to fear of retaliation. The conflict analysis predicts that an indirect form of aggression will occur, which may consist of verbal rather than physical attacks, displacement of aggression on to weaker people, or mere aggression in fantasy, such as watching western films or wrestling matches. Like sex, aggression is constantly aroused and restrained in social situations, and may be manifested very indirectly. The urge to aggress is also reduced by humour, e.g. funny cartoons, as long as it is not hostile.

7 *Self-esteem and ego-identity* Many psychologists have thought it necessary to postulate a need for self-esteem, i.e. a need to have a favourable evaluation of the self (e.g. Rogers, 1942).

Concern with the self-image is aroused under certain conditions – being in front of audiences, TV cameras and mirrors, and being assessed, in particular. Individuals differ in their level of self-esteem, and in their degree of confidence in what they are worth.

The origin of the need for self-esteem may be in the favourable evaluations made by most parents about their children. Children accept or partly accept these valuations, and seek to make later experiences and evaluations consistent with them (Secord and Backman, 1974). If the parents gave negative evaluations, in later life the child may accept this view of himself and show no sign of a need for self-esteem. There seem to be cultural differences in the extent to which self-esteem is important. In the East 'loss of face' is a much more serious matter than in the West.

A second type of motivation in this area which must be postulated is the need for a clear, distinct and consistent self-image. Part of this is a desire to regard oneself as a unique person, distinct from others. It will be shown later that adolescents often behave in deviant ways, or rebel against their families, simply in order to be able to see themselves as separate individuals. In addition to this there are pressures to establish a self-image that is consistent and integrated. There is plenty of evidence that people develop attitudes and beliefs that are consistent, and this is particularly true of attitudes towards the self. There are a number of processes involved – social pressure to conform to occupational, class and other roles, the effort to avoid motivational conflicts within the personality, and the effort to establish a clear and meaningful picture of the self and its ideals and goals. This affects social behaviour in much the same way as self-esteem – attempts are made to get others to accept and bolster up the self-image, and to avoid them or change their attitude if they do not (see Chapter 9).

8 *Other motivations which affect social behaviour* Achievement motivation leads to attempts to attain higher and higher standards of excellence, whether at examinations, competitive sports, or in other ways. In many social situations there is a task to be completed, as in committee work or in research groups. People high in achievement motivation are found to be most concerned with the task, while those in whom affiliative motivation is stronger are more concerned about getting on well with others. Achievement motivation is higher in first-born children, those who have been encouraged to be independent, and children with achieving parents. Weiner (1974) has produced evidence that high achievers differ mainly in attributing the likelihood of success to their own efforts, rather than to external factors. Achievement is unlike a drive in that it doesn't seem to satiate – the high-jumper who jumps as high as he hoped to simply revises his target upwards, and the same principle applies to other fields.

Achievement motivation in women is different in certain ways. 'Fear of success' is found in women likely to deviate from approved forms of female accomplishment, but men doing well at nursing, for instance, can have a similar problem. Women often need social approval, and this may prevent them taking a stand and risking unpopularity, which is necessary for some kinds of achievement.

There are also a number of acquired needs which affect social behaviour – for money, and needs related to interests, values, work or career.

In particular social situations, certain drives are likely to be aroused and satisfied. The immediate goals and plans which are formed are a complex product of a person's needs and the nature of the situation. Thus a dinner party may become the occasion primarily for sexual activity, affiliation, self-esteem, social contacts related to work or other interests, and so on.

Some of the social situations with which we shall be concerned later can be regarded as exercises of professional social skill – for example interviewing, teaching or selling. Here the performer of the skill is trying to affect the behaviour of others, not primarily because of his social needs but for professional reasons. He wants the others to learn, or buy, just as a person strong in affiliation wants others to respond in a warm and friendly manner. Of course the social-skill performer has other motivations – for achievement, money, etc. – which make him keen to do well at his job, but the *immediate* goals for him are those of getting the client to respond in the specific ways required by the situation. The social-skill performer will also in most cases be affected by social drives, and the client may be primarily affected by these.

FURTHER READING

Argyle, M., *Social Interaction*, Methuen, 1969, ch. 2.

Atkinson, J. W. (ed.), *Motives in Fantasy, Action and Society*, Van Nostrand, New York, 1958.

Baron, R. A., and Byrne, D., *Social Psychology: Understanding Human Interaction*, 3rd edn, Allyn and Bacon, Boston, 1981.

Devore, I. (ed.), *Primate Behavior*, Holt, Rinehart and Winston, New York, 1965.

Weiner, B., *Human Motivation*, Holt, Rinehart and Winston, New York, 1980.

Wrightsman, L. S., and Deaux, K., *Social Psychology in the 80's*, Brooks/Cole, Monterey, California, 1981.

CHAPTER 2

VERBAL AND NON-VERBAL COMMUNICATION

In Chapter 1 the goals which people seek in social interaction were discussed, and it was argued that these goals are satisfied by certain behaviour on the part of others. In order to get these responses people make use of a variety of verbal and non-verbal elements of behaviour. In conversation, for example, there are alternating utterances, together with continuous facial expressions, gestures, shifts of gaze and other non-verbal acts on the part of both speaker and listener. We shall start with the non-verbal elements, which communicate attitudes and emotions, as well as supplementing the verbal interchange in various ways.

The reader may feel that he is in the position of Molière's Monsieur Jourdain, who discovered that he had been speaking prose all those years. However, it is necessary to categorize and label the whole range of social acts, of different types and degrees of complexity, in order to move towards a scientific analysis of social behaviour.

NON-VERBAL COMMUNICATION

NVC (as it is usually called) is the only means of communication amongst animals. Similar signals are used by man, and the evolutionary origins of some of them have been traced. Showing the teeth by animals in anger, for instance, is derived from the act of attacking, but it is now used when there is no intention of actually biting. This is an example of a non-verbal signal having meaning, by being similar to or part of another act. Van Hooff (1972) has suggested the origins of human smiling and laughter: the lower primates have an expression known as the 'bared-teeth scream face', used in fear and submission, which has gradually evolved into our smile. Young primates also use a 'play-gnaw' accompanied by a kind of barking, which has become the human laugh.

All social signals are encoded and decoded by a sender and a receiver.

Often the sender is unaware of his own NVC, though it is plainly visible to the decoder. Sometimes neither is aware of it; an example is dilation of the pupils of the eyes in sexual attraction, which affects the receiver though he doesn't know why he likes the sender. Social skills training or reading this book will increase sensitivity to the NVC of others, and control over the NV signals which are emitted. We turn now to the main forms of NVC.

1 *Facial expression* As we have just seen, facial expressions have developed in the course of evolution, and are an important means of communication in apes and monkeys. Izard (1975) cut the facial muscles of some infant monkeys and their mothers, and found that the pairs failed to develop any relationship with each other.

One of the main functions of facial expression is to communicate emotional states, and attitudes such as liking and hostility. Ekman and others (1972) have found that there are seven main facial expressions for emotion:

happiness;
surprise;
fear;
sadness;
anger;
disgust or contempt;
interest.

Each involves a configuration of the whole face, though the mouth and eyebrows carry a lot of the information (see Figure 2, p. 32).

The seven emotions can be discriminated quite well, though similar ones can be confused, such as anger and fear, or surprise and

Descriptions	Neutral	Happy	Happy Sheepish	Angry1	Angry2	Fiendish	Sad1	Sad2	Sad3
Happy	33	81	36						
Neutral	39								
Sad	08								
Angry				58	03		42	06	
Furious				17	53		13	50	61
Amused	03	08	19	03	33	03			
Sheepish	03		25						
Mischievous			06	11		16			
Fiendish		08		03	11	75	03	03	
Depressed				03			17	08	24
Apprehensive	06		12	03			19	22	06

Figure 2. Emotions perceived in schematic faces (from Thayer and Schiff, 1969).

happiness. In addition, unlike monkeys, we often conceal our true feelings: it is not always easy to decode a smiling face, for example. These facial expressions seem to be much the same in all cultures, though Ekman has shown that there are 'display rules' which specify when an emotion may be shown – whether to cry at funerals, or to show pleasure when you have won.

Ekman also showed an unpleasant film, of a sinus operation. Both American and Japanese subjects displayed negative facial expressions, including ones of disgust, while watching the film, but at a subsequent interview the Japanese had happy faces, while the Americans did not.

Shimoda, Ricci Bitti and Argyle (1978) found that Japanese could decode British and Italian facial expressions *better* than Japanese ones (Table 1), probably because they are not supposed to display negative emotions like anger and sadness. They were probably helped by having seen Western films.

Judges	Performers		
	English	Italian	Japanese
English	63	58	38
Italian	53	62	28
Japanese	57	58	45

Table 1. Cross-cultural recognition of emotions (percentages correct; Shimoda, Ricci Bitti and Argyle, 1978).

Of the emotions listed above, surprise and interest are not really emotions, but cognitive reactions. The face gives a fast-moving display of reactions to what others have said or done, and a running commentary on what the owner of the face is saying. The eyebrows are very expressive in this way:

fully raised   – disbelief;
half raised   – surprise;
normal   – no comment;
half lowered   – puzzled;
fully lowered – angry.

The area round the mouth adds to the running commentary by varying between being turned up (pleasure) and turned down (displeasure). These facial signals lead to reactions from others; for example, looking puzzled may lead to clarification, and a smile acts as a reinforcement, encouraging the kind of act which led to it.

We are fairly aware of our facial expressions, and can control them. However, there may be 'leakage' of the true emotion to less well controlled parts of the body. A nervous person may control his face, but may perspire, clench his hands tensely together or have a shaky voice.

Facial expressions are perhaps social signals rather than direct expressions of emotion. Kraut and Johnston (1979) found that people at a bowling alley did not smile or frown at the pins when they hit or missed them, but smiled or frowned when they turned to face their friends. Furthermore, adopting a facial expression may affect the emotion experienced (see p. 100). On the other hand, people also make facial expressions which reflect their emotions while watching films alone (Ekman *et al.*, 1980), so it looks as if they are *both* social signals (which can affect the emotion experienced) *and* expressions of emotion.

2 *Gaze* Looking at other people in the area of their faces is primarily a means of collecting information about visible aspects of NVC, but it is also a signal itself – about direction of attention, attitudes to others and the synchronizing of speech (see Chapter 4).

3 *Gestures and other bodily movements* While a person speaks he moves his hands, body and head continuously; these movements are closely coordinated with speech, and form part of the total communication. He may:

1 display the structure of the utterance by enumerating elements or showing how they are grouped;
2 point to people or objects;
3 provide emphasis;
4 give illustrations of shapes, sizes or movements, particularly when these are difficult to describe in words.

Kendon (1972) found that these movements are synchronized with speech, the larger movements corresponding with the larger verbal units like long utterances.

Other gestures have conventional meanings, like our hitch-hike sign, nodding and shaking the head, clapping, beckoning, various rude signs, religious signs, and so on. These do not resemble their objects as closely as illustrative gestures do, and they have complex histories in the local culture. Italy is particularly rich in them, and here Desmond Morris and colleagues (1979) have studied a number, such as the hand purse, the cheek screw and the chin flick, which are only meaningful in certain Mediterranean countries. The signs for 'yes' and 'no' are interesting. In Southern Italy (i.e. that part of the country south of a line running east–west to a point somewhere between Rome and Naples), people toss their heads back to indicate 'no' as in Greece, instead of shaking them.

Head-nods are a rather special kind of gesture, and have two distinctive roles. They act as 'reinforcers', i.e. they reward and encourage what has gone before, and can be used to make another person talk more, for example. Head-nods can also play an important role in controlling the synchronizing of speech – in Britain a nod gives the other permission to carry on talking, whereas a rapid succession of nods indicates that the nodder wants to speak himself.

Gestures also reflect emotional states. When a person is emotionally aroused he produces diffuse, apparently pointless, bodily movements. People often touch themselves during certain emotions – fist-clenching (aggression), face-touching (anxiety), scratching (self-blame), forehead-wiping (tiredness) etc. These 'autistic' gestures are not normally used to communicate, since they are also used in private, and appear to express attitudes to the self such as shame and self-comforting.

4 *Bodily posture* Attitudes to others are indicated, in animals and men, by posture. A person who is trying to assert himself stands erect, with chest out, squaring his shoulders, and perhaps with hands on hips. A person in an established position of power or status, however, adopts a very relaxed posture, for example leaning back in his seat, or putting his feet on the table. Positive attitudes to others are expressed by leaning towards them (together with smiling, looking, etc.). Posture doesn't show specific emotions very

clearly, and mainly shows how tense or relaxed someone is. Some postures which do communicate fairly clearly are shown in Figure 3.

Figure 3. Some postures with clear meanings (from Sarbin and Hardyk, 1953).

People also have general styles of expressive behaviour, as shown in the way they walk, stand, sit and so on. This may reflect past or present roles – as in the case of a person who is or has been a soldier; it also reflects a person's self-image, self-confidence, and emotional state. It is very dependent on cultural fashions:

In a street market I watched a working-class mum and her daughter. The mother waddled as if her feet were playing her up. Outside a Knightsbridge hotel I watched an upper-class mum and her daughter come out from a wedding reception and walk towards Hyde Park Corner, the mother on very thin legs slightly bowed as though she had wet herself. She controlled her body as if it might snap if moved too impulsively. Both daughters walked identically. [Melly, 1965]

This last example shows the effect of cultural norms on expressive behaviour; style of walking may give information in this case about social class.

5 *Bodily contact* This is the most primitive kind of social behaviour, and is a very powerful signal. There are many ways of touching

people, but only a few are used in any one culture – in ours, for example, shaking hands, patting on the back, kissing, etc. Jourard (1966) has surveyed who has been touched by whom and where, and his results for American students are shown in Figure 4. It can be seen that there are great differences in who is touched by whom, and on which parts of their anatomy.

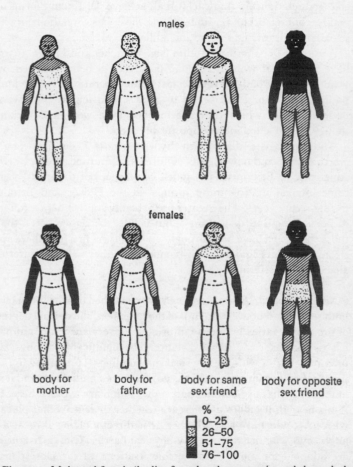

males

females

| body for mother | body for father | body for same sex friend | body for opposite sex friend |

%
0–25
26–50
51–75
76–100

Figure 4. Male and female 'bodies-for-others', as experienced through the amount of touching received from others (Jourard, 1966).

Bodily contact in our culture is controlled by strict rules, and is used mainly in the family, and by courting couples. Doctors, tailors and other professionals use it, but not as a *social* act. There is bodily contact with strangers in crowds, but in the absence of a social relationship. Bodily contact plays an important part in greetings and other ceremonies, and probably helps to bring about the changed relationship that such rituals achieve. Distinctive forms of bodily contact occur in some of the most basic relationships – sexual, nurturant, aggressive and affiliative.

A number of American studies (e.g. Whitcher and Fisher, 1979) have found that women respond positively to being touched by women. Female patients recover faster from operations, and mental patients talk more, if touched by nurses, and female borrowers prefer libraries where they are touched by a woman librarian, though men reacted in the opposite direction.

Anthropologists distinguish between contact cultures (e.g., North Africa) and non-contact cultures (e.g., Europe, India, North America). In Britain we use touch very little, but there has been some interest in 'encounter groups' in the U.S.A. and Britain during recent years. The greater use of bodily contact here is found to be exciting and disturbing – but it must be remembered that those concerned have been brought up in cultures in which there are strong restraints against bodily contact, and they will have internalized these restraints.

6 *Spatial behaviour Physical proximity* is one of the cues for intimacy, both sexual and between friends of the same sex. The normal degree of proximity varies between cultures, and every species of animal has its characteristic social distance. The significance of physical proximity varies with the physical surroundings – proximity to the point of bodily contact in a lift has no affiliative significance, and it is noteworthy that eye-contact and conversation are avoided here. If A sits near B, it makes a difference whether there are other places where A could have sat, whether he is directly facing B or at an angle, and whether there is any physical barrier. Closer distances are adopted for more intimate conversations: at the closest distances, different sensory modes are used – touch and smell come into operation, and vision becomes less important (Hall, 1966). It is

found that people sit or stand closer to people they like. There are also large cross-cultural differences – Arabs and Latin Americans stand very close, Swedes and Scots are the most distant (Lett *et al.*, 1969).

Orientation also signals interpersonal attitudes. If person A is sitting at a table, as shown in Figure 5, B can sit in several different places. If he is told that the situation is cooperative he will probably sit at B_1; if he is told he is to compete, negotiate, sell something or interview A, he will sit at B_2; if he is told to have a discussion or conversation he usually chooses B_3 (Sommer, 1965). This suggests (a) that one can become more sensitive to the cues emitted, often unintentionally, by others, and (b) that one can control non-verbal as well as verbal signals.

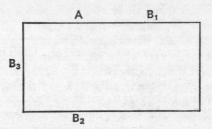

Figure 5. Orientation in different relationships.

Dominance, however, is signalled neither by proximity nor orientation, but by the symbolic use of space – sitting in the largest chair, or at the high table, for example. Movement in space is also important – to start or end an encounter, or to invade territory.

Manipulating the physical setting itself is another form of spatial behaviour – placing a desk to dominate the room, or arranging seats for intimate conversation.

Territorial behaviour is found in men as well as animals. There is the space immediately round the body, which we like to keep free – except in lifts and buses. Pairs or groups of people establish a claim to the space they are occupying, and others will keep out, or in the street will walk round them.

7 *Clothes and appearance* These also form part of social behaviour, and they communicate information about the self. Clothes, badges,

hair, skin, and physique can all be manipulated to a considerable degree. The information that is conveyed includes social status, occupation, attractiveness, attitudes to other people like rebellious-ness or conformity, and other aspects of personality. These signals are different from the others we have been considering, in that the code keeps changing as fashions change – long and short hair in males has had different significance at different dates. This will be discussed further in Chapter 8.

8 *Non-verbal aspects of speech* Emotional states, and attitudes to others, are conveyed by tone of voice. Davitz (1964) studied this by getting actors to read out an emotionally neutral passage in such ways at to express different emotions (see p. 98). A person who is depressed speaks at a low pitch, and slowly. Someone who is anxious speaks fast, but unevenly, in a raised pitch and a breathy voice, and makes a lot of speech errors. These 'paralinguistic' signals convey a message about the speaker, or his relationship to the listener.

Other non-verbal signals are closely linked to speech, and should perhaps be regarded as part of it. Timing is used to indicate punctuation, and short pauses (under ⅕ sec.) to give emphasis. The pattern of pitch indicates whether a question is being asked, and also 'frames' an utterance, to show, for instance, whether 'Where are you going?' is a friendly inquiry or a threat. Variations in loudness place stress on particular words or phrases – for example, on 'where' or 'you' in the question above. It can make clear which possible meaning an otherwise ambiguous sentence has, as in 'They are hunting *dogs*'. These 'prosodic' signals send a message about the message.

People speak in different accents, which are related to and convey information about their geographical origins and social class. Brit-ish accents are perceived along a single dimension of general prestige, with 'received pronunciation' at the top, Birmingham and Cockney accents at the bottom (Giles and Powesland, 1975). Experiments by Lambert in Canada and Giles in Britain show that if the same person records a passage in different accents, he is rated by different judges as possessing the stereotyped properties of the cultural or social groups in question. It is also found that speakers often accommodate to one another – shifting to a style of speech and accent similar to that of the other, perhaps in order to be approved of by him.

There are non-linguistic aspects of the conversation as a whole – the pattern of speech and silence – how much of the time each person talks, how fast, how soon after the other stops, and so on. Chapple (1956) has shown that people have characteristic ways of reacting to interruption and silence on the part of another. In his 'standard interview' the subject is first interviewed in a relaxed manner; later follows a period in which the interviewer fails to respond to twelve successive utterances by the subject, and another period during which the interviewer interrupts twelve successive speeches by the subject. Some people yield at once if interrupted, while others try to talk the interrupter down. Some people cannot tolerate silence, and will speak again if the interviewer is silent.

Sequences of NVC We have seen that NV signals come in combinations – a smile is commonly combined with a gaze and a friendly tone of voice, for example. They also occur in sequences of interaction between two or more people. Most social behaviour consists of verbal as well as non-verbal signals, and we shall see shortly how NVC operates in conversation. When there is little speech we can look at the NV sequences separately. For example, in greetings the following sequence has been found, by Kendon and Ferber (1973) and others:

1 person A waves, smiles, looks and says something like 'Hi.' B probably responds, and there is a brief mutual gaze;
2 A moves nearer to B, looks away, grooms himself, frees his right hand;
3 A and B shake hands, or make other bodily contact, second smile, second mutual gaze, second verbal greeting;
4 A and B stand at an angle, and conversation begins.

When a third person approaches two others, if they are willing to talk to him, they open up to give him the third side of a triangle to make what Kendon calls a 'facing formation'. The three move about, but maintain an equilibrium level of distance and orientation to each other. When one leaves he starts by a move away, revealing his intentions; this is followed by a move *in*, and then by his departure (Kendon, 1977).

Condon and Ogston (1966) and Kendon (op. cit.) have reported from detailed study of film that during a conversation two people coordinate their bodily movements with their own speech ('self-synchrony'), and with the bodily movements of the other ('gestural dance'). They also claim that this gestural dance is very finely tuned and can be observed at fractions of a second. A careful statistical study by McDowall (1978), however, failed to find such synchronizing at one eighth of a second. Self-synchrony and gestural dance *are* found at the level of utterances, and the main divisions of utterances: head-nods, shifts of glance and the beginning and ending of gestures are certainly coordinated at this time-scale (Rosenberg, 1981, and see pp. 83f).

DIFFERENT ROLES OF NON-VERBAL COMMUNICATION

Non-verbal communication functions in four rather different ways (Argyle, 1975).

1 *Communicating interpersonal attitudes and emotions*   Animals conduct their entire social life by means of NVC – they make friends, find mates, rear children, establish dominance hierarchies and cooperate in groups, by means of facial expression, postures, gestures, grunting and barking noises, etc. It looks as if much the same is true of humans too. Argyle *et al.* (1970) carried out an experiment in which superior, equal and inferior verbal messages were delivered in superior, equal and inferior non-verbal styles, nine combinations in all, by speakers recorded on videotapes. Two of the verbal messages were as follows:

1 It is probably quite a good thing for you subjects to come along to help in these experiments because it gives you a small glimpse of what psychological research is about. In fact the whole process is far more complex than you would be able to appreciate without a considerable training in research methods, paralinguistics, kinesic analysis, and so on.

2 These experiments must seem rather silly to you and I'm afraid they are not really concerned with anything very interesting or important. We'd be very glad if you could spare us a few moments afterwards to tell us how we

could improve the experiment. We feel that we are not making a very good job of it, and feel rather guilty about wasting the time of busy people like yourselves.

Some of the results were as shown in Figure 6. It can be seen that the non-verbal style had more effect than the verbal contents, in fact about five times as much; when the verbal and non-verbal messages were in conflict, the verbal contents were virtually disregarded. Much the same results were obtained in another experiment on the friendly–hostile dimension.

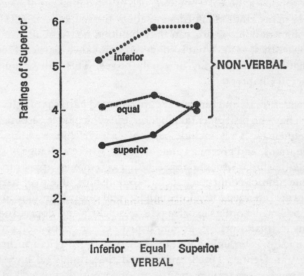

Figure 6. Effects of verbal and non-verbal cues (Argyle *et al.*, 1970).

A number of further investigators, though not all, have obtained similar results. Within NV signals, visual cues are stronger than vocal. Bugenthal *et al.* (1970) found that children reacted negatively to criticisms made with a smile and to negative messages whether verbal or non-verbal, especially from women. It should be emphasized that NV messages are only dominant for conveying emotions or attitudes – the verbal component is much more important for most other kinds of information (Friedman *et al.*, 1980).

The explanation of these results is probably that there is an innate biological basis to these NV signals, which evoke an immediate and powerful emotional response – as in animals. In human social behaviour it looks as if the NV channel is used for negotiating interpersonal attitudes, while the verbal channel is used primarily for conveying information.

2 *Self-presentation* As we have seen, clothes and other aspects of appearance, and accent, convey information about the self; the general style of behaviour also does this. In Britain and a number of other countries there is something of a taboo on the use of speech to convey many kinds of information about the self, especially favourable information, so this can only be done non-verbally, or very indirectly by speech. What is conveyed is not always true, of course, i.e. self-presentation may be partly bogus. This will be pursued further in Chapter 9.

3 *Ritual* Rituals and ceremonies are repeated patterns of behaviour which have no instrumental function, but which have certain social consequences. They include 'rites of passage' like weddings and graduations, and greetings and farewells, where a change of status or relationship is brought about. Other ceremonies appear to have the function of confirming social relationships, like drill parades; others are intended to heal, though by symbolic rather than medical methods, while others express religious beliefs and hopes. In these events, 'ritual work' is accomplished, i.e. a change of state or relationship is brought about by the ritual. The French anthropologist Van Gennep (1908) maintained that rituals all have three main phases, separation–transition–incorporation, which fit rites of passage quite well. Greetings, on the other hand, could be said to have a different structure – of moving towards and away from a climax. Exactly how the ritual work is done is not known, but it is clear that NVC plays an important part in it. Some NV signals here work by similarity or analogy – wine stands for blood; in some primitive rites to cure barrenness, red paint represents menstrual blood. Other signals have meaning through arbitrary associations, as in the case of flags, totem animals, or other objects representing social groups. Rituals are usually conducted by a priest or other official; at the height of the ceremony he usually looks at and

touches those who are being processed, which probably heightens the social impact of his work. The elements used may symbolize the state of affairs being brought about – putting on a chain of office, and the red paint which stands for menstrual blood, for example.

4 *Supporting verbal communication* Linguists recognize that timing, pitch and stress are integral to the meaning of utterances, e.g. by providing punctuation. A few linguists recognize that NVC plays a more extensive part – 'We speak with our vocal organs, but we converse with our whole body' (Abercrombie, 1968).

Completing the meaning of utterances In addition to the *vocal* signals of timing, pitch and stress, *gestural* signals also add to meaning – by illustrating, pointing, displaying structure, etc. Jean Graham and the author (1975) found that shapes could be conveyed much better, in one minute of speech, if hand movements were allowed. The effect was greater for those shapes for which there were no obvious words, and more information was conveyed in gestures by Italian than British subjects.

Information about honesty and dishonesty is also conveyed, unwittingly, by speakers. People who are lying tend to avert their gaze, make frequent speech errors, speak at a higher pitch and show bodily movements and tension – except, of course, practised liars (see p. 102 for the perception of honesty).

Controlling synchronizing When two or more people are conversing they must take it in turns to speak, and usually achieve a fairly smooth pattern of synchronizing. This is done by the use of non-verbal signals such as shifts of gaze, head-nods, and grunts (p. 62).

Obtaining feedback When a person is speaking he needs feedback on how the others are responding, so that he can modify his remarks accordingly. He needs to know whether his listeners understand, believe him, are surprised or bored, agree or disagree, are pleased or annoyed. This information is obtained from 'back-channel' signals from the listener: an early head-nod indicates understanding, a raised eyebrow signals surprise, and so on (Rosenfeld and Hancks, 1980).

Signalling attentiveness For an encounter to be sustained, those involved must provide intermittent evidence that they are still attending to the others. They should not fall asleep, look out of the window, or read the paper; they should be at the right distance, in the right orientation, look up frequently, nod their heads, adopt an alert, congruent posture, and react to the speaker's bodily movements.

Replacing speech When speech is impossible, gesture languages develop. This happens in noisy factories, the army, racecourses, and underwater swimming. Some of these languages are complex and enable elaborate messages to be sent, as in deaf languages, and the sign language used by some Australian aborigines. Some examples are given in Figure 7.

It has been suggested by some psychiatrists that the symptoms of

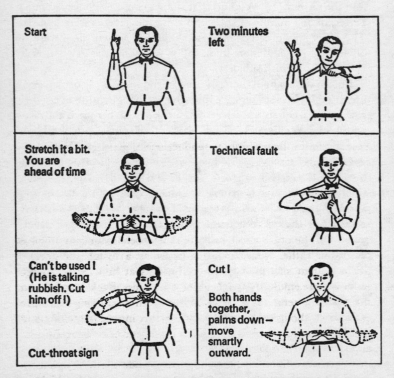

Figure 7. Non-verbal signals used in broadcasting (from Brun, 1969).

certain mental patients are a kind of NVC used when speech has failed – in pursuit of attention or love (pp. 223f).

Why do we use NVC? Animals use it because it is the only means of communication they have, but why do we? There are several reasons:

1 NV signals are more powerful for communicating emotions and interpersonal attitudes – they put the recipient in a state of immediate biological readiness, to deal with aggression, love or whatever. The power of ritual to change relationships is probably due to the NV components;

2 some messages are more easily conveyed by gesture than by words – shapes, for example – especially if we don't know the language well enough to describe things;

3 the verbal channel is often full, and it is useful to use another channel for feedback and synchronizing signals;

4 it would be disturbing to focus attention on some messages by putting them into words – such as certain aspects of self-presentation, or partly negative attitudes to others.

INDIVIDUAL DIFFERENCES IN NVC

People differ in their ability to send clear NV messages about their emotions and attitudes. Friedman *et al.* (1980) devised a scale with items like 'I am able to give a seductive glance if I want to', high scores being obtained by people with acting or lecturing experience, salesmen and doctors who have a lot of patients. We have found that socially inadequate patients are often very inexpressive (Trower, 1980). On the other hand, socially skilled behaviour may involve concealing rather than expressing emotions: a doctor who doesn't like a patient shouldn't make nasty faces at him. Some people express more emotion than they feel, others less. Buck (1979) found that women tend to be 'externalizers', in that their faces are expressive, though they report feeling less intense emotions and their autonomic reactions are weaker. Men tend to be 'internalizers' and show less than they feel.

People also differ in their ability to decode the NV signals of others. This can be measured from the accuracy with which an individual can decode photographs of facial expression or tapes of voices. It has often been found that women are better than men at decoding NV signals, but the reason for this is not known. Women are also more 'polite' in their perceptions – they see what they are intended to see and do not perceive what the other is trying to conceal (Rosenthal *et al.*, 1979). This sex difference increases with age during childhood (Blanck, 1981). Furthermore, in disturbed marriages it is found that the husbands are bad both at sending and receiving NV messages (Noller, 1980).

VERBAL COMMUNICATION

Speech is the most complex, subtle and characteristically human means of communication. Most animal noises simply communicate emotional states. Human speech is different in that it is learnt, can convey information about external events, and has a grammatical structure and sentences that can convey complex meanings. However, speech is used in a number of rather different ways, it is supported and elaborated by NVC, and utterances are put together in a sequence to form conversations.

Different kinds of utterance There are several different kinds of verbal utterance:

Egocentric speech This is directed to the self, is found in infants and has the effect of directing behaviour.

Orders and instructions These are used to influence the behaviour of others; they can be gently persuasive or authoritarian.

Questions These are intended to elicit verbal information; they can be open ended or closed, personal or impersonal.

Information This may be given in response to a question, or part of a lecture, or during a problem-solving discussion.

The last three above are the basic classes of utterance, but there are some other kinds:

Informal speech This consists of casual chat, jokes and gossip and contains little information, but helps to establish and sustain social relationships.

Expression of emotions and interpersonal attitudes This provides a special kind of information; however, this information is usually conveyed, and is conveyed more effectively, non-verbally.

Performative utterances These include 'illocutions' where saying the utterance performs something (voting, judging, naming, etc.) and 'perlocutions', where a goal is intended but may not be achieved (persuading, intimidating, etc.).

Social routines These include standard sequences like thanking, apologizing, greeting, etc.

Latent messages In these the more important meaning is made subordinate, e.g. 'As I was saying to the Prime Minister –'.

Language Language is possible only if there is a *shared vocabulary*. In order to talk about a particular topic, two people need to have common words for this area of activity or interest. The vocabulary may be quite small, as when serving tea or coffee, or very large, as for those working in botanical gardens or medicine. There are different technical vocabularies for cooking, sewing, cricket and many other activities. Criminals use special 'argots', or antilanguages, with alternative words from those used in straight society, e.g. for prostitutes and policemen. This is partly to prevent others understanding, partly a technical vocabulary and partly to maintain an alternative view of society (Halliday, 1978). As two or more people talk they build up common meanings and shared information, and the more they share the same concepts the better they can communicate (Moscovici, 1967).

A central feature of language is *syntax*, that is, the rules for combining verbs, nouns, etc. into sentences. Sometimes we can communicate without much syntax, for example, when ordering 'two pints of beer'. In order to convey information, a sequence of different kinds of word is needed – 'I [pronoun] ate[verb] the apple[noun].' The same applies to questions, orders and the other kinds of utterances listed above. In fact the structure of most sentences is much more complex than this, with subordinate clauses and other elaborations.

It is useful to distinguish between formal and informal speech, known as the High and Low forms of some languages, used in formal and informal situations.

Formal	*Informal*
planned, e.g. speeches	casual, e.g. chat
better grammar complex, with subordinate clauses	careless over grammar simple, fewer subordinate clauses
more nouns and adjectives	more verbs and pronouns

Formal speech is more efficient for conveying information accurately, but informal speech is better for sustaining face-to-face relationships. Examples of these two styles are the elaborated and restricted codes used in Britain (p. 188).

Some forms of informal or low speech are almost separate languages, such as Black English Vernacular (spoken by black Americans) and Scots, both of which follow grammatical rules of their own.

The use of pronouns and other *terms of address* is interesting. In many languages there is a choice of personal pronouns, e.g. the French *tu* and *vous*. In addition, people can be addressed as 'George' or 'Mr Smith'. This is partly a matter of intimacy, but also of status – subordinates are addressed by their first name, but this may not be reciprocated – so the use of first names can be rather ambiguous. It also depends on the situation: title and last name (Mr Smith) are used more in formal situations, such as in front of the customers in a shop, but much less at informal meetings, such as in the canteen (Staples and Robinson, 1974). Customs vary between organizations and cultures, Americans and Australians being very quick to move to first names, for example, unlike the British.

The *skilled use of language* requires more than knowledge of grammar. Polite and persuasive utterances are quite tricky. For example, to get someone to post a letter, 'If you're passing the letter box, would you mind posting this?', might do the job, while 'Post this letter' might not. Orders may be disguised as suggestions, or even questions.

There is an important non-verbal component in skilled utterances. The amount of warmth, directiveness or questioning is shown by the tone of voice and pitch pattern.

What is usually regarded as 'tact' requires more social skill. Tact could be defined as the production of socially effective utterances in difficult situations; these are usually utterances which influence others in a desired way, without upsetting them or others present. How do you congratulate the winner without upsetting the loser? What do you say to a child who has just been expelled from school? This is clearly an area of social skill, where the skill consists in finding the right verbal message; again it seems to have little to do with grammar.

Similar considerations apply to professional social skills. A selection interviewer needs tact to explore areas of failure, or to find out the truth where a candidate is concealing it. We shall discuss social competence further in the next chapter, and some professional social skills in Chapter 11.

FURTHER READING

Argyle, M., *Bodily Communication*, Methuen, 1975.

Harper, R. G., Wiens, A. M., and Matarazzo, J. D., *Non-verbal Communication*, Wiley, New York, 1978.

Knapp, M. L., *Nonverbal Communication in Human Interaction*, 2nd edn, Holt, Rinehart and Winston, New York, 1978.

Fraser, C., and Scherer, K. (eds.), *Social Psychology of Language*, Cambridge University Press, 1982.

Scherer, K. R., and Giles, H. (eds.), *Social Markers in Speech*, Cambridge University Press, 1979.

CHAPTER 3

SOCIAL SKILL

IN the last chapter we introduced the elements, verbal and non-verbal, of social interaction. The next problem is how to analyse this stream of events. In this chapter we shall show how this can be done.

We shall find that understanding social behaviour leads at once to an understanding of what one has to do in order to be socially competent. For example, as was shown in the last chapter, attitudes to other people, such as friendliness, and hostility, are communicated mainly by non-verbal signals. In our work with mental patients who have inadequate social skills we have found that they are often unable to use the normal signals for friendliness, in the face or voice. The social behaviour problems of mental patients will be discussed in Chapter 10, and the special skills of interviewers, teachers and other professionals, in Chapter 11. We shall bring the latest research on social interaction to bear on these practical problems.

Social interaction is a fascinating and baffling object of study: on the one hand it is immediate and familiar, on the other it is mysterious and inexpressible – there do not seem to be the words to describe it, or the concepts to handle it. An attempt has been made to dispel some of the mystery in previous chapters by describing the goals of social interaction (Chapter 1), and the elements of social behaviour which people use to attain these goals (Chapter 2).

In this chapter we shall try to break through the conceptual barriers which have held up the study of social interaction by introducing a theoretical model, and its associated language, for describing these events. The model is simply this: that the sequence of individual behaviour which occurs during social interaction can usefully be looked at as a kind of motor skill. By motor skills are meant the abilities required for such activities as cycling, skating, driving a car, playing the piano, typing, sending and receiving morse, performing industrial tasks, and playing tennis and other games. These have been extensively studied in the field and in laboratory experiments, and their psychological components are now well understood. Social interaction has many resemblances to other motor skills: the point of our suggestion is to pursue the basic psychological similarities in more detail, to see if the same processes operate.

We shall give a brief account of motor skills and show the parallels in social behaviour. This will direct attention to certain important aspects which might otherwise be overlooked, such as the perception of the right cues, the need for timing and anticipation, and the development of larger units of response. However, there are aspects of social behaviour which have no immediate parallel in motor skills, and which need special attention – such as seeing the other person's point of view and the projection of a self-image. This analysis enables us to handle the matter of degrees of social skill or competence. In later chapters we shall consider the closely related issues of training for social skills, and of the breakdown of skill – both of which have parallels in the case of motor skills.

SOME COMMON SEQUENCES OF BEHAVIOUR IN SOCIAL INTERACTION

Before presenting the social skill model, we need to describe some common sequences of social behaviour on which it depends.

1 *The effects of reinforcement* If Joan smiles, nods her head and agrees whenever George talks about politics, he will talk about politics more. If she wants him to talk about something else, she should frown and yawn whenever politics is mentioned. This process has been demonstrated in social situations by experiments on 'operant verbal conditioning'. A subject is interviewed by the experimenter; first there are ten minutes of relaxed, non-directive questioning on the part of the interviewer; for the second ten minutes the interviewer systematically rewards certain types of behaviour on the part of the client. For example, every time the client offers an opinion, the interviewer smiles, nods his head, agrees, looks him in the eye, or makes approving noises. For the third ten minutes the interviewer responds negatively to opinions – by disagreeing,

looking away, looking at his watch, or by making disapproving noises. The subject increases the frequency of giving opinions in the second period, and decreases it in the third period; this response is extremely rapid, and happens with a variety of types of social behaviour; the reinforcement may be any of the agreeable and agreeing social responses listed above. Some laboratory experiments have found that this process works only if the subject becomes aware of what the experimenter wants him to do; however experiments conducted under more natural conditions have found that the effect occurs without awareness – for example, during telephone conversations, where reinforcement is given and the effect on the other's conversation studied. Other experiments suggest that the person who delivers the rewards and punishments is not usually aware of what he is doing – he is merely reacting spontaneously to behaviour that pleases or displeases him. During social interaction each person is constantly reinforcing others and being reinforced himself, without either being aware of it (Argyle, 1969).

A large number of variations on this experiment have now been carried out, and the results are consistent with the idea that such conditioning occurs fastest when the subject is highly motivated to be accepted by the experimenter. Thus the subject should be anxious and compliant, and the experimenter should be prestigious, an attractive person of the opposite sex, or rewarding in other ways.

2 *Imitation* If Joan smiles, nods or folds her arms, it is likely that George will do the same – interactors tend to copy each other's styles of behaviour. This has been found for long and short utterances, the use of interruptions and silences, telling jokes and asking questions, the use of words like 'I', 'we', 'the', 'a', etc., smiles and head-nods, bodily posture, and revealing information about the self (e.g. Rosenfeld, 1967). This is probably a special kind of imitation, in which case we would expect it to occur under the normal conditions for imitation, e.g. B will imitate A when A is similar to B but of somewhat higher status, and when B is uncertain how he should behave. Again, this process is normally spontaneous and unplanned, but it can be deliberately controlled – in order to put a

nervous person at his ease, for example, one should avoid catching his nervousness, and adopt a visibly calm manner which he is likely to copy.

3 *The effect of non-verbal signals* As we showed earlier, non-verbal signals for friendly and hostile, superior and inferior, have a much greater impact than their verbal equivalents (pp. 42f). We showed that the relationship between two or more people is negotiated, established and sustained mainly by signals of this kind, normally in a spontaneous manner; those concerned do not usually attend to this process and are barely conscious of what is going on. Nevertheless NV signals are used in a highly skilled way, and social relationships may be negotiated by a series of small, tentative and ambiguous moves which can be withdrawn and disowned if necessary. A move to establish greater dominance, for example, could consist of a slightly raised voice level combined with a slight backward tilt of the head. Normally these moves are not the result of conscious planning, but they can be controlled in this way by those who know how NV signals work.

THE SOCIAL SKILL MODEL

We have said that interactors seek goals, consisting of desired responses on the part of others, and have shown that one social act leads to another. We have seen that social behaviour consists of a certain range of verbal and non-verbal signals.

I want to suggest that there is a useful analogy between motor skills, like riding a bicycle, and social skills, like making friends, conducting conversations and interviewing. In each case the performer seeks certain goals, makes skilled moves which are intended to further them, observes what effect he is having and takes corrective action as a result of feedback. Let us explore the parts of this model in more detail.

1 *The aims of skilled performance* The motor-skill operator has quite definite immediate goals – to screw a nut on to a bolt, to guide a car along the road by turning the steering wheel, and so on. He also has further goals, under which the immediate ones are subsumed: to

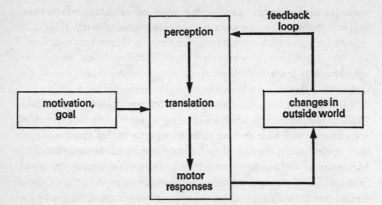

Figure 8. Motor skill model.

make a bridge or to drive to Aberdeen. He knows when each goal is attained by the appearance of certain physical stimuli. These goals in turn are linked to basic motivations; for example, he may be paid for each unit of work completed. In much the same way, a 'social-skill' operator may have quite definite goals, such as the following:

conveying knowledge, information or understanding (teaching);
obtaining information (interviewing);
changing attitudes, behaviour or beliefs (salesmanship, canvassing, disciplinary action);
changing the emotional state of another (telling joke, dealing with hostile person);
changing another's personality (psychotherapy, child-rearing);
working at a cooperative task (most industrial work);
supervising the activities of another (nursing, child-rearing);
supervision and coordination of a group (chairmanship, foremanship, arbitration).

These aims are linked in turn to more basic motivations in the performer, connected with his work. In everyday non-professional social situations the actors are motivated too, but this time simply by basic social motivations of the kind discussed in Chapter 1. We showed how motivation can be described in terms of the goals sought, and that strong positive affects are associated with these goals. Emotions and motivation are involved in social performance. In professional situations the social-skill operator will, in fact, be motivated by a combination of professional and social motivations – he may for example want the client both to learn and to be impressed by his knowledge.

2 *The hierarchical structure of social acts* Commands go from the brain to the appropriate muscles, producing a pattern of movements, of feet, hands, and face. In fact there is a hierarchy of commands, so that larger goals are linked to larger patterns of movements, in a hierarchical structure. There is also a series of sub-goals: when one sub-goal has been reached the sequence leading to the next sub-goal begins, until the main goal is attained. Driving a car from Oxford to Cambridge has sub-goals like starting the car, getting onto the Banbury Road, and getting to Bicester and Buckingham. One of the interesting findings about motor skills is that the series of responses leading to sub-goals become more or less automatic, and can be regarded as larger response units; for example, words rather than letters become the units for morse or typing. When a motor skill has been perfected, it is faster, movements are more accurate, unnecess-ary movements are eliminated, conscious awareness is much re-duced, tension is reduced or sometimes focused at points of difficul-ty, there is less need for feedback together with a danger of becoming mechanical, and the whole operation is smoother, effort-less and more effective.

The pattern of motor responses has a hierarchical structure, where the larger, high-level units consist of integrated sequences and groupings of lower-level units. An interview has a number of phases (pp. 233f), each with a certain sequence of questions, each question consisting of a number of words, and accompanying non-verbal signals. The sequences making up small units tend to become habitual and 'automatized', i.e. independent of external feedback; more attention is given to the performance of the larger units on the other hand – they are carefully planned, and are controlled by rules and conventions. Even quite large units may become habitual; a lecturer reported that he could 'arise before an audience, turn his mouth loose, and go to sleep'.

Harré and Secord (1972) have argued persuasively that much of human social behaviour is the result of conscious planning, often in words, with full regard for the complex meanings of behaviour and the rules of situations. This is an important correction to earlier social psychological views, which often failed to recognize the complexity of individual planning and the different meanings which may be given to stimuli, for example in laboratory experiments. However, it must be recognized that much social behaviour is *not* planned in this way: the smaller elements of behaviour and longer automatic sequences are very often outside conscious awareness, though it is possible to attend to patterns of gaze, shifts of orientation, or the latent meanings of utterances. The social skill model, in emphasizing the hierarchical structure of social performance, can incorporate both kinds of behaviour.

There is another important implication of this line of thought: the moves, or social acts, made in social behaviour are rather different from the actions in a motor skill. Social acts, like shaking hands, bidding at an auction sale or asking questions at a seminar are signals with a shared social meaning in a given context. They are like the moves in a game: in any particular game there is a repertoire of possible moves, which is quite different for chess, polo or wrestling; each move has a generally accepted meaning in the context of the game and the move can be made by alternative physical actions.

It is an interactor's *behaviour* which affects other people, but the model also applies to the control of thoughts and feelings. Hochschild (1979) has argued that social-skill performers, especially those in professional jobs like doctors and nurses, are expected to have the right feelings – to be happy, sad, etc. where appropriate, and need to be able to control the emotion as well as their expression of it.

3 *The perception of the other's reactions* An experienced motorist concentrates his attention on certain stimuli: outside the car he attends to the movement of other traffic and the position of the edge of the road, rather than the architecture of the houses; while inside he is aware of the speedometer rather than the upholstery of the seats. He knows where to look for the cues, and what they mean; he can interpret road signs and can anticipate what is going to happen next. Part of the training for some industrial skills consists in

teaching performers to make finer discriminations, to learn the significance of cues, concentrating on particular cues and suppressing irrelevant ones.

The selective perception of cues is an essential element in serial motor skills. The performer learns which cues to attend to and becomes highly sensitive to them. Vision is the most important channel. The performer makes a rapid series of fixations, each lasting a fraction of a second – as, for instance, in reading. The pattern of fixation is itself part of the skill; ideally, information should be collected just before it is needed. The performer also learns where to look at each point, in order to obtain the necessary information: perception is highly selective. The incoming data are actively organized into larger units which are recognized as objects, signals, or cues. These in turn are interpreted, i.e. used to predict future events, as with dial-readings or road signs.

The perceptual channels used in social interaction include hearing the literal content of speech, hearing the paralinguistic, emotive aspects of speech, observing the other's facial expression and other bodily cues. It seems likely that the more skilled performer can make more use of the last two channels. A rare fourth channel is touch – used in parts of the world where interaction often involves bodily contact. Hearing the emotive aspects of speech is very important, but it appears that many people fail to make use of this part of the message. Visual perception of the other consists mainly of scanning his face with a series of short glances in the area of the eyes. This area not only provides information about the other's emotional reactions, but also about the direction of his attention, for which his direction of gaze is a cue. Visual attention is finely timed and coordinated with speech, so that perceptual information, for example, to immediate reactions to what has just been said, is received when it is needed. Failure of social performance can result from not looking in the right place at the right time, or not being able to interpret what is seen or heard.

The motor-skill performer gets quite a lot of information from perceiving his own movements, either by sound, vision or kinaesthetic sensations. Do social interactors receive any direct feedback in a similar way? As we shall show in Chapter 9, people are very interested in the image they are projecting: one of the goals of interaction is to present oneself in a certain light to others. The main source of direct feedback is the sound of one's own voice. Some people are said to be very fond of this, but the sound they hear is quite different from what other people hear, since they hear the sound as transmitted through their bones. Many people fail to recognize tape-recordings of their voices, and are very startled the first time they hear one. People are often quite unaware of the emotive, paralinguistic aspects of their speech – they do not realize how cross they sound, for instance. They may also be unaware of the timing aspects of their speech – such as how often they interrupt. Posture, gestures and facial expression cannot be perceived visually by the actor: it is very difficult to *see* ourselves as others see us. The only way to do this is to have a lot of mirrors or to study films of oneself.

4 *Feedback and corrective action* In a continuous skills or 'tracking' task feedback can be seen very clearly. A beginner motorist tries to steer the car down the road, he sees that he is about to hit the kerb, so he corrects the steering to the right. When he is more competent the same process takes place with greater speed and accuracy. The social-skill performer corrects in a similar way. A teacher who sees that her pupils have not understood the point will repeat it slowly in another way; a person who realizes that he is annoying someone by his behaviour will usually change his style of behaviour. If someone is steering a boat he must learn which way to turn the rudder to go in the desired direction. There has to be some central store of 'translation' processes in the brain, which prescribe what to do about any particular perceptual information. This may be in the form of verbalized information, e.g. 'pull the rope on the side you want to turn towards', in the case of a rudder. Often the translation processes are completely unverbalized and lead to automatic sequences of behaviour with little conscious awareness – as in riding a bicycle. Or they may start as conscious rules and deliberate decisions but become automatic later, as with changing gear in a car. The output consists of a plan, i.e. the decision to make a particular series of motor responses, which has been selected from a range of possible alternatives. This involves some prediction about how external events are likely to develop while the response is being

organized – as when a tennis or squash player, while he is shaping his shot, anticipates exactly where the ball will be.

Social interaction also depends on the existence of a learnt store of central translation processes. In the course of socialization people learn which social techniques will elicit affiliative or other responses from those they encounter. Research has shown how these can be improved upon in many cases. For example, to get another person to talk more the best techniques are (a) to talk less, (b) to ask open-ended questions, (c) to talk about things he is interested in, and (d) to reward anything he does say. In Chapter 11 an account will be given of the rather specialized styles of response for professional social skills.

Taking the right corrective action may require knowledge and understanding of cars or cricket balls, or of people and social situations. The information contained in this book may help you to get your social performance right. The skills needed to deal with social encounters may be quite subtle. Here is Goffman's description of the way in which a surgeon will keep down the level of anxiety among his assistants during an operation.

Thus at a point of high tenseness, when a large renal tumour had been completely exposed and was ready to be pierced by a draining needle, a chief surgeon lightly warned before he pierced, 'Now don't get too close'.

Since the surgeon's own self-control is crucial in the operation and since a question concerning it could have such a disquieting effect upon the other members of the team, he may feel obliged to demonstrate that he is in possession of himself.

During quite delicate tasks, he may softly sing incongruous undignified tunes such as 'He flies through the air with the greatest of ease'. [Goffman, 1961, pp. 124–7.]

5 *The timing of responses* An important feature of motor skills is the achieving of correct timing, and often of rhythm. Without correct anticipation of when a response will be required the performance is jerky and ineffective. This can be seen in the intermediate motor/ social skill of tennis: each player moves alternately in a regular rhythm, all the time adjusting to the reactions of the other. The same is true of the simplest type of interaction – a conversation between two people. They must speak in turns, and there must be synchronizing of tempo, as described later (pp. 131f). There must be

some adjustment of each person's characteristic tempo, length of speeches, speed of reaction, and tendency to interrupt, for a synchronized set of responses to develop.

The synchronizing, or smooth handing-over, of the floor when speaking, can be achieved by most people although they have no idea how they do it. To hand over the floor one can simply end a sentence, or better, ask a question. A long gaze at another at this point makes him more likely to reply, especially during a period of hesitant speech. To *keep* the floor, on the other hand, one should not pause at the end of a sentence or look at the other at this point, but keep a hand in mid gesture, and if interrupted, speak louder! If the listener doesn't want to speak, he should respond by nodding, smiling and saying 'Uh-huh' in an encouraging tone of voice. If he wants to break in he should interrupt smoothly at the end of a clause.

By such signals the 'battle for the floor' is conducted, and a smoothly timed sequence of speech attained (Kendon, 1967; Duncan and Fiske, 1977; Beattie, 1980). Not all interruptions are intended to shut the other person up: some are to help him finish a sentence, some are intended as simultaneous speech – 'How interesting' – others are due to incorrect anticipation of the other coming to the end of an utterance. Thus one aspect of verbal behaviour, and of gaze-direction and other bodily movements, is the control of who shall hold the floor. Silences and interruptions become rare as the two become more adjusted to one another, and an equilibrium pattern develops.

What is the use of the social skill model? It makes some rather general predictions – e.g. that feedback is essential for effective performance, and that social behaviour depends on a set of learned responses to different situations. It provides an analogy with motor skills, which provides another set of hypotheses – that the empirical laws governing motor skills will apply to social skills. For example, there may be one or more 'plateaux' in acquiring social skills, i.e. periods of training where there is no improvement, and periods of sudden improvement. This and other more specific theories or hypotheses about social performance can be stated in the language provided by the model. It also provides us with a conceptual map of social behaviour and a list of the main components and processes involved – this will be used later as a guide to methods of training, and a means of classifying failures of social performance in mental patients.

One objection which has been made to the social skill model is that when people are engaged in relaxed, informal chat they do not appear to be trying to influence or control the others. My analysis of this kind of situation is that those concerned are trying to sustain a certain type of interaction, and that this *does* involve the control of others' behaviour – keeping them relaxed and happy, preventing them from leaving, or getting too serious, keeping the intimacy level right, and so on.

However the social skill model does require some amplification, since there are several features of social performance which are absent from the performance of a motor skill. These are discussed in the next section.

SPECIAL FEATURES OF SOCIAL SKILLS

We have considered social skills on the analogy of serial motor skills. We will now look at what appear to be special features of social skills, which are not obviously present in manual skills.

1 *The independent performance of the other(s)* A car or bicycle may have unique idiosyncrasies, but it does not exercise independent initiative in an attempt to control the driver. In social situations however the influence on A and B is not a one-way affair, and can better be represented as a system in which each accommodates to the other:

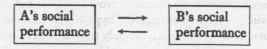

Sometimes one person can direct operations – teachers, interviewers, therapists and doctors; the dominant person has a plan which he follows, and the other reacts to his series of moves. The social skill model fits this kind of situation very well – though sometimes pupils and patients exercise some initiative, in which case things become more complicated. We shall discuss the problems of interaction where *both* parties have plans below.

2 *Taking the role of the other* A cyclist is not constantly wondering how the bicycle is feeling, or whether it thinks he is riding it nicely. Interactors, however, are concerned with what others are thinking, and to a greater or lesser degree imagine how the others are reacting. An interactor may be worried about what sort of impression he is making (if being interviewed or assessed), what the other person really wants (if he is a salesman), or what the other's problems are (if he is a psychiatrist). He may do this in an external, calculating way, or he may find himself identifying with the other and sharing his emotions and problems (Turner, 1956). A selection interviewer or social worker may start by doing the first, and end up by crossing over to the client's side, and trying to get him the job, or defending him against all comers. In many social skills a balance has to be kept between sympathy and some degree of detached objectivity.

There are tests for the ability to 'take the role of the other'. In the 'As-if' test, subjects are asked to describe how their life would have been different if they had (a) been born a member of the opposite sex, and (b) been born a Russian (Sarbin and Jones, 1956). It is found that people who do well on such tests also perform better at laboratory interaction tasks. It is supposed that one will interact better with another person X if one can imagine correctly what X's point of view is – the problems he faces, the pressures he is under, etc. On the other hand most people seem able to deal perfectly well with the opposite sex, and with older people – roles of which they have no experience, and which they probably imagine very inaccurately.

Taking the role of the other is one source of 'altruism', and of helping others. It has been found that a child is more likely to help a second child in distress if the first child has experienced this state of distress himself (Lenrow, 1965).

3 *Self-presentation* The presenting of information about the self is a normal and essential part of our social behaviour. This information is needed by others in order to know how to deal with us appro-

priately. We have seen that the desire to have self-image and self-esteem confirmed by others is a common form of social motivation, and that it has to be done in a way that is acceptable in the culture. In social skill situations where there is a more specific task, such projection of images may be a distraction from the proper task – the teacher should be concerned with getting his pupils to learn rather than with impressing them.

On the other hand, it may be important that the client should have the right attitudes towards and perception of the performer: it has certainly been found that learning takes place more readily when pupils respect and trust the teacher – and the same is true of clients in all social skill situations. Perhaps the answer is that skilled social performers should provide subtle evidence of their competence and expertise, but particularly by their expert performance in the role. Self-presentation can go wrong in a number of ways – by putting too much effort into it, by revealing too little or by presenting an image which is false or misleading (p. 227).

4 *Rewardingness* We described above how small rewards and punishments during the course of interaction are able to increase or reduce the behaviour reinforced. However, the overall balance of rewards and punishments which is emitted has a second effect – attracting the other person, and keeping him in the situation. A person can be rewarding in a large variety of ways – by being warm and friendly, taking an interest in the other, admiring him, being submissive, showing sexual approval, helping with his problems, or by being interesting and cheerful. What is rewarding to one person may not be rewarding for another. However if B is to be kept in the situation at all, A must keep it sufficiently rewarding for him. While A is free to use any social techniques he likes on B, in fact he is constantly restricted by what B will put up with. If A is not extremely careful, B will either withdraw from the situation entirely, e.g. by slamming the door on a political canvasser, or he may become sullen and uncooperative. If Joan can talk to David or Peter at a party, she drifts towards the one who is more rewarding to her.

We shall show later that rewardingness is the key to popularity – the main way in which popular people differ from others is in being more rewarding. Rewardingness is also the key to effective social influence: if A is sufficiently rewarding to B, he has more influence over B, because there is the possibility that the rewards may be withdrawn (p. 144).

5 *The rules of social behaviour* When we think of the skills involved in playing tennis, or any other game, it is obvious that the performer has to keep to the rules of the situation. The same is true of social situations. Some rules are 'intrinsic' – if broken, interaction is completely disrupted: for instance, playing cricket with a football, bidding less than the last person at an auction sale, or saying goodbye at the beginning of an encounter. Other rules are matters of fashion and convention, like what clothes are worn.

SEQUENCES OF INTERACTION

We showed above that each interactor's behaviour is like a motor skill. This analysis is very useful for situations where the person in question is in charge, like an interviewer or a psychotherapist. We shall now discuss situations where two people are both able to exercise some initiative.

First we must decide on a set of categories of social acts. The twelve categories devised by Bales (1950) are a good example. The first three and last three refer to 'socio-emotional' acts, the middle six to task behaviour. They are grouped in pairs, so that for example 8 (asks for opinion) often leads to 5 (gives opinion). Observers record interaction from behind a one-way screen, or from videotape, on a special machine. However, different social acts are used in different situations, so that different categories are needed for behaviour in the classroom, during psychotherapy, or elsewhere. Indeed, different sets of categories can be used in the same situation – there are many sets in existence for teaching (Simon and Boyer, 1974). Some include 'pupil initiation', or 'higher-order questions', while others do not; the only way to choose between them is to know which social acts are most important, and need to be emphasized in training, for example.

Two-step sequences These are the simplest sequences. We can find the probability of one kind of act leading to another, in a so-called

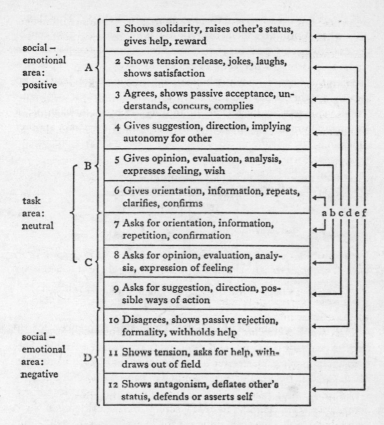

social –
emotional
area:
positive

A

1 Shows solidarity, raises other's status, gives help, reward

2 Shows tension release, jokes, laughs, shows satisfaction

3 Agrees, shows passive acceptance, understands, concurs, complies

B

4 Gives suggestion, direction, implying autonomy for other

5 Gives opinion, evaluation, analysis, expresses feeling, wish

task
area:
neutral

6 Gives orientation, information, repeats, clarifies, confirms

7 Asks for orientation, information, repetition, confirmation

C

8 Asks for opinion, evaluation, analysis, expression of feeling

9 Asks for suggestion, direction, possible ways of action

social –
emotional
area:
negative

D

10 Disagrees, shows passive rejection, formality, withholds help

11 Shows tension, asks for help, withdraws out of field

12 Shows antagonism, deflates other's status, defends or asserts self

a b c d e f

KEY:

a Problems of Communication   A Positive Reactions
b Problems of Evaluation   B Attempted Answers
c Problems of Control   C Questions
d Problems of Decision   D Negative Reactions
e Problems of Tension Reduction
f Problems of Reintegration

Table 2. The Bales categories (Bales, 1950).

Markov chain. The basic layout is shown in Table 3. This shows that when A produces social act type 1, it is followed in 15 per cent of cases by B using type 1, on 75 per cent of occasions he responds with type 2, and on 10 per cent of occasions with type 3. This is a 'reactive' sequence, showing how an act by one person leads to an act by another. It is also necessary to consider 'pro-active' sequences, where an act by A leads to another act by A: for example, a teacher comments on an answer by a child and then asks another question.

		next act by B		
		1	2	3
	1	15	75	10
last act by A	2	20	15	65
	3	70	15	15

Table 3. Example of reactive Markov chain, with three categories.

There are a number of important two-step sequences, for instance:

question→answer
open-ended question→long answer
smile, head-nod, etc.→smile, head-nod, etc. by other
gives order or request→it is carried out
is rude→is aggressive
and so on.

In order to make the second move correctly it should be *relevant* to the previous one (Grice, 1975), though this rule is quite often broken by topic changes. The second move should not repeat the first, should take for granted what has gone before and should add something to it (Rommetveit, 1974). Two people must have some shared objects of attention, shared knowledge and shared concepts. Each utterance uses and adds to this shared material, as when I say, 'Professor Rommetveit did this research in Oslo.' Minsky (1975) has shown that to take part in a conversation at all, one must build up a mental picture of what the other has said; answering a question may be an example of a two-step sequence, but it can also be a very complex intellectual operation.

Social skill sequences I shall now discuss sequences of more than two steps. The social skill model generates a characteristic kind of four-step sequence:

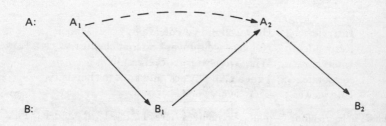

This is a case of asymmetrical interaction with A in charge. A's first move, A_1, produces an unsatisfactory result, B_1, so A modifies his behaviour to A_2, which produces the desired B_2. Note the link A_1-A_2, representing the persistence of A's goal-directed behaviour. This can be seen in the research interview:

Interviewer₁: asks questions
Respondent₁: gives inadequate answer, or does not understand question
Interviewer₂: clarifies and repeats question
Respondent₂: gives adequate answer

or

Interviewer₁: asks question
Respondent₁: refuses to answer
Interviewer₂: explains purpose and importance of survey; repeats question
Respondent₂: gives adequate answer

The model can be extended to cases where both interactors are pursuing goals simultaneously, as in the following example, from a selection interview:

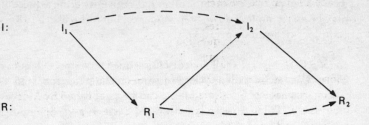

Interviewer$_1$:	How well did you do at physics at school?
Respondent$_1$:	Not very well, I was better at chemistry.
Interviewer$_2$:	What were your A-level results?
Respondent$_2$:	I got a C in physics, and an A in chemistry.
Interviewer$_3$:	That's very good.

There are four two-step sequences here: I_1, R_1, I_2, R_2 and R_1, I_2, R_2, I_3. There is persistence and continuity between R_1 and R_2, as well as I_1 and I_2. Although I has the initiative, R can also pursue his goals.

Another set of sequences are the 'social routines' described by Goffman (1971). An example is the 'remedial sequence' – the behaviour which takes place when someone has committed a social error of some kind:

1 A commits error (e.g. steps on B's toe);
2 A apologizes, gives excuse or explanation ('I'm frightfully sorry, I didn't see your foot');
3 B accepts this ('It's OK, no damage done');
4 A thanks B ('It's very good of you to be so nice about it');
5 B minimizes what A has done ('Think nothing of it').

Other such routines are those of greeting, opening conversations with strangers, introductions, thanking and parting.

Repeated cycles Sometimes the two-step links form repeated cycles. In an interview there is a very simple cycle:

| Interviewer: | asks question |
| Respondent: | answers |

Teachers often use the cycle:

Teacher: lectures
Teacher: asks question
Pupil: answers

More elaborate teaching cycles are given on p. 257.

The existence of a repeated cycle can be established by Markov analysis: in Table 3 there is a repeated cycle 1–2–3. Sometimes husbands and wives have a repeated cycle, always ending in a row in the same way. Sometimes *cycles* follow each other in a regular manner, as when a teacher starts with one style of instruction and then shifts to another. There can even be a cycle of cycles (Dawkins, 1976b).

Different types of sequence It is useful to distinguish four kinds of interaction sequence, as in Figure 9.

In the first kind, *pseudo-social,* the whole sequence is totally predictable, since neither interactor is really reacting to the other,

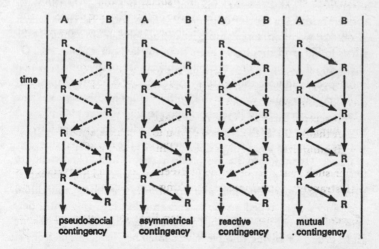

Figure 9. Classes of social interaction in terms of contingency (Jones and Gerard, 1967).

except in timing. The ritualized sequences just described are like this, except that there is some variation and interaction. Formal ceremonies and acting in a play are better examples.

Reactive contingency occurs when each person reponds mainly to what the other person did last, as in a rambling conversation with no particular goal. This kind of sequence can be analysed as a 'first-order Markov chain'.

Asymmetrical contingency describes instances in which one person has a plan, and the other fits into it, as in teaching, interviewing, etc. The social skill model fits these situations quite well, except that it does not say anything about rules of sequence.

Mutual contingency occurs when each interactor has plans and exercises initiative, as in negotiation and discussion. This is the most difficult kind of sequence to analyse. We shall try to do so further by investigation of the rules of sequence, by taking account of the plans of both parties, and by showing how these are integrated into a series of 'episodes'.

Rules of sequence There are rules for putting words together in sentences in the right order. Are there similar rules for putting utterances, smiles or other units of social behaviour in the right order? Is there a 'social grammar'? There could be rules which people know about; for example, at an auction sale they should take turns to bid, and should bid more than the last person, not less. Or there could be more obscure rules, like those of grammar, which most people follow, though they don't know what the rules are. There are various ways of trying to find rules of this sort, such as Markov analysis (and its elaborations to find longer chains), and modelling, i.e. rules are postulated and studies done to see how far actual sequences can be reconstructed from the suggested rules.

Clarke (1975) found that people do have an implicit knowledge of rules of sequence. He recorded and transcribed actual conversations, which were informal and apparently rambling; individual utterances were typed on cards and shuffled into random order; another group of subjects could put them back into more or less the right order – showing that we have some knowledge of the rules of sequence, even though we cannot state them very readily. Try putting the following sequence in the right order:

A: No, bloody awful.

A: Well, what's been happening at home?

B: Did you have a good day at the office, dear?

B: Nothing much.

A: Hello.

In another study he found that 'nested' sequences are quite acceptable, e.g.:

A: Would you like a drink?

B: What have you got?

A: Sherry – or gin and tonic.

B: I'd like some sherry please.

On the other hand Clarke has found that people don't seem to plan very far ahead, though they may be aiming for a particular goal, e.g. getting another to agree to something, or ending a class at a certain time. He has found that there are two kinds of rule: (1) two-step rules of the kind we discussed above; and (2) rules giving the opportunity to make a certain move *after* certain other moves have been made, and *before* another kind of move has occurred (Clarke, 1983).

What are the rules of sequence for verbal utterances? They probably include the following:

1 An utterance by A should be responded to by B or C, without too much delay and without interruption;

2 B's response should be on the same subject, unless some explanation is given;

3 B should keep to the same social episode, e.g. interview, polite conversation, psychotherapy; or he should negotiate a change of episode;

4 People should not suddenly arrive or leave, or start a new activity, without appropriate greeting or farewell rituals.

If rule 3 was broken there would be conversations like:

A: Shall we deal with item 7 on the agenda now?

B: Have you heard the one about the Japanese rabbi?

C: The trouble is I get these terrible impulses to rape my sister.

Each of these belongs to different contexts, or to episodes in a developing situation.

We have confined discussion so far to sequences of verbal utterances. Similar principles apply to social acts consisting of non-verbal as well as verbal components, or of non-verbal elements alone. Bidding at an auction sale, for example, can be done verbally or non-verbally. This is different from the Markov chain described earlier: here we are concerned with what is allowed, not with probabilities. We here need a three-step rule, to prevent a customer bidding again after the auctioneer has stated last bid. Most situations have special rules of sequences – auction sales, psychoanalysis, at the pub and so on.

To study a game or a social situation we need to find the rules. But rules are only part of the story – there is also play within the rules. To predict the course of events in a game, we need to know how hard each person is trying to win (plans), and also the skills and the strategies used by each player. There is cooperation over keeping to the rules, even in boxing and management–union bargaining, and there is often competition within the rules, whereby each person is pursuing his particular goals (Collett, 1977).

Social episodes The stream of social behaviour can be divided up into episodes, during which a particular kind of action is taking place. The episodes of a church service or a dinner party are fairly obvious. A selection interview has four fairly clear episodes – greetings and introduction, interviewer asks questions, candidate is invited to ask questions, ending and farewell. The second part of an interview might be divided into the different areas of questioning – school career, previous jobs, etc. The division of an encounter into episodes can be made by showing a videotape and asking observers to indicate where they think the main periods of action start and stop (p. 103). Episodes differ in the main activity, topic of conversation, environmental setting or spatial arrangement, and so on. They also differ in characteristic sequence of events. Figure 23 (p. 257) shows several different cycles of classroom interaction, which would constitute different episodes. Other episodes are one-off affairs, with no repetition, such as greetings and the 'remedial sequence' described above.

How does an episode start? Sometimes it is part of a familiar sequence of events, which may be written down somewhere – like committee agendas and church services. Sometimes there is a person in charge who can decide on the next episode; a teacher, for example, can introduce the next part of a lesson by saying, 'Now we are going to start on fractions.' Sometimes an episode change can be made non-verbally, as when a hostess rises from the table, or an interviewer gathers his papers together, puts his spectacles on and starts to look businesslike. In less formal situations anyone can try to introduce a new episode, but it has to be negotiated and agreed to by the others. Someone might start serious discussion of politics at a party, but the others reject this and go back to gossip or golf.

How do episodes end? If there are repeated cycles, when do they stop? Clearly there is more to episodes than going round in circles: episodes are also goal-directed, and when the goal has been reached, the episode ends. An interviewer plans to find out a certain amount about the candidate's school career, and when that has been done moves on to the next topic. Another factor is time, and there are usually conventions about how long certain episodes should last.

Episode sequence Most social encounters consist of a number of distinct episodes, which may have to come in a particular order. For example, the doctor–patient interview is said to have six phases, while negotiations have three.

We have found that encounters usually have five main episodes or phases:

1 greeting;
2 establish relationship;
3 central task;
4 re-establish relationship;
5 parting.

The task in turn may consist of several sub-tasks, e.g. a doctor has to conduct a verbal or physical examination, make a diagnosis and carry out or prescribe treatment (p. 247). Often, as in this case, the sub-tasks have to come in a certain order. At primarily social events, the 'task' seems to consist of eating or drinking accompanied by the exchange of information.

A successful interactor, then, needs to be able to use the repertoire of social moves for whatever situation he is in. Take a teacher, for example: he needs to be able to ask higher-order questions; he needs to know what leads to what, in order to control the other's behaviour, and how to set in motion various cycles of events; he should behave in accordance with the appropriate contingencies – if he is the main performer in an asymmetrical encounter, he should be responsible for the direction of behaviour; and he should follow the rules.

SOCIAL COMPETENCE

By social competence I mean the ability, the possession of the necessary skills, to produce the desired effects on other people in social situations. These desired effects may be to persuade the others to buy, to learn, to recover from a psychological problem, to like or admire the actor, and so on. These results are not necessarily in the public interest – skills may be used for social or anti-social purposes – and there is no evidence that social competence is a general factor: a person may be better at one task than another, e.g. interviewing *v*. lecturing, or in one situation than another, e.g. parties *v*. committees. In this section I shall discuss a variety of social competences. Professional social skills are mainly about performances in set-piece situations, like teaching, interviewing and public speaking. Social skills training (SST) for students and other more or less normal populations has been directed to the skills of dating, making friends and being assertive. SST for psychiatric patients has been aimed at correcting failures of social competence, and also at relieving subjective distress, such as social anxiety.

Social competence is easier to define and agree upon in the case of professional social skills: an effective therapist cures more patients, an effective teacher teaches better, an effective salesgirl sells more. When we look more closely, it is not quite so simple: examination marks may be one index of a teacher's effectiveness, but usually more is meant than just this. A salesgirl should not simply sell a lot of goods, she should make the customer feel she would like to go to that shop again. The general idea is clear, however: an effective performer of a professional skill is one who gets better results than another of the kinds relevant to the task. A combination of different skills is required and the overall assessment of effectiveness may involve the combination of a number of different measures or ratings. The range of competence is quite large: the best salesmen and salesgirls regularly sell four times as much as some others behind the same counter; some supervisors of working groups produce twice as much output as others, or have 20–25 per cent the labour turnover and absenteeism rates (Argyle, 1972).

For everyday social skills it is more difficult to give the criteria of success, whereas lack of competence is easier to spot – failure to make friends, or opposite-sex friends; quarrelling, and failing to sustain cooperative relationships; finding a number of situations difficult or a source of anxiety; and so on.

Perhaps the best way of measuring social competence is to assess actual effectiveness: a salesgirl's sales over a period in relation to those of others in the same department; the output, absenteeism, labour turnover, accidents, etc., of a foreman's work-group. Or, individuals can be rated by observers, who watch their performance on the job. These ratings can include detailed aspects of behaviour, such as facial expression, and other non-verbal signals, as well as details of verbal performance.

An alternative is to observe performance at standard role-playing of, for example, situations requiring assertiveness. In order to reduce the artificiality of this procedure some investigators have observed performance at staged encounters in the waiting room. Interview and questionnaire methods are less trouble, and we are often interested in a person's level of subjective comfort or distress as well as in his behaviour and his effect on others. There are rating scales for assertiveness (e.g. Rathus, 1973). It is also useful to discover the situations a person finds difficult; rate yourself from Table 4, scoring 5 if you find a situation very difficult, 1 if you find it very easy. You can then see the situations which cause you most trouble.

Rate according to degree of difficulty (1–5)

1   Dealing with someone who is cross or aggressive
2   Getting to know people in depth, intimately
3   Going to parties
4   Mixing at work
5   Making friends of your own age
6   Dealing with awkward members of the family
7   Making decisions in a group
8   Entertaining at home
9   Meals with the family
10 Attending a formal dinner
11 Going into a crowded room
12 Meeting strangers
13 Apologizing to a superior
14 Seeing doctors, solicitors or bank managers
15 Being a chairman at a committee or other meeting
16 Dealing with people who are older or of higher status
17 Reprimanding a subordinate (e.g. for being late)
18 Complaining to a neighbour whom you know well about constant noisy disturbance
19 Taking a person of the opposite sex out for the first time for an evening
20 Going for a job interview
21 Going to a close relative's funeral
22 Going round to cheer up a depressed friend who asked you to call
23 Being a host or hostess at a large party (e.g. twenty-first birthday)
24 Giving a short formal speech to a group of about fifty people that you don't know
25 Taking an unsatisfactory article back to a shop where you purchased it
26 Introducing yourself to new neighbours
27 Going to a function with many people from a different culture
28 Playing a party game after dinner (charades, musical chairs)
29 Attending a distant relation's wedding ceremony when you know few people
30 Mixing with people from another racial group
31 Being the leader of a small group

Table 4. Difficult situations.

Research into these difficult situations has found that they can be put into one of several categories, notably:

1 intimate situations, e.g. with the opposite sex;
2 situations requiring assertiveness or being the focus of attention;
3 formal social occasions;
4 meeting strangers.

(Argyle, Furnham and Graham, 1982)

The processes which have been described in this chapter enable us to understand the different ways in which people can be socially inadequate. In addition, a number of different kinds of training can be used. First, it is important to find out which are the situations an individual finds difficult, i.e. feels anxious in, perhaps avoids, or simply feels he is not making a success of. The next step is to find out what an individual is getting wrong. The different processes which we have described in this chapter each correspond to common forms of social inadequacy, which we will elaborate further in later chapters.

FURTHER READING

Argyle, M., *Social Interaction*, Methuen, 1969.

Trower, P., Bryant, B., and Argyle, M., *Social Skills and Mental Health*, Methuen, 1978.

Bellack, A. S., and Hersen, M. (eds.), *Research and Practice in Social Skills Training*, Plenum, New York and London, 1979.

Singleton, W. T., Spurgeon, P., and Stammer, R. B. (eds.), *The Analysis of Social Skill*, Plenum, New York and London, 1980.

CHAPTER 4

EYE-CONTACT AND THE DIRECTION OF GAZE

GAZE is of central importance in human social behaviour. It acts as a non-verbal signal, showing, for example, the direction of the gazer's attention. At the same time it opens a channel, so that another person's non-verbal signals can be received. Gaze is a signal for the person looked at, but it provides a channel for the person doing the looking. It is linked with the social skill model, since this channel is the main one for receiving feedback. Consequently the *timing* of gaze, in relation to speech, for example, is important.

During conversation and other kinds of interaction, individuals look at each other, mainly in the region of the eyes, intermittently and for short periods – this will be referred to as 'gaze' or 'looking at the other'. For some of the time, two people are doing this simultaneously – this will be called 'mutual gaze' or 'eye-contact' (EC). Figure 10 shows how these phenomena can be studied.

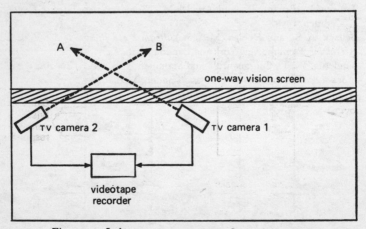

Figure 10. Laboratory arrangements for studying gaze.

Two subjects, A and B, are seated and asked to discuss some topic. A's gaze is recorded on a split-screen videotape recorder via TV camera 1, B's via camera 2, and the videotapes are later analysed by trained raters who press buttons which activate some kind of interaction recorder. The raters may also record periods of speaking. One kind of interaction recorder marks periods of looking or speaking as deflections of inked lines on a paper tape, as shown in Figure 11. It is also possible to record electronically, on equipment that summates periods of button-pressing and number of presses. A and B may both be real subjects, or one of them may be a trained confederate whose behaviour has been programmed by the experimenter.

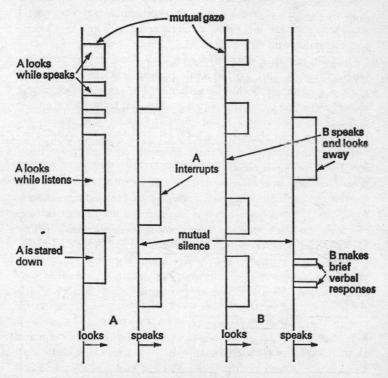

Figure 11. Record of looking and speaking (Argyle, 1969).

Several different aspects of gaze can be recorded, and typical figures from one of our experiments are given below.

Total individual gaze	61%
Looking while listening	75%
Looking while talking	41%
Average length of glances	2·95 secs
Mutual gaze	31%
Average length of mutual glances	1·18 secs

(From Argyle and Ingham, 1972.)

When two people are talking, they look at each other between 25 per cent and 75 per cent of the time (61 per cent in the experiment above), though we have seen the full range from 0 to 100 per cent; I shall discuss these individual differences later. They look nearly twice as much while listening as while talking, except interactors of high power or status, who are found to look as much while talking as when listening (p. 90). Mutual gaze is less than individual gaze; if two people both look 50 per cent of the time, we should expect 25 per cent EC. Individual glances can be anything up to 7 seconds or so (average 2·95 seconds in the above experiment), and mutual glances are rather shorter.

Interactors can tell with some accuracy when they are being looked at, as can observers of the interaction. On the other hand, Von Cranach and Ellgring (1973) have found that interactors cannot tell with much accuracy which part of their face is being looked at. What is being recorded as gaze is really gaze directed to the face; studies with eye-movement recorders show that people scan each other's faces with repeated cycles of fixation, each fixation being about a third of a second long, though they fixate on the eyes more than anywhere else. Interactors look at the eyes because there is an innate interest in eye-like patterns, which leads to early focusing on the mother's eyes; eyes provide crucial information about where the other is looking, since the area round the eyes is extremely expressive. The main exception to this is that deaf people focus on another person's mouth while he is speaking. When not looking at the face most people look right away, either at objects under discussion or blankly into space.

In addition to the amount and timing of gaze, the eyes are expressive in other ways:

pupil dilation (from 2–8 mm. in diameter);
blink rate (typically every 3–10 seconds);
direction of breaking gaze, to the left or right;
opening of eyes, wide-open to lowered lids;
facial expression in area of eyes, described as 'looking daggers',
    'making eyes', etc.

GAZE DURING CONVERSATION

Gaze is closely linked with speech, and plays several important roles in face-to-face conversation. People look nearly twice as much while listening as while talking, for example, and they look at particular points of an utterance. Gaze is part of a total communication system, which includes speech and non-verbal signals.

There is more gaze in some kinds of conversation than others. If the topic is difficult, people look less in order to avoid distraction. If it is intimate, they look less in order to avoid undue overall intimacy, as explained below. If there are other things to look at, interactors look at each other less, especially if there are objects present which are relevant to the conversation. Argyle and Graham (1977) found that gaze at the other fell from 77 per cent to 6·4 per cent if a pair of subjects were asked to plan a European holiday and there was a map of Europe in between them; 82 per cent of the time was spent looking at the map. Even a very vague, outline map was looked at for 70 per cent of the time, suggesting that they were keeping in touch by looking at and·pointing to the same object, instead of looking at each other. There was little gaze at the map if it was irrelevant to the topic of conversation.

It is found that glances are synchronized with speech in a special way. Kendon (1967) found that long glances were made, starting just before the end of an utterance, as shown in Figure 12, while the other person started to look away at this point.

The main reason why people look at the end of their utterances is that they need feedback on the other's response. This may be of various kinds. A wants to know whether B is still attending – his direction of gaze shows if he is asleep or looking at someone else. A

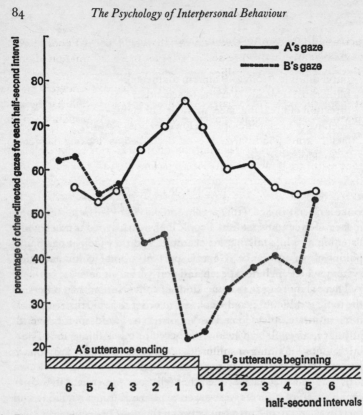

Figure 12. Direction of gaze at the beginning and end of long utterances (Kendon, 1967).

also wants to know how his last message was received – whether B understood, agreed, thought it was funny. At pauses in the middle of long speeches, A will look for continued permission to carry on speaking, and B will nod or grunt if he is agreeable to this. However, gaze is only a minor full-stop signal for synchronizing purposes; verbal and vocal cues are more important.

In another experiment strong support was obtained for the hypothesis that looking is used to gain information on the other's response. Vision between A and B was interfered with in various ways, e.g. B wore dark glasses, then a mask with only eyes showing, and finally went behind a one-way screen. In these conditions A was increasingly uncomfortable, was increasingly less clear about how B was reacting, and expressed a desire for more information about B's responses (Argyle, Lalljee and Cook, 1968).

Rutter and Stephenson (1979) found that pairs of strangers look at each other more than pairs of friends, especially while listening; they interpret this in terms of the greater need for information with strangers.

Gaze is also used to *send* information, though this is not usually done with conscious intent. An experiment was carried out at Oxford in which pairs of subjects were separated by a one-way screen (Argyle *et al.*, 1973). A could see but not be seen, while B could be seen but not see. The person who could see looked directly at the other 65 per cent of the time, compared with 23 per cent for the other. This study confirms the obvious but very important point that people look at each other in order to receive information, mainly non-verbal signals. However, the act of looking is itself a signal. In the experiment above, those who could not see through the screen looked directly at their partner (23 per cent of the time), they looked at certain moments, to give emphasis and to indicate interest or approval – evidently to *send* information. They did this while nodding or smiling, and Exline and Fehr (1978) found that people also look while gesturing.

In the Kendon study it was found that the terminal glance conveyed information to the other, that the speaker was about to stop speaking; if this glance were omitted, a long pause followed. In the one-way screen experiment there was much less gaze when subjects were asked to exchange monologues – where no signals for synchronizing speech were required.

So gaze does three main jobs during conversation – it enables non-verbal reactions to be seen, it sends information, and it helps with synchronizing of utterances.

We can also observe which direction a person looks away. Ask someone a question and he will look away – either to left or right. There is a tendency for people to look right (and downwards) if asked a question about words, spelling, etc., and to look left (and upwards) if asked a spatial question such as asking the way. This is because verbal processes take place primarily in the left hemisphere and produce a gaze shift in the opposite direction, while spatial issues are dealt with by the right hemisphere. There is some evidence that 'verbal' people tend to look right, while 'spatial' people like artists look left (Bakan, 1971).

We have just seen the main ways in which gaze is coordinated with speech. In any kind of encounter, gaze is also used to show interest in and involvement with the others present. It is used to start encounters – one person catches the other's eye and receives a signal that he is willing to have some conversation. Kendon and Ferber (1973) found, in their study of greetings, that there were two periods of mutual gaze – in the 'distant salutation' and the 'close phase' (p. 41). Other studies suggest that gaze is used at boundaries of episodes, perhaps because it is necessary to monitor the other's reactions very carefully at these points.

During encounters, those present should show their continued involvement by looking frequently at the others – rather than at other people (during a party, for example), since the direction of gaze indicates the direction of attention. It is interesting that we can tell where someone is looking by looking at his eyes. Infants of 11–14 months can follow their mother's line of regard (Scaife and Bruner, 1975). Shifts of gaze are sometimes used by adults as an alternative to pointing. Cycles of looking are used in most kinds of interaction. The earliest kinds of social behaviour between infants and their mothers consist of simple cycles like 'peek-a-boo' in which gaze is one of the main components.

Gaze fits into the sequence of social behaviour in another way: it acts as a reinforcer. Like nods and smiles, glances act as reinforcers of what another person has just said or done – particularly if the person doing the looking is an attractive female or a high-status male. This is not exactly reinforcement like giving a rat a piece of cheese; glances also carry meaning, that the gazer is interested and attentive. People are found to make use of this principle. For example, if one individual is trying to extract a favour from another – 'ingratiation' – he smiles and looks more in the softening-up stage, where he is being nice preparatory to asking the favour (Lefebvre, 1975). Gaze is itself affected by reinforcement: if Joan smiles and nods whenever George looks at her, George will look at her more.

It is found that the synchronizing of speech is quite good without vision, e.g. over the telephone. There are longer pauses but *fewer* interruptions. This is less surprising now we know that the main synchronizing cues are verbal and vocal, rather than visual. On the other hand, there is more 'listening behaviour' over the telephone – 'I see', 'How amazing', 'Uh-huh', etc. These replace feedback expressions. People have to learn a somewhat different style of social performance in which visible signals are transferred to the auditory channel.

Conveying information and solving problems can be done just as well over the telephone, provided visual materials like maps or charts are not needed. However, vision does make an important difference in certain kinds of interaction. People get to like and trust each other more if they can see one another, and cooperate more readily. If bargaining is done over the telephone, the person with the better case wins; when two people can see each other, they become concerned about being approved of by each other and sustaining the relationship, with the result that the person with the weaker case sometimes wins (Short, Williams and Christie, 1976).

GAZE AS A SIGNAL FOR INTERPERSONAL ATTITUDES AND EMOTIONS

We have seen how gaze is used to collect information and do various jobs during interaction. It is also under the influence of more basic motivational forces, and comes to act as a signal for attitudes to other people, and for emotional states. For example, we look more at those we like. Exline and Winters (1965) arranged for subjects to talk to two confederates, and then to state their preference for one or the other; in subsequent interaction they looked much more at the one they preferred. Rubin (1973) found that couples who were in love (as measured by his questionnaire) spent a higher proportion of time in mutual gaze. Of course liking or loving are communicated by a combination of cues: as well as looking there is smiling, a friendly tone of voice and the contents of speech.

Although gaze and EC are pleasant, especially with those we like, EC is unpleasant and embarrassing if there is too much of it, and if mutual glances are too long. This may be because unpleasantly high levels of physiological arousal are generated, or it may be because of the fact that there are also avoidance components connected with EC. One of these is that mutual gaze is distracting and adds to the cognitive load. If subjects are asked to look continuously there are more speech disturbances of various kinds (Beattie, 1981). It is more comfortable watching others from behind a one-way vision screen than watching others who can look back.

If there are forces both to engage in EC and to avoid it, there will be a state of conflict of the kind described earlier (p. 18). It follows that there is an equilibrium level of looking for each person and of EC for any two people, and that when the approach forces are relatively strong there will be more EC. We will now consider some implications of this equilibrium when the positive forces for EC are mainly affiliative or sexual, as opposed to dominant or aggressive.

We suggest that intimacy is a function of the following:

physical proximity;
eye-contact;
facial expression (smiling);
topic of conversation (how personal);
tone of voice (warm);

etc.

If we suppose that there is an overall equilibrium for intimacy, it follows that when one of these component elements is disturbed there will be some complementary change among the others to restore the equilibrium. Several examples of this have been observed.

Argyle and Dean (1965) tested the hypothesis that greater proximity would result in less EC. Subjects took part in three three-minute discussions with stooges trained to stare, at distances of two, six and ten feet. The amount of EC was recorded by observers in the usual way (Fig. 13). In later experiments it was found that the same results were obtained with pairs of genuine subjects. The effect is greatest for male–female pairs; the change is mainly in looking while listening, and changes of EC are due to amount of individual gaze, not changes in coordination.

The gaze-distance effect has been widely confirmed, as have a

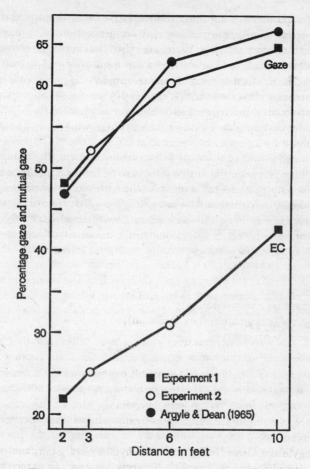

Figure 13. The effects of distance on gaze and mutual gaze (from Argyle and Ingham, 1972).

number of other derivations from the affiliative balance theory (Patterson, 1973). There is less gaze at the points where a person is smiling and when intimate topics are discussed. The theory works best for externally imposed changes to an established relationship, but it does not allow for changes of intimacy during an encounter.

Under certain conditions another person's moves, e.g. towards greater proximity, are reciprocated – which is the very opposite of what the theory predicts. Patterson (1976) has extended the theory to allow for this, proposing that a move towards greater intimacy leads to increased arousal in the target person: if the move is interpreted as a pleasant event (e.g. friendly) there will be reciprocity, whereas if it is interpreted as unpleasant (e.g. embarrassing) there will be withdrawal. In other words, equilibrium is being maintained.

If two people of different power or status meet, the low-power person looks at the other much more as he listens, than as he talks, while there is no such difference for the high-power individual, who looks as much whether talking or listening. There is no difference in gaze for low-power and medium-power individuals, suggesting that for humans there is no submission display. Those with high and low needs to control others behave in a corresponding way (Ellyson, Dovidio and Fehr, 1981). This may reflect the 'attention structure', whereby monkeys keep an eye on their leaders. Dislike may result in the 'cutting' of one person by another, or use of the 'hate stare', directed, for example, by some blacks towards whites in the southern states of the U.S.A.

It has also been found by Exline and colleagues that when someone recounts a happy experience he looks at the listener a lot, while he does so much less, casting his eyes mainly downwards, when telling of a sad experience. During an angry confrontation, intermediate behaviour is to be observed.

Exline and others (1970) carried out an ingenious experiment in which subjects became implicated in cheating on the part of a confederate. When they were interviewed by the experimenter and lied to defend the confederate, their level of gaze fell to nearly half what it had been before, except in the case of subjects with high scores in 'machiavellianism' (cold, calculating manipulators), who looked frankly and fearlessly as before. When people look at others a lot they are usually taken to be more sincere and credible. When they are embarrassed, for example by unsuitable self-disclosures from another person, they gaze less, as well as producing more speech disturbances and bodily movement (Edelmann and Hampson, 1979).

How much a person looks at others appears to depend on a balance of approach and avoidance forces. There are positive forces driving us to look at those we like, at those with whom we are involved and to collect information. There are avoidance forces to avoid seeing negative reactions, to avoid too much distracting input, and to avoid undue intimacy. The actual amount of gaze is a result of the balance between these two sets of forces.

THE PERCEPTION OF GAZE

If someone looks at us, how do we decode this signal? Very often we don't even notice – some subjects do not notice variations of gaze level from 15 per cent to 85 per cent. If A becomes aware that B is looking at him, the main message received is that he is the object of B's attention, that B is interested in him and willing to be involved. If they are not already interacting, gaze indicates that something is about to start. The nature of the action which is likely to occur varies with the situation, e.g. boy–girl, chairman–committee member, diner–waiter.

In addition, when B looks, A feels observed, that he is the object of another's attention. There are those who find this a disturbing experience, and some mental patients feel that they are being transformed into objects, observed as if they were insects, and, for some psychotics, turned into stone. We shall discuss this experience further in Chapter 9.

When there is mutual gaze, this is experienced as a special kind of intimacy and union, in which each is attending to and receptive to the other. Mutual gaze produces an increased level of physiological arousal, e.g. higher heart rate.

Gaze also conveys more specific meanings, indicating the nature of the other's interest. If A looks a lot at B, B often thinks (correctly) that A likes him, and B will like A in return. Argyle, Lefebvre and Cook (1974) found that people were liked if they looked more, up to the normal amount, but that too much gaze was liked less (Figure 14).

If A loves B, his or her pupils will dilate, and B will decode the signal correctly, though without awareness. In Italy, girls used to enlarge their pupils with drops of belladonna. The eyes are used a

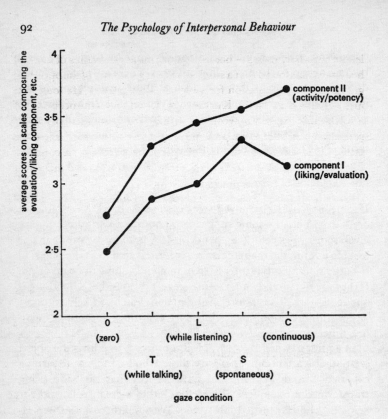

Figure 14. The meaning of five patterns of gaze (from Argyle, Lefebvre and Cook, 1974).

lot in courtship, and girls both make up their eyes and enlarge their eye display by dark glasses.

In animals gaze is often used as a threat signal. Exline and Yellin (1969) found that a monkey (in a strong cage) would attack or threaten an experimenter who stared at him, but would relax if the experimenter averted gaze – which is an appeasement signal. A number of experiments show that gaze can act as a threat signal for humans too. Ellsworth (1975) found that staring confederates on motorcycles caused motorists to move off more rapidly from stop lights; other studies found that people stared at in libraries either left or built barricades of books. Marsh, in recent studies of football hooligans, has found that a single glance at a member of the opposing group can be an occasion for violence, with cries of 'He looked at me!' (Marsh *et al.*, 1978). Kurtz (1975) found that if the occupant of a work table greeted newcomers with a long gaze, this was interpreted as a hostile stare and prevented the newcomer using the table, i.e. it was successful in defending the territory. In contrast, Ellsworth found that a mere glance from a person in need increased the likelihood of help being given.

Gaze is also used as a cue for personality. Those who avoid gaze are seen as nervous, tense, evasive, and lacking in confidence; people who look a lot are seen as friendly and self-confident. In the next section we will examine the real relationships between personality and gaze.

Decoding gaze is a two-stage process, rather like deciding which emotional state one is in (pp. 16f). There is a general factor of awareness of the other's attention, heightened concern with the other, and readiness for action. The specific meaning and response, however, depends on other contextual cues, such as the other's facial expression and the nature of the relationship.

INDIVIDUAL DIFFERENCES

Some people look consistently more than others. Kendon and Cook (1969) studied the gaze of fifteen subjects who each met between four and eleven others; they found a high degree of consistency across different partners, though gaze was also affected by the partner. We have already seen that several aspects of the situation affect gaze, and we shall see that not everyone reacts to situations in the same way.

The most striking link between personality and gaze is found in autistic children, for whom gaze aversion is one of the defining symptoms. They look very little, in very short glances of up to 0·5 seconds, and have various ways of avoiding mutual gaze, such as turning other people round and pulling hats over their eyes; sometimes, however, they look with a blank and unresponsive stare. One theory is that they have a high level of arousal and find mutual gaze very arousing, for which there is some evidence, though it is not known how this comes about. Clancy and McBride (1969) suggest that autism is due to a failure to form the initial attachment to the mother, leading to the development of cut-off skills for maintaining isolation. Good results are reported for children treated to improve the mother–child relationship by feeding and play routines.

Schizophrenia will be discussed more fully in Chapter 10. It has often been noticed that schizophrenics seem to avert gaze, and this has been confirmed in a number of studies in which the gaze of schizophrenics was recorded while they talked to a psychologist, or a partner provided by him – they look on average about 65 per cent as much as normals. However, a study by Rutter (1976) has shown that when schizophrenics are talking to another person, whether a patient or a nurse, about impersonal problems, their gaze level is normal. It appears from this and other studies that schizophrenics avert gaze only when interviewed about personal matters by psychologists or their assistants. Depressive patients avoid gaze to about the same extent as schizophrenics when interviewed, and also look downwards. Those neurotic patients who are socially inadequate look at others less than is normal; they also talk and smile less (Trower, 1980). A few, however, stare inappropriately.

Turning now to variations in the normal population, it has often been found that extraverts have a gaze level higher than that of introverts. They look at others more frequently, especially while talking, and they also look for more of the time. This variation is greater among females than males. Need for affiliation has some overlap with extraversion. Individuals high in need for affiliation look more, although only in non-competitive situations, and again this is more pronounced among females (Exline, 1963). The explanation of these findings is probably that gaze is part of a broader, affiliative pattern of behaviour, which establishes friendly relations with others.

Females look more than males, on all measures of gaze. A difference between the sexes has been found at the age of six months, but it increases up to adulthood, so is probably not innate. The experiment by Exline on affiliative motivation suggests that gaze is used more by females as an affiliative signal, though we don't know why. Mutual gaze, and being looked at, may be less disturbing for females, if they interpret this as affiliative rather than as threatening. And for a female to be looked at by a male may be seen as sexual choice: Argyle and Williams (1969) found that females often felt 'observed' by males, which is probably part of the normal relationship between the sexes in our culture.

Gaze is used as a social signal very early in life: mutual gaze with the mother first occurs at the age of three or four weeks. Visual interaction between mother and infant plays an important part in forming the bond between them: by six months, infants are upset when EC is broken, by eight months it plays an important part in games with the mother. Mothers often instruct their children in proper gaze behaviour – 'Don't stare at people', 'Look at me when I am talking to you' (Sue Vickers, unpublished study). The amount of gaze increases during childhood, falls during adolescence and rises again in early adulthood. The habit of looking away at the beginning of an utterance and returning one's gaze at the end develops during childhood (Levine and Sutton-Smith, 1973).

There are some interesting cultural differences in gaze. In 'contact cultures', like those of the Arabs, Latin Americans and Southern Europeans, level of gaze is high; here, too little gaze is seen as insincere, dishonest, impolite, etc. The affiliative balance theory predicts *less* gaze in contact cultures. The reason that there is more is probably that a given level of gaze has a different meaning in these cultures, though it is possible that relationships are more intimate in contact cultures. In non-contact cultures, like Britain, Europe and Asia, too much gaze is seen as threatening, disrespectful, insulting, etc. (Watson, 1972).

There are often rules about gaze: not to look at your mother-in-law (Luo in Kenya), at a high-status person (Nigeria), not to look at the other but at outside objects during conversation (some South American Indians), or to look at the neck, not the face (Japan). In a number of Mediterranean countries there is still a belief in the Evil Eye – that priests or old women with squints or other facial abnormalities cast a curse on anyone they look at. This depends on an outmoded theory of vision – that the looker sends a radiation to the object, together with the often disturbing experience of being looked at.

We can summarize some of the main findings in this way: if A gazes at B a lot, this may be because:

they are placed far apart;
they are discussing impersonal or easy topics;
there is nothing else to look at;
A is interested in B, and in B's reactions;
A likes B;
A loves B;
A is of lower status than B;
A is trying to dominate or influence B;
A is an Arab, Latin American, etc.;
A is an extravert;
A is affiliative (and female, in a cooperative situation);
A is low in affiliation (and female, in a competitive situation).

When an interactor tries to decode the meaning of another's gaze pattern, he can recognize some of these factors, as we have seen. Others are more obscure, and were not recognized until the relevant research was done. The ways in which people perceive each other will be discussed in the next chapter.

FURTHER READING

Argyle, M., and Cook, M., *Gaze and Mutual Gaze*, Cambridge University Press, 1976.

Exline, R., and Fehr, B. J., 'Application of semiosis to the study of visual interaction', in Siegman, A. W., and Feldstein, S. (eds.), *Nonverbal Behavior and Communication*, Erlbaum, Hillsdale, New Jersey, 1978, ch. 5.

Harper, R. G., *et al.*, *Nonverbal Communication*, Wiley, New York, 1978, ch. 5.

CHAPTER 5

PERCEPTION OF OTHERS

IN order to 'perceive' other people and social events, interactors use visual and auditory signals, verbal as well as non-verbal. Sherlock Holmes was very good at it. He perceived that Watson had returned to his medical practice in this way:

> If a gentleman walks into my rooms smelling of iodoform, with a black nitrate of silver upon his right forefinger, and a bulge on the side of his top hat to show where he has secreted his stethoscope, I must be dull indeed if I do not pronounce him to be an active member of the medical profession. [*A Scandal in Bohemia*]

We need to perceive features of persons, their emotional states and the attitudes of others to ourselves, and to understand the flow of events. It was shown in the last chapter that gaze is important because it opens the channel of receiving NVC. In fact we make use of auditory as well as visual information, verbal as well as non-verbal, to perceive events and other people. However, more than 'perception' is involved; I am referring to the whole process of interpreting and making sense of other people and the social events in which we are involved. This is important, because the way in which a person perceives (and interprets) events affects how he will behave. In an experiment by Kelley (1950), subjects who expected a person presented by the experimenter to be 'warm' interpreted his behaviour differently from those who expected him to be 'cold', and members of the first group talked to him more. The 'perception' of people is quite different from the perception of physical objects: objects are seen as being pushed and pulled by physical laws, while people are seen to some extent as being responsible for events and initiating action; the perceiver does his best to understand why they do it. Inadequate social performance is often due to faulty perception – simply not attending enough, or making inaccurate interpretations. It is particularly important for interviewers, doctors, personnel officers and others, to avoid the various sources of error here.

THE PERCEPTION OF EMOTIONS

Apes and monkeys keep up a continuous running commentary on their emotional states for other members of the group to see and hear. From their facial expressions and shrieks and grunts, it is clear whether they are angry, relaxed, want to play, want to copulate or are in fear of attack. In man, the face is the main source of information about emotional state. As we have seen, the face displays seven main emotions – happiness, surprise, fear, sadness, anger, disgust/contempt, and interest (p. 31). How accurately can these faces be decoded? If photographs of posed facial expressions are used, the success rate is about 60 per cent. Some emotions are more easily confused than others; for example, anger may be confused with fear or disgust, but not with happiness or surprise. Facial expressions can be recognized more readily when there is a word to describe them, like 'frown' or 'sneer'.

There is now evidence that the face plays a central part in the experience of emotion (see below). However, in most cultures there are restraints or 'display rules' on what may be shown in the face. This makes it difficult to tell what someone is really feeling, and we have to make use of other cues. Some of these are found in the face itself: an anxious person perspires at the temples, sometimes people smile with the lower half of the face only, and the area round the eyes has been found to convey curiously mixed emotions like pleasure and anger.

The second main cue to emotions is tone of voice. Davitz (1964) carried out experiments in which neutral statements were tape-recorded in different emotional styles. One of these statements was, 'I'm going out now. I won't be back all afternoon. If anyone calls, just tell them I'm not here.' The average accuracy of identification of emotions, from many studies of this kind, is 56 per cent, and the emotion most easily recognized from voice is anger, followed by sadness, indifference and happiness (Scherer, 1979). The cues in the voice which convey emotions have been found; for example, sadness is conveyed by a low pitch and slow speed, anxiety by a breathy tone of voice with many speech disturbances. These and other dimensions have been produced on a synthesizer and the 'emotions' judged correctly (Scherer, 1974).

Some information about emotions is conveyed by the rest of the body below the head, but not very much. Graham, Ricci Bitti and Argyle (1975) showed videotapes of people enacting emotional scenes, with different parts of the screen covered up. The body, including gestures, conveyed as much information about level of emotional intensity as the face, but was a poor source of information about specific emotions.

A further source of information is the situation the other person is seen to be in. If he has just been given a nice present, it is very likely that he will be pleased; if something very unexpected has happened, it is likely that he will be surprised. A number of experiments have tried to find out how facial expression is combined with information about the situation. The relative impact of non-verbal and situational cues depends on how clear and strong such cues are. Furthermore, perceiving emotions is quite a complex process, which may include inference and the application of principles acquired in the course of experience – for example, that people often pretend to be happy when they are not, but do not often pretend to be sad.

As well as interpreting the emotional states of others, we also interpret our own. The experiment by Schachter and Singer described earlier showed that people use situational cues to interpret a state of physiological arousal – 'misattribution' of a physiological condition (p. 16). Valins (1966) played amplified sounds of heart-beats to subjects, and found that he could influence how much young men thought they liked slides of nude females by speeding up the heart-beats they heard – making them think that they were more emotionally aroused than they were. In another experiment he made subjects feel less afraid of snakes, by the same method. While misattribution techniques can certainly reduce anxiety in laboratory experiments, they have not been found so successful in patients; and there is an alternative explanation – that subjects in the feedback experimental groups are simply better informed about which symptoms to expect, which reduces their anxiety (Cotton, 1981).

Facial expression also affects the emotions we experience. Izard (1971) has put forward the view that it plays an important part in this process: a situation produces a biological response at lower levels of the nervous system, causing a facial expression which provides information resulting in the subjective experience of emotions. This theory has been supported by a number of experiments in which subjects adopt a facial expression for a few minutes, and are then found to be experiencing the appropriate emotion (Laird, 1974) – 'Smile, and you will feel happy'! Lanzetta *et al.* (1976) found that subjects asked not to show pain in their faces felt less pain from electric shocks and experienced a smaller physiological reaction.

Leventhal (1974) has carried out some amusing experiments on what makes people laugh, i.e. decide that they are amused. If funny films are accompanied by canned laughter, subjects find them funnier. However, it makes a difference which ear the laughter is administered to: for males the right ear, for females the left ear, is better. This suggests that males process jokes in a verbal way, since verbal activities are concentrated in the left brain hemisphere, which is activated more by the *right* ear. Females perhaps process jokes intuitively, using brain processes which are concentrated in the right hemisphere.

PERCEPTION OF INTERPERSONAL BEHAVIOUR

We have seen that animals establish their social relationships entirely by means of non-verbal signals, and that, to a surprising extent, so do human beings. There are two main dimensions of attitudes to others which are communicated (see opposite page). There are also combinations of these, such as friendly dominance, and friendly combined with sexual attraction – the difference between loving and liking will be discussed later (p. 152). These attitudes are expressed by a wide range of non-verbal signals. Thus, a *friendly* attitude may be shown by some or all of the following:

bodily contact;	open arm position;
close proximity;	high level of gaze;
side-by-side orientation;	smiling face;
leans towards;	soft tone of voice.

We have done a number of experiments on the decoding of verbal and non-verbal cues for interpersonal attitudes, which were described on pp. 42f. A number of other experiments have been

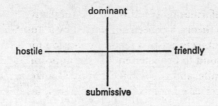

carried out on the perception of conflicting cues for interpersonal attitudes. Shirley Weitz (1972) found that white American students sometimes used friendly words towards a black subject, but in an unfriendly tone of voice. These subjects chose less intimate joint tasks and less close proximity, showing that their tone of voice showed their real attitude, not their words.

How accurate are these perceptions of others' attitudes to ourselves? Tagiuri (1958) surveyed likes and dislikes in sixty groups of people who knew each other well. He found that most people knew who liked them, but made quite a lot of mistakes about who did not like them – nine per cent of dislikes were seen as likes. The reason is that we very rarely make overt signals of rejection, so that politeness is mistaken for liking.

It is particularly difficult to interpret interpersonal attitudes when a person is in a dependent or subordinate position. In an act of ingratiation, one person is nice to another and then asks for a favour. Experiments by Jones (1964) and others have found that ingratiators agree with the other, flatter him, look and smile more; they do this strategically, such as disagreeing on unimportant matters. It is found that observers of these events interpret them as ingratiating if the actor is in a dependent position. In real life, the boss or other recipient of ingratiation may find it very difficult to tell whether his subordinates like and admire him or not.

Ingratiation and politeness are two of the main sources of error in judging interpersonal attitudes. Another is the tendency to form 'balanced' sets of attitudes and beliefs. For example, if A likes B, he will think that B likes A more than he actually does, and if A dislikes C, he will think that C dislikes A more than he really does. Of course, B will tend to like A, since such choices are reciprocated – but on average not as much as A thinks. Again, if A likes B and C, he will assume that B and C like each other, while if he likes one and not the other he will expect them not to like each other. (In the figure below, ⟶ = 'likes'; ⟶ = 'does not like'.)

This perception of another's attitudes is an example of *meta-perception*, that is, perceiving another's perception of oneself. As we will see later, there are certain conditions under which people become concerned about the perception of others – for example, when being interviewed for a job, or other occasions of self-presentation. Laing and his colleagues (1966) have developed a more elaborate set of measures of interpersonal attitudes. They find out how A perceives B, how A thinks B perceives A (the meta-perspective) and how A thinks B thinks A perceives B (the meta-meta-perspective). The last one is important if A dislikes or thinks ill of B, but does not want B to know this – A is then concerned with assessing how B thinks A sees B. From combining the perceptions of both parties it is possible to obtain further measures, e.g. accuracy of metaperceptions. The various accuracy scores were found to be greater in happy compared with disturbed marriages.

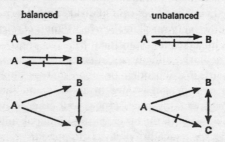

It is important to be able to tell whether someone is being *honest*. A number of ingenious experiments have been carried out; for example, one by Kraut and Poe (1980) in which customs officers tried to detect experimental 'smugglers'. The cues which people use are mainly non-verbal, such as aversion of gaze, speech disturbances, postural shifting and other signs of nervousness, but include some verbal ones, like evasiveness.

After a traffic accident, a family row or any other social event, it is often found that people report what happened differently, or have different ideas about whose fault the accident was, who started the row or why people acted as they did. Hastorf and Cantril (1954) studied a football game between Dartmouth and Princeton. The game became very rough and several players were injured. After the match, 36 per cent of Dartmouth students and 86 per cent of Princeton students interviewed thought that the Dartmouth team had started the rough play. This shows that interpretations can be different in important respects, and are influenced by group memberships or attitudes of perceivers. A study of British football fans by Marsh *et al.* (1978) found that they see their behaviour on the terraces as an orderly, rule-governed affair, where they have fun making threats and rude gestures at supporters of the other side, but have no intention of inflicting any bodily harm. The press and authorities, on the other hand, see football 'hooligans' as extremely violent, uncontrolled savages, who need to be kept in order by large numbers of police, wire cages and £1,000 fines. This situation has become complicated by the fact that the fans pretend to themselves and others that the official theory is true, and gain some satisfaction from the enhanced image of themselves as a frightening menace to society.

One thing we do when observing a series of social events is to divide it up into chunks or episodes. This can be done by showing videotapes to judges and asking them to press a button whenever they see a boundary between two chunks; or they can sort cards describing small pieces of the action into chunks. It is found that judges agree quite well on these boundaries, though they use different scales and find units of different sizes (Newtson, 1977). There is some evidence that people choose as units the actions leading to a particular goal (Dickman, 1963). If there are major changes of activity or spatial position, as at a dinner party or a seminar, the chunks can be quite easy to spot.

We only see a certain amount of what is going on if we are taking part in an encounter ourselves, because we are busy planning our own performance and are looking only some of the time. Repeatedly playing the videotape of an encounter can reveal a great deal more about what was happening, especially at the level of minor non-verbal signals like head-nods, frowns, interruptions and so on. More still can be revealed by asking experts on social interaction to analyse different aspects of the encounter. However, the expert view can be greatly augmented by asking the participants how they themselves saw the events and, in particular, what they were trying to do. These accounts can be quite difficult to handle. The football fans referred to above often described their behaviour on the terraces in terms of extreme violence, half-killing people, blood and so on. However, they also admitted that it was very rare for anyone to be actually injured.

There is some disagreement between social psychologists here. Some think that they should stick to an analysis of behaviour; some think that they should take the perceptions or accounts of participants as their data, and think that the social scientists' interpretation is simply another point of view with no special validity. My view is that the social scientist should use *both* observational and interview data, and try to piece together an objective and verifiable interpretation. This is particularly important when endeavouring to understand our own behaviour. Freud showed long ago that human actions are often motivated by earthier drives than we suppose, as in the case, for example, of the young man who wants to help a young lady with her mathematics, spiritual problems, etc. We are often unaware of non-verbal signals from another which influence our behaviour, e.g. their physical orientation and pupil dilation (pp. 91f). We do have some conscious access to our intentions, beliefs and so on, but this insight is woefully incomplete and distorted.

ATTRIBUTING RESPONSIBILITY AND ALLOCATING BLAME

Does a polite subordinate really like and respect his boss? Did a person fall because he was clumsy or because it was slippery? Under certain conditions, we decide that a person acted as he did from internal causes, i.e. as a result of his intentions or personality, rather than from external causes, such as social pressure. 'Attribution theory' puts forward the factors which indicate someone is acting from internal causes:

1 if he behaves in a way which deviates from the norms or is against his interests, such as being rude to the boss;
2 if he appears to be free of social pressures. For instance, when a high-status person conforms, he is seen as freely deciding to change

his mind; when a low-status person conforms, he is seen as yielding to social pressure (Thibaut and Riecken, 1955);

3 if his behaviour is consistent, e.g. he is nice to the secretary in a variety of ways and places;

4 if his behaviour is distinctive, e.g. he is nicer to one important person than to another with whom he has the same formal relationship;

5 if a number of different kinds of behaviour lead to the same goal, e.g. making money. In such an instance we are likely to infer that he is motivated towards that goal (Kelley, 1967; Jones and Davis, 1966).

Attribution is part of a wider process of explanation of behaviour, especially that of other people. If the behaviour is thought to be due to causes from within the individual rather than to pressures from the external situation, it could be as a result of his ability (e.g. in cases of success and failure), his intentions or purposes, his psychological state (e.g. depressed or elated), his disposition (e.g. aggressive or submissive), his past experience, or other sources (Schneider *et al.*, 1979).

There are a number of common errors of attribution.

1 Performers think that their behaviour is mainly due to situational factors ('I fell over because it was slippery'), while an observer is more likely to attribute it to the performer's personality ('She fell over because she's clumsy') (Jones and Nisbett, 1972). This is because the performer is attending to the environmental situation, while an observer is attending to the performer's behaviour.

2 Success is attributed by an actor to his own ability or efforts, while failure is attributed to the difficulty of the task (Weiner, 1980).

3 An example of underestimating situational factors is the tendency to overlook our own influence on another person's behaviour. If another person is bad-tempered or competitive, this may be partly because of our own behaviour.

Under certain conditions people who are not to blame are held responsible and punished for their part in events. Observers are found to blame the perpetrator of an accident more if a lot of damage is done, if they believe that they are similar to the perpetrator or if they are likely to cause a similar accident themselves. It has been suggested that this is a means of defence, a way of avoiding blame for possible events in the future (Burger, 1981). Another factor is equity, the belief that the world is basically fair and just: if the perpetrator of an accident suffers himself, jurors and others are more lenient towards him (Kalven and Zeisel, 1966).

FORMING IMPRESSIONS OF OTHER PEOPLE

When we form impressions of other people's personalities, we categorize them in various ways. Since we behave somewhat differently towards males and females, old and young and other divisions of people, it is necessary to categorize them as soon as possible.

The actual occasion of meeting may be accidental, by introduction or through belonging to the same group. At this point A experiences his first perception of B. An important aspect of this perception is that A will categorize B in terms of social class, race, age, intelligence or on whatever dimensions of people are most important to him, and this will activate the appropriate style of social behaviour in A.

Everyone has a number of dimensions, or sets of categories, which are most important to him and which affect his behaviour. He may not bother about social class, but may be very concerned about whether another person is Catholic or Protestant (e.g. in Belfast), or how intelligent he is. One way of finding out which categories are important to a person is the 'repertory grid' devised by George Kelly (1955). The technique is as follows: the subject is asked for the names of ten to fifteen people in certain relationships, e.g. 'a friend of the same sex', 'a teacher you liked'. The names are written on cards and presented to him three at a time. The subject is asked which two of the three are most similar, and in what way the other one differs, thus eliciting one of his 'constructs'. When a number of constructs have been found, a 'grid' is made up in which all the target persons are rated on all the constructs. Statistical methods can be used to find the general dimensions which are most used by the subject.

It is found that people use three kinds of construct – roles (e.g. class, occupation), personality traits (e.g. intelligent, extraverted) and physical characteristics (e.g. attractiveness, height). The most commonly used personality traits are:

extraversion or sociability;
agreeableness or likeability;
emotional stability;
intelligence;
assertiveness.

It is now very clear, however, that these traits are more in the mind of the beholder than in the behaviour of the target person. Different people use different traits. Women (and psychologists) tend to look for personality traits and social style; men on the other hand are more interested in status and achievement. People become most accurate at assessing whatever qualities concern them most – anti-semites are better at identifying Jews, for example. The categorization needs to be made, because an anti-semitic person will use quite different social techniques with Jews and Gentiles, and he wants to know which to select. Precisely the same is true of a person for whom differences of social class, or of intelligence, are of importance.

All person perception is highly selective, and salient traits direct attention to relevant cues. To detect social class, intelligence, Jews, Labour sympathies or sexual availability all require special cues, well known to those interested in these categories of people – accents, wedding rings and so on.

The constructs an individual uses may be extremely weird and private. Whole groups have their constructs, like *saved – not saved*. Some people use very simple category systems, with only one or two dimensions, such as *nice – nasty, in the Army – not in the Army*. Others may use a considerable number of independent dimensions. A teacher might classify pupils as *intelligent – unintelligent, creative – uncreative, hard-working – lazy, neurotic – stable, socially-skilled – socially-unskilled*, etc. Those who use only a few dimensions will collapse the other possible ones, and suffer from 'halo effect'. A more complex impression makes it possible to handle the other person in a more effective way; for example, if a teacher decided that a pupil was *intelligent, lazy* and *unstable*, this would enable her to select appropriate social skills. Thus people differ in 'cognitive complexity', which may be defined in terms of the number of independent dimensions they use.

It is found that schizophrenics do not have adequate constructs for persons and their emotional states. It has been suggested that this is a factor in their inadequate social behaviour – just as a gardener needs an adequate classification of plants and weeds, so for purposes of social behaviour we need adequate constructs for people (pp. 216f).

Individuals also differ in 'implicit personality theories', that is their ideas about the ways in which personalities work and fit together. How, for example, does one trait correlate with another? Bank managers believe that impulsiveness and carelessness go together, but students do not (Warr and Knapper, 1968).

Different constructs are used in different situations. Forgas, Argyle and Ginsburg (1979) found that members of a psychology research group, for informal chat over coffee, used *extraversion* and *evaluation*. At seminars, on the other hand, they categorized each other in terms of *dominance, creativity* and *supportiveness*. Furthermore, different traits are used to describe different groups of people, such as girlfriends, children, sporting friends and professors (Argyle, Forgas, Campbell and Ginsburg, 1981).

Children, as they get older, come to perceive people in more complex ways. If asked to give free descriptions of those they know, older children make greater use of traits, values and motives, discover more regularities of behaviour and use organizing ideas about how traits work (Livesley and Bromley, 1973).

It has recently been discovered that people categorize physical objects and persons in fuzzy sets, without clear boundaries, the sets being defined by a variety of prototypes. Thus we may have an idea of a typical extravert, with sub-sets such as 'PR type' or 'practical joker'. These categories contain a lot of stereotyped information about the properties of members of the set, which helps us to predict their behaviour and to deal with them (Cantor and Mischel, 1979).

Stereotypes and physical cues Impressions of others' personalities are partly based on stereotypes. If we know someone to be a *female Oxford psychology undergraduate*, this draws our attention to four sets of stereotyped information, based on our past experience and contact with popular culture. Katz and Braly carried out a classic study in 1933, which was repeated in 1951 and 1967, on the stereotypes of Princeton students: 84 per cent thought negroes were superstitious, 79 per cent thought Jews were shrewd and 78 per cent thought Germans were scientifically minded. The percentage of Princeton students holding these views has fallen a lot since 1933. (The method in these studies was not entirely satisfactory, since subjects were *invited* to express such stereotypes.) However, many people do hold stereotyped beliefs about the characteristics of, for example, old Etonians, sociology students and policemen. Although psychologists usually say that it is very wicked to hold stereotypes, these often contain useful summaries of the typical attributes of different sections of the population. Stone, Gage and Leavitt (1957) found that stereotyped ratings of a number of individuals simply described as 'students' were *more* accurate than the ratings given after interviewing them. On the other hand, there is a lot more variation among, say, sociology students than the stereotype would suggest, and it is important to be able to recognize variations from the statistical average.

Our impressions of others are partly based on inferences from their appearance. People who wear spectacles are thought to be intelligent, though Argyle and McHenry (1970) found that the effect disappears after a person has been seen in action for a few minutes. The same may be true for the other traditional findings of this type, such as:

thick lips	– sexy;
thin lips	– conscientious;
high forehead	– intelligent;
dark or coarse skin	– hostile;
	and so on.

There is certainly no concrete evidence that the individuals with these characteristics possess the qualities in question.

Voices are decoded mainly in terms of stereotypes: a person's accent is used to allocate him to a particular social class or nationality, and stereotypes are applied accordingly. Clothes raise other problems: they are completely under voluntary control, and play an important part in self-presentation. We learn how the other person wants us to see him, which is not quite the same as how he really is (see Chapter 9).

Physical attractiveness This is a way of classifying people which is very widely used; a person's physical attractiveness has important effects on the way he or she is treated. It can be measured very easily by asking judges to rate an individual on a five- or seven-point scale, like this:

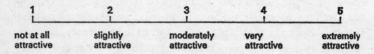

1	2	3	4	5
not at all attractive	slightly attractive	moderately attractive	very attractive	extremely attractive

There is a high level of agreement between different judges of either sex on a person's physical attractiveness (p.a.) score. The individual, however, may not have a very accurate idea of his or her attractiveness (as seen by others); there are quite low correlations, of the order of 0·25–0·30, for p.a. as rated by self and others: some people are over-modest, others the reverse. There are individual differences in preferences which are related to the personality of the beholder; extraverted males like pictures of girls with large bosoms and few clothes. It is possible that they are more prepared to admit these preferences than introverts. There are cultural differences in preference for thin or fat women and so on.

Attractiveness in females for many people in our society today appears to be based on the following elements (Wilson and Nias, 1976):

1 *Height* – shorter than the beholder, otherwise medium: Miss World winners average 5′8″;

2 *Physique* – 36–24–35 is the ideal; each of the three components is important; fatness is a very negative feature;

3 *Face* – regular features, full lips, clear skin, smiling expression;

4 *Hair and grooming* – long hair; 'frizzy wig' often used in experiments to make unattractive; careful grooming of skin;

5 *Health* – apparent healthiness, vivaciousness and arousal;

6 *Clothes* – in current fashion;

7 *Self-esteem* – people with high self-esteem get more attractive mates.

It is interesting that most of these features are under voluntary control, if we include ways of increasing height and changing real or apparent physique. To a large extent, personal appearance is a style of behaviour, which can be indulged in by those who choose to do so. Sex therapy and social skills training often include suggesting improvements to appearance, which are easier to make than improvements in social behaviour.

Attractiveness in men is not as important as in women, but it has its effects. It has similar components to those for females, but height is important and dominance is found attractive.

Experiments have shown that those who are physically attractive, of either sex, are thought to possess all kinds of other desirable attributes – they are seen as more sexually warm and responsive, sensitive, kind, interesting, strong, modest, sociable, altruistic, warm, sincere, poised and outgoing; it is thought that they are more likely to get married, would have greater marital happiness, get more prestigious jobs and be happier, but be *less* competent parents (Dion *et al.*, 1972). This is known as the 'physical attractiveness stereotype', the assumption that those who are beautiful are good.

Perception leads to action, and those who are seen as attractive are treated differently. The most celebrated study is the 'computer dance' at which Elaine Walster and colleagues (1966) invited 752 new students to a dance at which they were paired at random, except that the male was always taller than his partner. Ratings of attractiveness were made by the experimenters, and these proved to be the only predictor of how much each person was liked by their partner, for both sexes, but especially for females. Berscheid and colleagues (1971) found that attractiveness correlated 0·61 with the number of dates in the last year for females, 0·25 for males. It has been found that attractive females at an American university got better grades, and that they did it by staying behind afterwards and using their charms on the instructors (Singer, 1964). Other studies show that taller men get better jobs and attractive girls are less likely to be found guilty in law courts (see Berscheid and Walster, 1974a).

Names and nicknames Rom Harré (1976) has recently drawn attention to the importance of names in social behaviour. People think of themselves and each other by their names, as when asked 'Who are you?' A person's name often has clear indications of social class (Sebastian Digby-Vane-Trumpington), race (Moses Levi) or regional origins (Stuart McGregor). First names, though usually given by parents, also carry certain images – Charity, Horace, Robin, and Joan, for example.

Children are given nicknames by their parents, sometimes as many as eight different ones being used in the family. They are also given nicknames by their peer group, and this signifies acceptance into a social group and often some social role within it. These names may be based on personal qualities, e.g. Fatty; on particular incidents, e.g. Sneaky; or on the person's real name, e.g. Sherlock (surname Holmes). The society of childhood contains a number of traditional roles, perpetuated by school stories and comics, such as that of Piggy the fat boy, Twit and Thinker. In these various ways a person's name and nickname contribute to impressions formed about him.

A title is a kind of appellation which is achieved – for instance, ranks in the army, Dr and Professor, Sir and Lord. The niceties of British titles, of the different kinds of Lady, are most important to those concerned, as are such German academic labels as 'Dr Dr'. In a number of countries, such as Wales, it is the custom to refer to people by their profession, e.g. 'Jones the Spy'.

The combination of cues How do we arrive at an overall impression of someone's intelligence, neuroticism, etc., when we have a number of bits of information to go on, e.g. several instances of behaviour? When the evidence points in the same direction, an observer *averages* the bits; he doesn't *add* them. Thus a candidate for an important job who adds that he can ride a bicycle (an actual case) will probably reduce rather than increase his chances of getting the position. When the cues are conflicting, the observer may do one of several things. He may simply ignore some of the evidence or opt for certain bits and discount others. Taking more account of non-verbal than verbal cues for emotions is an example of this (pp. 42f). (In fact using the correct weights corresponds to a linear regression model, and is the best way of combining predictors.) On the other hand, he may make inferences using his knowledge or implicit personality theories.

The order in which bits of information are presented affects the way they are combined. If a person is said to be *kind* and then *dishonest*, this may conjure up a kind of Robin Hood figure, while someone who is said to be *dishonest* and *kind* may be thought of as a special sort of con-man. The first item changes the way the second is interpreted.

The accuracy of person perception Forming accurate impressions of others is important in all social situations, because we need to know how to handle people and how they will react. For professional interviewers and clinical psychologists, however, forming accurate impressions is their job. What is meant by 'accurate' here? It is possible to compare the judgements of interviewers or observers with the results of psychological tests. One problem here lies in separating *differential* accuracy from simply knowing the right average score for the population. Cook (1979) measured differential accuracy and found that judges could place target persons in nearly the right order for extraversion, after seeing a short sample of their behaviour on videotape, but could not do the same for neuroticism, which evidently is not so easily visible.

A more basic problem is that people vary greatly in their behaviour in different situations, as will be shown in the next chapter: extraverts are not extraverted all the time. Cline and Richards (1960) showed judges films of target persons being interviewed and asked them to predict, or rather *post*dict the behaviour of these rather carefully studied target persons in a number of situations. They found that some judges were consistently better than others.

One kind of prediction of great practical importance is that of success at jobs, each job involving a range of situations. We shall discuss the accuracy of personnel-selection interviewers later (p. 234). These results can be summarized by saying that interviewers can add a lot to other sources of information, but that their predictions are far from perfect and that interviewers disagree a lot with each other.

The main sources of error in person perception in general are as follows:

1 assuming a person will behave in the same way in other situations, overlooking situational causes of his observed behaviour, including the behaviour of the observer himself;

2 trying too hard to construct a consistent picture of the other; thinking all good things go together; being unwilling to recognize that he may be intelligent *and* lazy, neurotic *and* generous;

3 being influenced too much by first impressions, in particular by physical appearance and accent, and applying corresponding stereotypes;

4 making positive evaluations and giving favourable ratings to people from the same town, school, social class, etc. as oneself;

5 being influenced too much by negative points, and not enough by positive features, of the other;

6 making constant errors, whereby everyone is regarded as second-rate, aggressive or whatever;

7 simply not looking enough at, paying enough attention to or being sufficiently interested in, other people, a common problem among socially inadequate patients.

FURTHER READING

Cook, M., *Perceiving Others*, Methuen, London and New York, 1979.
Schneider, D. J., Hastorf, A. H., and Ellsworth, P. C., *Person Perception*, Addison–Wesley, Reading, Massachusetts, 1979.

CHAPTER 6

THE EFFECT OF PERSONALITY AND SITUATION ON SOCIAL BEHAVIOUR

SCHIZOPHRENICS, children, old people, extraverts and criminals all have distinctive styles of social behaviour (some of these will be described in Chapter 10). It is possible to predict, to some extent, whether a person will be helpful, aggressive or anxious, or whether he will conform or be assertive, from knowledge of his personality. In other words, social behaviour is, in part at least, a function of personality.

Social behaviour also varies between situations – people are noisier and more talkative at pubs than in church, and they engage in quite different behaviour at seminars, Scottish balls and cricket matches. It is sometimes easier to influence behaviour by changing the situation than by trying to change the people. A prison governor stopped inmates fighting by finding out where conflicts occurred – in this instance, at the corners of corridors – and modifying these areas – by rounding off the brickwork so that hurrying prisoners didn't bump into one another, a prime cause of fights.

In this chapter we shall examine how features of persons combine with features of situations to generate social behaviour.

THE INTERACTIONIST MODEL OF PERSONALITY

For many years psychologists believed that personality traits could enable them to predict an individual's social behaviour. It was gradually discovered that tests give extremely poor predictions of individual social behaviour (correlations usually 0·25 or less). As will be shown below, there is now extensive evidence that situational factors are at least as important as personality, if not more so. To give an example of what this means, consider three mythical people, Tom, Dick and Harry, who have different tendencies concerning lateness. If persons and situations are equally important, their typical lateness might be like this (Argyle, 1976):

minutes late for	lecture	tutorial	coffee	person means
Tom	0	3	6	3
Dick	3	6	9	6
Harry	6	9	12	9
situation means	3	6	9	6

However, there is a further problem. The table above shows our three friends as consistently late – Tom is always earliest, Harry always latest. We now know that people are not nearly as consistent as this. Tom might be keen on lectures and always arrive early, while Harry is very bored by lectures and is always late. Their average lateness might be more like this (Argyle, 1976):

minutes late for	lecture	tutorial	coffee	person means
Tom	−6	3	12	3
Dick	3	6	9	6
Harry	12	9	6	9
situation means	3	6	9	6

This is known as *interaction* between personality and situation (P×S interaction), and is reflected in low correlations between different situations or tests. Similarly, Tom may be more anxious than Dick when confronted by physically dangerous situations, but *less* anxious than Dick in difficult social situations (Endler and Okada, 1975).

What has caused many psychologists to abandon the traditional trait model of personality is the realization that personality tests simply do not predict behaviour in actual situations with any accuracy; if there are low correlations between situations it follows that a test could not predict behaviour in all of them.

The traditional trait model has been replaced by the interactionist model of personality (Endler and Magnusson, 1976). This model recognizes the existence of stable, underlying features of personality, but says that these interact with the properties of particular situations to produce behaviour. This is quite different from the earlier model: it is not saying that a person has a typical or average tendency to dominance which he generalizes across situations, for example, but that he has certain drives and other aspects of personality which may or may not produce dominant behaviour on a particular occasion. Authoritarian personalities illustrate the point: an authoritarian bullies less powerful or important people and is submissive to more powerful people – there is no question of the generalization of similar behaviour.

Attempts have been made to test these two models by finding the relative importance of persons, situations and P × S interaction. This is done by observing, or asking for reports of, the behaviour of a number of individuals in a number of situations, and calculating how much of the variation can be explained by persons and situations. A typical study is that by Moos (1969) on the observed behaviour of mental patients.

		Source		
Category	Persons	Settings	P × S	Within
Hand and arm movement	17·2	13·8	29·6	39·3
Foot and leg movement	27·3	13·0	31·2	28·6
Scratch, pick, rub	26·3	18·2	27·6	27·9
General movement and shifting	23·1	4·4	48·2	24·3
Nod yes	4·6	56·5	21·3	18·5
Smile	33·4	8·3	36·1	22·3
Talk	7·4	60·1	19·9	12·5
Smoke	36·5	12·2	10·2	41·1

Table 5. Percentage of variance accounted for by persons and situations (Moos, 1969). (The last column refers to variation between different occasions of observation.)

This general pattern of results has been confirmed by a series of studies of different populations, and using different variables (Bowers, 1973). The overall results are very clear: situations are at least as important as persons, and P × S interaction is more important than either. It is now recognized that this kind of research cannot establish whether personality or situation is more important, for various reasons (Argyle, 1976). Nevertheless, the results clearly favour the interactionist position.

In order to predict how a particular person will behave in a particular situation, we need to know something else – the equation showing how P and S interact, which is of the general form

$$B = f(P, S)$$

This states that the amount of some form of behaviour is a mathematical function of personality and situation variables. Such equations can be given by graphs showing how behaviour is a function of person and situation. Below is an example, from a study of reactions to role conflict (Figure 15). Notice that only people with high neurotic anxiety are affected by role conflict. Notice also that experienced conflict is greater when actual role conflict is high (situation), and for people with high neurotic anxiety (personality), but is most affected by an interaction between the two (P × S).

It has been suggested that perhaps people really are consistent across situations, but only in those traits which are important to them (Bem and Allen, 1974). This has been confirmed by studies in which subjects were invited to nominate traits relevant for them, or in which they thought they were consistent. Those most frequently

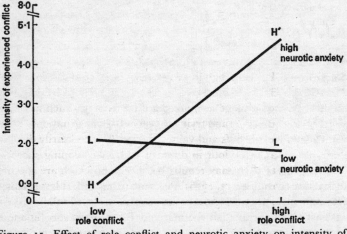

Figure 15. Effect of role conflict and neurotic anxiety on intensity of experienced conflict (Kahn *et al.*, 1964).

nominated included 'friendly' and 'assertive', while 'relaxed' was
rarely put forward (Kenrick and Stringfield, 1980).

Which people are most consistent? Is it not the case that some people are
more consistent across situations than others, so that there are at
least some individuals for whom the trait model works? Mental
patients, perhaps surprisingly, are found to be *more* consistent. Moos
(1968), for example, studied twenty-two patients and ten staff in
nine situations in the hospital, observing five aspects of their
behaviour. The percentages of P, S and P × S variance for patients
and staff are shown below:

Source	Patients	Staff
Persons	30·0	6·8
Situations	1·7	12·6
Persons × Situations	17·0	25·4

Snyder (1979) found that people who monitor their own behaviour carefully, and who are consequently very aware of their
effect on others, are less consistent, but generally more highly
skilled, than those who make a point of their straightforwardness
and sincerity (p. 208). Consistency is greater among those who are
high in 'internal control' and more resistant to situational pressures. This dimension of personality can be measured by a questionnaire which asks how much an individual feels that he can control
what happens in situations, as opposed to the effects of chance or
other people. Persons high in internal control are found to be less
affected by social pressures, though they are influenced by reasoned
arguments; they engage in more cognitive activity, such as being
alert, asking questions and trying to find out about situations. They
will stick to their beliefs and values, but do not necessarily display
the same social behaviour in different situations; coping successfully with a situation may require social moves which are specific
to that situation (Phares, 1976). Women are somewhat less consistent than men, thus confirming an ancient piece of folklore, and
we found that the British are more consistent than the Japanese
(Argyle, Shimoda and Little, 1978), mainly because of the elaborate
rules of etiquette for particular situations in Japan.

Limitations of the interactionist model This model has a number of limitations arising out of certain features of social behaviour. In the first place, people do not usually enter situations because psychologists put them there, but because they choose to enter them, and their choice reflects their personality. An example of this is the choice of situations made by extraverts: they select leisure occasions involving social interaction, like parties and dances, much more often than do introverts, and they spend more time playing games, walking and pursuing other physical activities (Furnham, 1981). Another example of choice is the selection of occupation: people decide on jobs where they can be creative, help others or make money, and this reflects their pattern of interests and values (Argyle, 1972). Authoritarian students at American universities often leave to join military academies.

When a person has chosen a situation or a series of situations in this way, it also affects his personality. Runyan (1978) has shown how the stages through which a person becomes a drug addict can be traced as a series of choices of situations, each of which has implications for the next condition of the personality. For instance, at the period of regular use, the drug is readily available, most friends are drug users, and the desire for the drug is intense. Each step that is taken creates a quite new $P \times S$ equation, by changing the situation, and eventually changing the state of the personality. It is possible to anticipate such changes, or to bring them about deliberately, by committing oneself to a series of situational experiences, such as going to one kind of educational establishment or another, one kind of job or another, or a course of encounter group meetings.

A second problem is that as well as choosing situations, people can change them once they are there. Some people turn every situation into a party, or try to. Informal situations, where a wide range of behaviour is permitted, can be modified, or 'redefined', quite a lot in this way; more formal situations cannot be changed much. Very often, individuals are not aware of the extent of their impact on others. They think that they are constantly encountering others who are bad-tempered, shy or very friendly, for example, without realizing that they themselves are the real cause of this behaviour (Wachtel, 1973). We will discuss below the problems of predicting the behaviour of two people in combination.

Behaviour sometimes cannot be understood apart from the situation in which it occurs, and the same is true of the personalities of those involved. The behaviour of, for example, Mrs Thatcher and Mrs Billy Jean King, takes place in certain very distinctive settings, like Parliament and Wimbledon. In order to understand or predict their behaviour we need to appreciate the properties of these settings. Traits like extraversion, or categories of behaviour like amount of talk, don't help very much.

Our task is to understand the ways in which properties of persons interact with properties of situations. The interactionist approach has uncovered some of these ways. We now turn to the analysis of social situations, and then finally to the analysis of personality.

THE ANALYSIS OF SITUATIONS

It is now clear that the situation is an important factor in the generation of social behaviour. We need to measure, classify or otherwise analyse situations, in order to explain and predict the behaviour that occurs in them. One way of doing this is to find the dimensions along which people discriminate situations one from another. In multi-dimensional scaling, subjects rate the similarity of pairs of situations, as well as their scores, on a number of marker scales, which are used to interpret the dimensions extracted. Wish and Kaplan (1977) have found the following dimensions of situations, using this approach:

cooperative and friendly – competitive and hostile;
dominant – equal;
intense – superficial;
formal and cautious – informal and open;
task-oriented – social.

While these dimensions are obviously useful and important, they tell us only part of the story about situations. Take a particular combination – task-oriented, dominant, formal and intense: this includes a wide variety of situations which are quite different – religious confession, psychotherapy, selection interview, teaching, supervision of work and so on. Each is quite different in terms of the goals of the participants, the behaviour that occurs and the rules which must be followed. I would suggest that situations cannot entirely be reduced to dimensions (as in physics), but are in some ways more like the discrete discontinuous elements of chemistry, each with its own internal structure.

Social situations are like games: they have goals, rules and repertoires of moves, and they require special skills. If someone wanted to play, for example, American football, he would want to know how to win, what the rules are and so on. Clients for social skills training often seek similar instructions about parties, interviews or other occasions which they find difficult.

Social situations probably exist as regular events in the culture because they enable common needs to be met. The rules and other component features of situations are functional because then they make this process easier. The main components of situations are listed and discussed below.

Goals In all situations there are certain goals which are commonly obtainable. It is often fairly obvious what these are, but socially inadequate people may simply not know what parties are for, for example, or may think that the purpose of a selection interview is vocational guidance.

We have studied the main goals in a number of common situations by asking samples of people to rate the importance of various goals, and then carrying out factor analysis. The main goals are usually:

    social acceptance;
    food, drink and other bodily needs;
    task goals specific to the situation.

We have also studied the relationships between goals, within and between persons, in terms of conflict and instrumentality. This makes it possible to study the 'goal structure' of situations. An example is given in Figure 16, showing that the only conflict between nurses and patients is between the nurses' concern for the bodily well-being of the patients and for the well-being of themselves (Graham, Argyle and Furnham, 1980).

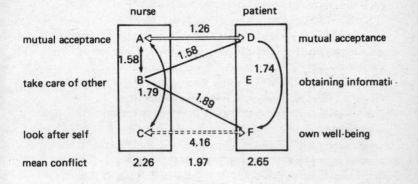

Figure 16. The goal structure for nurse and patient (from Graham, Argyle and Furnham, 1980).

Rules All situations have rules about what may or may not be done in them. Socially inexperienced people are often ignorant or mistaken about the rules. It would obviously be impossible to play a game without knowing the rules and the same applies to social situations.

By a rule we mean a shared belief that certain things should or should not be done. Figure 17 shows a cluster analysis of the rules we found for Oxford psychology students. The top cluster consists of those which apply to nearly all situations – should be friendly, should be polite, etc. The last cluster shows those for sherry parties and similar occasions – should dress smartly, should keep to cheerful topics of conversation, etc. There were two specific rules for going to the doctor – make sure you are clean and tell the truth. Some of these rules are clearly functional in relation to the goals of situations.

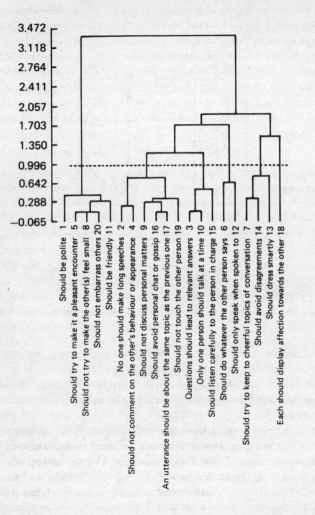

Figure 17. Clusters of rules for Oxford psychology students (from Argyle *et al.*, 1979).

Repertoire of elements Every situation defines certain moves as relevant. For example, at a seminar it is relevant to show slides, make long speeches, draw on the blackboard, etc. If moves appropriate to a cricket match or a Scottish ball were made, they would be ignored or regarded as totally bizarre. We have found 65–90 main elements used in several situations, like going to the doctor. We have also found that the grouping of elements varies between situations. For example, asking questions about work and about private life are quite similar on a date, but totally different in the office (Argyle *et al.*, 1982).

Environmental setting Environmental psychologists sometimes assess situations in purely physical terms. It has been found, for example, that if people meet in a room at a temperature of 93·5°F, or with four square feet per person, they will like each other less than in a larger and cooler room (Griffitt and Veitch, 1971). However, the physical features of the environment work in another way, by their symbolic meaning. A room decorated in red and yellow suggests a warm emotional mood; placing some people at a greater height, as on a high table, suggests dominance; a room with a concrete floor, battered furniture and a bare light bulb suggests prison or interrogation, not love, work, social life or committee meetings. Many situations involve special props – a lecture needs a blackboard and slide projector, while a party needs quite different equipment.

Concepts In order to play cricket one must know the meaning of 'innings', 'over', 'out' and so on. In order to carry out psychotherapy one needs to know about 'resistance' and 'transference'. As a chess player becomes more experienced, he acquires more elaborate concepts, like 'fork', 'discovered check' and so on. Similar knowledge is needed in social situations proper, and perhaps the kinds of concepts introduced in this book provide what is necessary for many of them. Examples are 'mutual gaze', 'terminal gaze', 'synchronizing', 'reinforcement', 'remedial sequence', 'informal speech', and 'self-presentation'. There are concepts to describe different kinds of person, and different kinds of situation, as well as ongoing social interaction. There are also concepts related to the task, such as 'amendment', 'straw vote' and 'nem con' for committee meetings.

Roles In most situations people adopt roles specific to the occasion, like those of doctor and patient, salesman and customer. The goals can be similar, but the rules different, for those in distinct roles, like the chairman, secretary or treasurer of a club. There may be roles created by the situation, like those of guest and host, and also more general ones, such as age and sex.

Special skills In order to play a game like ice-hockey, polo or water-polo, certain skills have to be mastered. Many social situations require special skills, as in the case of various kinds of public speaking and interviewing or such everyday situations as dates and parties. A person with little experience of a particular situation may find that he lacks the necessary skills.

This method of analysing situations opens the way to a number of useful applications. Some forms of crime are most easily tackled by situational modifications; for example, shoplifting can be greatly reduced by closed-circuit TV and by chaining up the goods, vandalism by buildings which have better lighting and surveillance, stronger materials and rougher surfaces (Clarke and Mayhew, 1980). Social skills training for mental patients can be focused on the situations which they find troublesome (p. 283). Difficult situations anywhere can be modified by altering the physical setting, the rules or other components (Argyle, Furnham and Graham, 1982).

THE MAIN FEATURES OF PERSONS

There is no denying the existence of personality. Everyone has a distinct biography as well as relatively stable underlying properties – some of them physiological – which generate distinctive behaviour in every situation they enter. These properties also generate a very wide range of behaviour in different situations. When familiar personality variables are mentioned in this section, it should be understood that they operate in conjunction with properties of situations, including the properties of others present. There are many features of persons which affect their behaviour on certain occasions, but the following have frequently been found to be important.

1 *Motivation* Several kinds of motivation were described in Chapter 1. A person can be analysed in terms of the main goals he seeks and the structure of sub-goals. If a person is high in affiliative motivation for example, he will seek out situations where it can be gratified; when he is in a suitable situation this need system will become aroused, and he will try to establish warm and intimate relationships. To simplify things, a person's motivations can be expressed in terms of the two dimensions *friendly–hostile* and *dominant–submissive* (p. 143).

2 *Biological core* Research on personality has consistently yielded the two dimensions *introversion–extraversion* and *neuroticism* (or *anxiety*)–*stability*. These are partly inherited, and are related to physique and the way in which the brain functions (Eysenck and Eysenck, 1969). They correlate with many aspects of social behaviour, though the relationships are not very strong. For example, extraverts tend to talk, look at others and conform more, but also to be chosen as leaders and to be more persuasive. They engage in more sex, aggression, drinking and smoking, and they choose situations where social activity takes place. This can be explained in terms of their *lower* level of arousal, i.e. they seek further stimulation (p. 15) and have a greater need for affiliation (Morris, 1979).

It is now possible to measure *state* anxiety, i.e. how anxious people feel at a particular moment, as distinct from *trait* anxiety, i.e. how anxious they usually feel (Spielberger, 1972).

3 *Intelligence and other abilities* Intelligent people are more likely to become leaders of groups of children or students but not of groups of delinquents or anti-school cliques. This depends on the situation, in that the individual with the greatest ability at the group task is most likely to become the leader. If the task changes, the leader may change also: for example, delinquent gangs have different leaders

when playing football from when being delinquent. Intelligence fits the earlier trait model quite well, since if A is more intelligent than B, we know that A will do better at a wide range of tasks, but there is usually *something* that B can do better through possessing special abilities.

Another quite different area of ability is social competence. It is not yet known how far there is a general factor affecting competence in all situations. There are certainly a number of special social skills which can only be used in specific settings, such as making speeches, teaching, interviewing and carrying out psychotherapy. Methods of measuring social competence are described on pp. 76f.

4 *Demographic variables* Age, sex, class and race each affect behaviour in two quite different ways. In the first place, older people really are different from younger ones in a number of measurable respects, and their social behaviour is different. The same is true of males and females and members of different social classes, though most of these differences are learnt aspects of sub-cultures, like having different accents and attitudes. In addition, males and females, and the old and the young, occupy different positions in society, and others treat them accordingly.

5 *Physique and appearance* These also affect social behaviour in two ways. Correlations have been found between physique and temperament – muscular individuals tend to be aggressive and extraverted, thin people to be tense and intelligent; fat people to be placid and happy (Parnell, 1958) – and as we have seen, people react towards tall men and attractive girls in special ways (p. 110).

6 *Cognitive structure* We have seen that individuals perceive and interpret events in accordance with their system of cognitive categories; different ways of labelling and interpreting events lead to different patterns of behaviour. Attitudes, beliefs and ideology represent larger systems of interpretation of events. They include values and the broader goals which an individual considers worthwhile – medical, moral, aesthetic, political or religious, for example. One of the most important pieces of cognitive structure is the

self-image, which affects social behaviour in a number of ways (see Chapter 9).

7 *Situation-linked features of persons* One way of describing persons is to list the situations which they most enjoy or in which they spend most time. Joan is happiest in church, museums and libraries, and is clearly different from George, who prefers pubs, noisy parties and football grounds. It is also interesting to know the range of situations a person avoids or finds difficult.

People have a wide range of relationships and exhibit different styles of interaction in each of them. Figure 20 (pp. 148–9) shows the averaged results obtained by Wish, Deutsch and Kaplan (1976) for eighty-seven students of teaching and management. The relationships are plotted onto four of the dimensions found. Any individual will have his own pattern of variation and grouping of relationships.

The seven areas of personality listed above provide much information relevant to social behaviour, and numerous studies have shown that social performance can be predicted from them. We have said nothing about the internal 'dynamics' of persons, that is, their motivational conflicts and the ways they are resolved; these must affect social behaviour too, in ways mainly unknown. I shall discuss one area of personality dynamics in Chapter 9, in connection with the self-image.

SELECTING SOCIAL BEHAVIOUR TO DEAL WITH THE OTHER

We have already seen that the same person varies his behaviour from one situation to another – parties, interviews, etc. – in keeping with their different rules and conventions. People also vary their behaviour according to the age, sex and social class of those present, and in accordance with other role-relationships. Some people behave so differently towards men and women that they seem to undergo a personality change when moving from one kind of encounter to the other. A young man may be very relaxed with other men, but terrified of women, or aggressive and competitive towards men and very amorous and at ease with women. Such differences of behaviour are learnt in the course of relations with parents, and later with male and female members of the peer group during adolescence.

Age is a more differentiated variable than sex: some people have alternative ways of behaving towards young children, older children, teenagers, young adults, etc., with any number of fine variations; others may use broader divisions, e.g. between those who are older or younger than themselves.

Social class, especially in Britain, is an important dimension for the classification of others for most people. Authoritarians in particular treat those of greater or less status and power quite differently – deferring to the one, and dominating the other. It is found that salesgirls in retail stores categorize the customers in terms of class, and feel nervous and apprehensive about the upper-middle-class ones, because of the haughty manner they are felt to adopt (Woodward, 1960).

Social class and age each have two separate effects on the social techniques adopted. Firstly there is the question of whether the other person is higher or lower, secondly of how great the social distance. There may be certain age or class groups for which a person has virtually no social techniques at all – he is simply unable to interact with members of them. This can be observed among some adults in relation to children, some upper-middle-class and working-class people in relation to each other, some adolescents in relation to adults, and many children in relation to adults outside the family circle. This no doubt reflects a lack of experience with the groups in question, combined with the discovery that the familiar social techniques are completely useless.

Introverts and extraverts need to be handled differently. Experiments with schoolchildren show that introverts respond better to praise, while extraverts respond better to blame. Variation of motivation in others means that they will strive for different goals in social situations and can be rewarded in different ways. One may need a strong leader, another a submissive follower, a third needs acceptance of his self-image, and so on. For those very low in affiliative needs the usual social rewards will not be satisfactory.

Variations in anxiety, or neuroticism, mean that some people will be very ill at ease in social situations. When with them it is important to adopt social techniques which will reduce their anxiety (pp. 54f). Experienced interviewers may spend a large part of an interview doing just this.

Attitudes to authority and to the peer group are important. Juvenile delinquents are often very hostile to authority but behave quite differently with members of their peer group. Those in authority can only handle such boys and girls if they adopt the manner of an older member of the peer group, and make special efforts to win their confidence, such as taking them into their confidence or granting special privileges.

THE COORDINATION OF SOCIAL BEHAVIOUR

Two people may meet, each with his own social drives and his own social skills, but there will be no proper interaction unless the two sets of techniques mesh together in a synchronized and coordinated manner. If both talk all the time, or if both shout orders or ask questions, to give three obvious cases, there cannot be said to be social interaction at all. Between such extreme cases and a well-conducted interview or a conversation between friends, there are degrees of coordination of behaviour. Rather low on the scale, for example, would be conversation with a schizophrenic, with long pauses, irrelevant remarks and inappropriate emotions being expressed. Synchronization is necessary along a number of different dimensions for smooth and motivationally satisfying interaction to take place.

1 *Amount of speech* In most conversations between two people, there is enough talk for nearly all of the time to be filled. If they speak more than this, there will be interruption and double-speaking; if they speak less than this, there will be periods of silence.

There also has to be synchronizing of the speed or tempo of interaction – the actual rate of speaking in words per second, the shortness of the interval before replying and the rate of movements of eyes, facial expression and other parts of the body.

2 *Dominance* This is a matter partly of who speaks most, and partly of the degrees of deference with which A and B treat each other – of

whose ideas are to be taken most seriously and of who shall for purposes of the encounter be regarded as the more important person. If A and B both want to be the dominant member, there is incompatibility of styles – both may give orders, but none are obeyed.

3 *Intimacy* This we have discussed previously (p. 88) and shown to be a matter of physical closeness, eye-contact, conversation on personal topics and so on. If A uses techniques corresponding to greater intimacy than B, A will feel that B is cold, formal and stand-offish, while B will feel that A is intrusive and over familiar.

4 *Emotional tone* If A is elated and euphoric while B is anxious or depressed, there is incongruity. To everything that happens A and B are likely to react in quite different ways, involving incompatible reactions and remarks.

5 *Role-relations and definitions of the situation* Two people must agree on the role-relation between them. If one is to be a teacher the other must behave like a pupil, if one is to be an interviewer then the other must behave like an interviewee.

6 *Task, topic and definition of the situation* Two people must agree on what the encounter is for, just as they must agree to play the same game, not different ones. They also have to agree on the different phases or episodes of the encounter.

As we have seen, however, everyone has a wide range of styles of interaction to suit a range of different relationships. Individuals also have preferences for certain styles, while there may be some they cannot manage at all.

To begin with a simple case, can we predict how much A and B will each talk when they meet? It is found that A's talkativeness is related, rather weakly, to his talkativeness in other similar situations; it is also *inversely* related to the normal talkativeness of B, i.e. a normally silent person talks more with silent people, a normally talkative person talks less with normally talkative people (Borgatta and Bales, 1953). Clearly people often have to shift from their average behaviour in order to accommodate others. But who will shift the most? There may be a 'struggle for the floor', in which they interrupt or try to shout each other down. When A does this he frustrates B; he may make B less friendly or even cause him to leave the situation. However, A can interrupt B safely under two conditions:

1 if A has sufficient power over B;
2 if A has sufficient skill to interrupt without upsetting B.

How can we predict the dominance relations between A and B? Dominance includes taking decisions, influencing the other, controlling the pattern of behaviour, as well as usually talking more. Simply measuring A's 'dominance' gives a rather poor prediction of his dominance in relation to B. A better prediction can be made from role variables: the person who is older, male rather than female, or of higher social class, is likely to be dominant (Breer, 1960), though the dominance of males seems to be diminishing. If these variables are held constant, the person with the highest score on questionnaire measures of extraversion, intelligence and dominance, or who knows most about the task in hand, will dominate.

Let us consider a more complex prediction of both dominance and intimacy. We will take account of the motivations of A and B in the figure below. This shows that A is strong in both dominance and affiliative needs, and prefers to be in a warm and superior relation to others. B prefers a warm and submissive relation, so they would get on smoothly together. C and D are also in equilibrium – both are hostile and C is slightly superior to D.

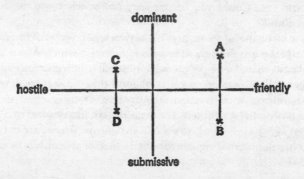

On the other hand, in the next diagram X and Y are not in equilibrium – X is friendly while Y is hostile, and both want to dominate. If Y is able to get more of his way than X, they might move to X'Y'.

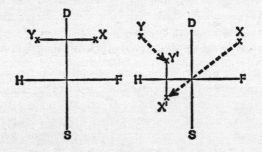

Let us take another case, where A and B play incompatible roles. For example an inexperienced interviewee thinks he has come for a pleasant chat, or to receive free vocational guidance. If one person adopts a certain role, it may force the other to adopt the complementary role that goes with it, particularly if the first person is powerful, and is in charge of the situation. If one person plays the role of interviewer the other person is more or less compelled to behave like a candidate. An interviewer can use other methods to modify a candidate's behaviour. The interviewer can modify the candidate's behaviour by (a) using non-verbal signals and reinforcements to control the candidate, (b) explaining the normal procedure, and (c) controlling the candidate by the content of his remark, e.g. 'Could you tell me, *very briefly*, what you do in your spare time?'

It may be useful to distinguish between two levels of interaction here. There are the *alternative styles of behaviour* which A can adopt, and as we have seen people have quite a wide repertoire of such styles. At a more microscopic level are the *negotiating signals* used to communicate with B about the pattern of interaction or role-relationship to be adopted. For example, an interviewer may use a verbal negotiating signal to explain the normal procedure to B; or A may use non-verbal signals for dominance or friendship to modify B's behaviour.

When A is in charge he can use explicit, verbal negotiating signals about how he wants the other to behave. In most other situations such instructions would be unacceptable and ineffective – it is not usually possible to tell one's friends or colleagues to talk less or to be less dominating. Here non-verbal negotiating signals are normally used; they have the advantage that they are small and tentative, can be easily withdrawn, can be used to explore other possible relationships without embarrassment, and operate away from the focus of conscious attention of either party (cf. Mehrabian, 1969).

Sometimes the style of behaviour acts also as a negotiating signal. This happens if A firmly adopts a particular role and pushes B into the complementary role ('altercasting'), as when a doctor behaves like a doctor so that the patient has to behave like a patient. Here is an example of someone *not* accepting the proffered role:

PLAYBOY: How do you get your kicks these days?

DYLAN: I hire people to look into my eyes, and then I have them kick me.

PLAYBOY: And that's the way you get your kicks?

DYLAN: No. Then I forgive them, that's where my kicks come in.

PLAYBOY: Did you ever have the standard boyhood dream of growing up to be President?

DYLAN: No. When I was a boy, Harry Truman was President. Who'd want to be Harry Truman?

PLAYBOY: Well, let's suppose that you were the President. What would you accomplish during your first thousand days?

DYLAN: Well, just for laughs so long as you insist, the first thing I'd do is probably move the White House. Instead of being in Texas it'd be in the East Side of New York, McGeorge Bundy would definitely have to change his name and General McNamara would be forced to wear a coonskin cap and shades.

[Brackman, 1967]

How can we tell which person will have to adjust most in a situation where the interaction styles of the two people are initially incompatible? There are a number of ways in which a person may acquire the power to control the way in which the interaction proceeds:

1 A may have formal power over B, so that he is able to deliver major rewards and punishments, as in the case of foremen or parents;

2 A may be less attracted towards the situation, and therefore less dependent on it, than B: this is the reason that performers in some situations avoid close friendships with those they have to deal with;

3 A can provide large rewards for B in that he can help B to attain some goal, whether social or otherwise;

4 if A for some reason is able to initiate the interaction, as in the case of waiters or salesmen, this gives him the chance to control the course of interaction;

5 if A is less sensitive than B to minor negative reactions from the other, or is less concerned about them, he will adjust his behaviour less; however, if he goes too far in ignoring B's responses and does not provide large enough rewards for B in compensation, B may simply withdraw.

It has been seen how everyone has a profile of motivation, so that certain drives are particularly strong and certain goals will be sought in social situations. The more a person can succeed in establishing the pattern of behaviour which meets his needs, the more he will enjoy the situation; the more he has to move away from his preferred interaction pattern, the less he will like it. On the other hand, there may be other compensatory rewards provided by a particular situation or person, in which case he will on balance still be drawn towards it or him, but in a conflicting way, generating internal tension.

FURTHER READING

Argyle, M., Furnham, A., and Graham, J. A., *Social Situations*, Cambridge University Press, 1982.

Furnham, A., and Argyle, M. (eds.), *The Psychology of Social Situations*, Pergamon, 1981.

CHAPTER 7

TWO-PERSON RELATIONSHIPS

IN this chapter we move from the study of short-term encounters to long-term relationships. Much of our social behaviour, and most of that which is important to us, is with family, friends, work-mates, neighbours or others whom we have known for some time. Many problems which mental patients and clients for social skills training present are in this area. Many people can't make friends, and a third of marriages in Britain end in divorce.

We will start by looking at two important features of all relationships – attraction and influence, anticipated by Dale Carnegie in the title of his famous book *How to Win Friends and Influence People* (1936). It is interesting that in the U.S.A. the most popular form of social skills training is in assertiveness, while in Britain it has been directed more towards making friends.

HOW TO WIN FRIENDS AND INFLUENCE PEOPLE: I MAKING FRIENDS

A number of conditions affect the chances of two people liking one another. This may result in friendship, love or simply enjoying each other's company at work.

Proximity and frequency of interaction Frequent interaction can come about from living in adjacent rooms or houses, working in the same office, belonging to the same club and so on. Interaction can lead to liking, but liking leads to more interaction; in other words, a positive feedback cycle is started, which is halted by competing attractions and the increasing difficulties of accommodation with greater intimacy – like two hedgehogs trying to keep warm. Only certain kinds of interaction lead to liking, as has been shown in research on inter-racial contacts. Two people should be of equal status and members of the same group, cooperating in the pursuit of identical goals. This is the first stage in forming a relationship; the next is finding out if those involved have enough in common.

Similarity People like others who are similar to themselves in certain respects. They like those with similar attitudes, beliefs and values, who have a similar regional and social class background, and who have similar jobs or leisure interests, but not necessarily those who have similar personalities. Again there is a cyclical process, since similarity leads to liking and liking leads to similarity. The effects of similarity on liking have been shown experimentally; for example, Griffit and Veitch (1974) paid thirteen male subjects to spend ten days in a fall-out shelter, and found that those who shared opinions liked each other most by the end of the ten days. Similarity in attitudes important to those concerned has most effect. Duck (1973) has produced evidence that similarity of cognitive constructs is important, i.e. the categories used for describing other people (pp. 106f.). As far as other aspects of personality are concerned, it now seems that neither similarity nor complementarity have much effect on friendship.

Reinforcement The next general principle governing liking is the extent to which one person satisfies the needs of another. This was shown by Jennings (1950) in a study of four hundred girls in a reformatory. She found that the popular girls helped and protected others, encouraged and cheered them up, made them feel accepted and wanted, controlled their own moods so as not to inflict anxiety or depression on others, were able to establish rapport quickly, won the confidence of a wide variety of personalities and were concerned with the feelings and needs of others. The unpopular girls, on the other hand, were dominating, aggressive and boastful, demanded attention and tried to get others to do things for them. This pattern has been generally interpreted in terms of the popular girls providing rewards and minimizing costs, while the unpopular girls tried to get rewards for themselves and incurred costs for others. The activities of the popular girls could also be interpreted in terms of 'social support'. It is not necessary for the other person to be the actual source of rewards: Lott and Lott (1960) found that children who were given model cars by the experimenter liked the other children in the experiment more.

Equity There is evidence that people like their relationships to be equitable, i.e. of such a nature that each gets satisfaction in proportion to what he or she puts in. If this is not the case, participants are likely to withdraw. These inputs and outputs can cover a wide field; for example, being young and attractive, of high status and contributing most of the money are inputs, while being cooked for, given lifts or helped with work are outputs. It has been found among young couples that individuals who feel they are under-benefiting *or* over-benefiting are less happy than those who think matters are equitable (Figure 18).

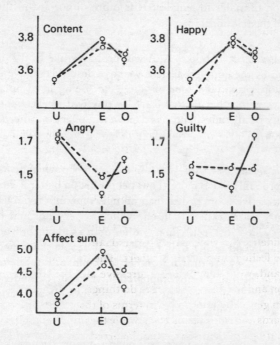

Figure 18. Mood measure as a function of the perceived equity–inequity in marriage. ♂ = men; ♀ = women; U = underbenefited; E = equitably treated; O = overbenefited (Hatfield *et al.*, 1979).

There is doubt, however, as to whether equity is equally important in other relationships – mother and child or long-married couples, for example. We have seen that kin may care for each other in order to promote their own genes (p. 19), and it has been suggested that equity may apply to friends while altruism applies to kin (Alexander, 1979). Experiments have shown that where two people are seen to engage in reciprocation of a reward by a very similar one, the relationship is perceived as less close (Clark, 1981). In an intimate relationship, if A provides some gratification for B, A finds it rewarding too, as when a mother gives her child a present.

Physical attractiveness As we showed above (pp. 110f.), this is important for friendship as well as love, though particularly in the attraction of males to females. It is more important in the early stages of the relationship.

Reciprocated liking If B likes A, A will probably like B. B's liking is signalled by the non-verbal signs we have described above – facial expression, proximity, tone of voice, etc. Being liked by another combines with other factors, such as physical attractiveness and similarity of attitudes, and has a powerful effect on interpersonal attraction.

Emotional state of the chosen If A is in a good mood when he meets B, he will probably like B more. Thus people get on better if they meet in an attractive room rather than an ugly one, in a room which is pleasantly warm rather than one which is very hot and humid, when they have just seen a funny rather than a sad film or when they have heard good rather than bad news. If people share emotional experiences they are drawn together. The most dramatic cases of inter-racial attitudes being improved have occurred under conditions of high arousal, such as fighting side-by-side and serving on ships together (Amir, 1969).

Need for affiliation Some people simply want more friends and social contact than others. Affiliative motivation can be measured by a scale with items like 'I join clubs because it is such a good way to make friends' (Mehrabian, 1970). Extraversion is a similar dimension; we have seen that extraverts seek out social situations (p. 120). There is a sex difference here: women spend more time than men with friends or in the company of others.

Self-disclosure As two people get to know one another more, they disclose increasingly intimate information about themselves. Self-disclosure can be measured on a scale (1–5) with items like:

the types of play and recreation that I enjoy (1·01);
how often I have sexual experiences and the nature of these experiences (4·31)

(Jourard, 1971)

Taylor (1965) studied pairs of students who shared rooms at college. The amount of self-disclosure increased during the first nine weeks and then levelled off, but at quite different degrees of intimacy for different pairs (see Figure 19). The main increase was at the most superficial level; there was not much increase of disclosure about intimate matters and basic values. Other studies show that intimate disclosure is increased when two people are isolated, and that if A discloses to B, B will disclose to A. More disclosure is possible when people come to trust each other – they know that another will not laugh at or reject them, or pass on their confessions to others or use them to his or her own advantage (Naegele, 1958).

Self-disclosure is more important to females than males: they disclose more and are disclosed to more, as in the case of pairs of female friends.

Building a shared life In the case of marriage and the other long-term relationships there are further sources of attachment, arising out of shared activities.

1 In addition to self-disclosure, there is also a great deal of talk, in the course of which a shared cognitive world is built up, in which there is confidence because it is shared. Women friends talk a great

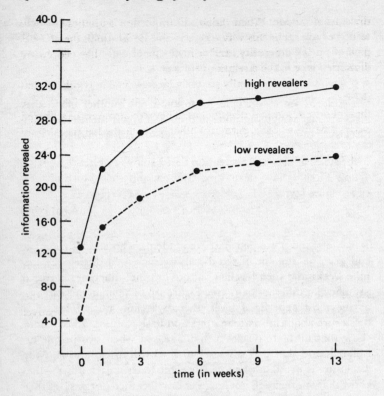

Figure 19. Amount of disclosure over time of high- and low-revealers (Taylor, 1965).

deal, disclose more and drink a lot of tea and coffee together; so do most married couples and people at work, though the range of topics here is more limited. This is perhaps the main female form of attachment.

2 Many activities which are important to us, at work, in the home or for leisure, require the cooperation of other people: their behaviour is needed in conjunction with our own, so they become necessary to us. Male friends *do* things together, e.g. play golf or squash; married couples share domestic jobs; and at work there is

division of labour. When daily and important activities are sustained regularly in this way, there is a sense in which the other is part of one's personality, and it is not surprising that people are distressed when such a relationship is ended.

3 Two people are usually part of a larger social network, so that their relationship is supported by the others in the network, e.g. their children, kin and neighbours. They are also part of a shared environment – a house, garden or office – which also helps to sustain their relationship.

HOW TO WIN FRIENDS AND INFLUENCE PEOPLE:
II INFLUENCING PEOPLE

In any relationship it is not enough to agree with the other person all the time, since this would lead to frustration and eventual discontent. Special skills are needed to be sufficiently assertive without damaging the relationship. These are suggested by Table 6, which shows how dominant and affiliative styles are related. It is the top right-hand corner, warm and dominant, which is most effective.

	dominance	
	analyses	advises
	criticizes	coordinates
	disapproves	directs
	judges	leads
low affiliation	resists	initiates
	evades	acquiesces
	concedes	agrees
	relinquishes	assists
	retreats	cooperates
	withdraws	obliges
	dependency	high affiliation

Table 6. Combinations of dominant and affiliative techniques (Gough, 1957).

One of the keys to successful leadership is consultation; it is found that people act with more enthusiasm if they have been consulted and have helped to make a decision. This principle applies to all face-to-face social influence, and means that the other person has to be persuaded and agree with what he is to do.

Non-verbal signals Requests need to be made in a sufficiently assertive manner. We discussed these non-verbal cues earlier – talking loudly and most of the time in a confident tone of voice, interrupting others, adopting an attentive but unsmiling facial expression, and an erect posture with the head tilted back, shoulders squared and hands on hips. For most situations rather small amounts of these signals will be enough, and again these social techniques must be combined with sufficient warmth and rewardingness to keep the other in the situation. There is a clear difference between assertive and aggressive behaviour: aggressive behaviour may or may not produce the desired influence, but it also damages the relationship.

Reinforcement It is possible to influence another's behaviour in the immediate situation by systematic rewarding of the desired behaviour immediately it takes place, and non-reward or punishment of other behaviour. Rewards based on the need for affiliation include smiling, looking, agreement, head-nodding, etc. Punishment could consist of frowning, looking away, looking bored, looking at a watch, disagreeing, etc. It may be easier to influence another person in this way if he is of higher status, where direct influence might be inappropriate. Members of groups often conform because they want to be accepted rather than rejected. Endler (1965) found that conformity could be increased if the experimenter reinforced it, and reduced if the experimenter reinforced nonconformity.

Using the personal relationship It is easier to influence another person if they like you, because they do not want to lose your approval or damage the relationship. This is the basis of ingratiation.

Reciprocation of favours This is similar to the above. If A does something for B first, B is more likely to do what A asks. Regan

(1971) found that subjects bought twice as many raffle tickets from a confederate who had previously bought them a Coke, compared with other confederates. This kind of reciprocity or exchange of gifts plays an even more important part in African countries, where officials often have to be bribed (as we call it) before they will be helpful.

Persuasion The design of persuasive messages has been studied most in connection with the mass media, but some of the principles apply in face-to-face situations. It is necessary to appeal to the needs, values or interests of the other in some way, and then show that what you want him to do will satisfy one of those needs: 'Come and do the washing-up while I change, then we will be able to go out to the pub earlier'; 'If you do some work during the holidays, you'll get better A levels and be more likely to get into university.' This may require some initial exploration of what the other does want, as when a salesman tries to find out the customer's needs. The objections to the behaviour being requested may be neutralized, by appealing to higher loyalties, denying that injury will result, or other ways of changing the way the act or the situation is perceived (Sykes and Matza, 1957): 'It's nothing, just a matter of taking a small present to a friend of mine in Amsterdam.' Moral exhortation on the other hand is no good if the exhorter is seen not to be behaving in this way himself (Bryan and Walbek, 1970). The very words used can create certain assumptions or ways of defining the problem – politicians may manage to make the public think primarily in terms of unemployment and the problems of social inequality, or alternatively of national prosperity and the creation of collective wealth. Similarly, face-to-face persuasion may be achieved by using the right rhetoric, making the other think in terms of your concepts.

Power Persuasion is more effective if the source of it is regarded as an expert – on university entrance, to take the earlier example. There are other kinds of power, such as the power to reward and punish, possessed by most formal leaders. This makes influence easier, particularly if the influencer is thought to be a *legitimate* source of directions, in view of his ability, experience, or his sheer rank in a hierarchy. In the well-known experiments by Milgram (1974) it was found that 65 per cent of subjects gave what they thought were 450-volt shocks to what they thought were other subjects, who gave signs of intense suffering and apparent collapse, because the experimenter ordered them to do so as part of a learning experiment. The most likely interpretation is that subjects assumed that the experimenter was in charge and knew what he was doing, therefore it was all right to do what he said. The experiment shows the very high degree of obedience which can be commanded by a legitimate leader, with no power to reward or punish.

Persuasive strategies By a 'strategy', I mean a planned sequence of at least two moves. These may be conscious and deliberate, as in some sales techniques, but they may also be acquired and used with little conscious awareness of what is being done. Interviewers commonly ask questions in a carefully prepared order; the more intimate ones come last, the most harmless ones first. A salesman may offer the most expensive objects first, and then produce cheaper ones, depending on the customer's reaction. This is similar to starting negotiations with exaggerated claims, with the intention of making concessions and extracting reciprocal concessions from the other party; this doesn't work if the initial demands are seen as bluffing. The foot-in-the-door technique consists of making a small request which is followed by a larger one. Freedman and Fraser (1966) found that if housewives had been asked to answer a few questions earlier, 53 per cent agreed to allow a survey team into their houses for two hours, compared with 22 per cent who had not been asked those questions. Another technique, known in the U.S.A. as 'low-balling', involves obtaining an initial agreement and following it with a series of extra charges or conditions. Cialdini *et al.* (1978) found that 55 per cent of subjects turned up for a 7 a.m. experiment if they had already agreed to take part without knowing at what time it would be, compared with 25 per cent of those who were invited directly to come at this hour.

THE RANGE OF RELATIONSHIPS

We will start by looking at the range of relationships and at the results obtained by Wish, Deutsch and Kaplan (1976). They carried out multidimensional scaling of ratings of a number of relationships as experienced and observed by American graduate students of teaching and management. The relationships are plotted against the four main dimensions which were obtained (see Figure 20). These results show clear differences between relationships, and I believe that there are quite basic distinctions between, for example, spouse and friends, and that these are not just matters of degree.

Argyle and Furnham (in press) carried out a study of the main sources of satisfaction and conflict in a wide range of relationships. Fifty-two subjects varying in age and sex, and generally of lower middle class, completed scales for fifteen sources of satisfaction and fifteen sources of conflict. There were three satisfaction factors:

1 instrumental reward, e.g. financial support: spouse and parents were highest;

2 emotional support: spouse highest, followed by siblings and friends, with neighbours and work-mates lowest;

3 shared interests: all were fairly high, but spouse was again highest.

There were two main sources of conflict:

1 emotional conflict: spouse and work superior were highest;

2 criticism: spouse, siblings and adolescent child highest.

It was interesting that spouse was highest on all three satisfaction factors and also on both conflict factors. Siblings, for young females, were also very high on both. Neighbours were the lowest source of satisfaction, followed by work-mates.

Can one relationship substitute and compensate for the absence of another? People certainly engage in substitution, but we don't know how satisfying this is. For example, unmarried people spend three times as much time as married people with friends, relatives and neighbours (Schneider, 1972), while old people who are unmarried are more likely to live with a child (usually a daughter) and

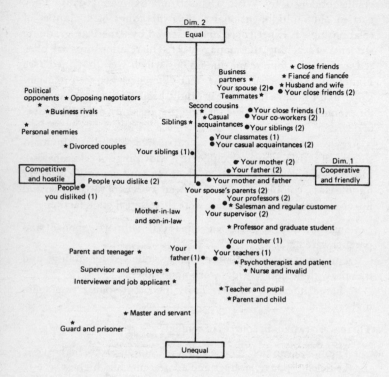

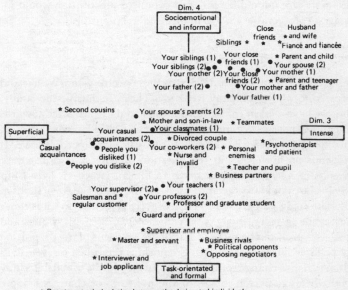

Figure 20. Four dimensions of relationships. There are twenty-five 'typical' (*) and nineteen 'own' (●) relationships (Wish, Deutsch and Kaplan, 1976).

to have seen one of their children or siblings in the last two days (Townsend, 1968). Only children are more likely to have an imaginary companion, and having a pet does not affect this (Manosevitz *et al.*, 1973). On the other hand, the activities normally carried out with spouse, friends and neighbours, for example, are quite different, and complete substitution would involve a considerable change in the usual relationship.

THE MAIN TYPES OF RELATIONSHIP

Friendship Friends can be defined as those people whom we like and trust, and whose company we enjoy. They are outside the family, but we have a lot in common with them and are attracted towards them. Friends are symmetrical and equal, unlike kin who are often of different age or social class. How many friends do people have? It depends on how you put the question, but if asked to list their friends people give around seven to fifteen. However, friendship choices are not always reciprocated. In Wellman's survey (1979) in Toronto only 36 per cent of choices were returned. Friends don't just come in pairs, though; they form networks, with cliques and chains, which can be more or less dense, in terms of the proportion of possible linkages taken up. Friendships don't last forever; children's friends change quite fast, and among adults friendships may end when one person moves to another town or changes his job. However, close links formed during adolescence may last a long time, and are also found to be the most intimate.

The nature of friendship can be understood by finding out what friends do together. In the survey by Argyle and Furnham described below it was found that friends talk, eat and drink, and engage in joint leisure, e.g. sport and dancing (p. 161).

Here, as in many other studies, a sizeable sex difference was found: women friends *talk*, drink coffee, disclose confidences and provide social support; men friends play squash, help each other and in a number of ways *do* things together – there is less disclosure and intimacy, though men often drink together and talk about work. As well as having fewer intimate friendships, men have fewer friends altogether, especially in middle age. The reason for these sex differences is not agreed upon: it could be male fear of homosexuality, male competitiveness at work and sport, or the fact that work contacts meet the same needs; or it may be that women have greater need of social support and greater skills at providing it.

There are even greater age differences. Between adolescence and the age of twenty-five friends may spend hours a day together; in middle age they may only meet once a month, family and social contacts at work seeming to have replaced friendships. Middle-aged people also find it more difficult to make new friends than when they were younger (Nicholson, 1980). Old people who are widowed or retired may spend time with their friends, but they are more likely to take up with their siblings or grown-up children. Allan (1979) found that, in the early 1970's, there were class differences in the nature of friendship. Working class people in Britain met acquaintances in specific settings, such as at work, the pub, the club or church, but did not usually see them in more than one setting and tended not to ask them home. They had fewer friends in the middle class sense, while kin were more important to them and did get asked home, or asked themselves.

The nature of friendship is shown in the study by Wish and colleagues: close friends are *equal*, *cooperative* and *friendly*, *socioemotional* and *informal*, and fairly *intense*. Our own study of the satisfactions derived from friendship found three main sources. (1) *Shared interests* (doing things together/joint leisure, talking about things of mutual concern, sharing common beliefs and values) provided nearly as great a source for same sex friends as for spouses, with all other relationships well behind in this respect. (2) *Emotional support* among friends was less important than between spouses but just more so than in other relationships, e.g. with members of the family or people from work. (3) On the *instrumental reward* scale, however (financial support, advice, working together, etc.), friends were quite low compared with spouses and parents. There are different kinds of friends, too. Bochner *et al.* (1977) found that foreign students in Hawaii had Hawaiian friends (for instrumental reasons, e.g. showing them the ropes) and friends from the same country (probably for emotional support and shared values).

Friends are expected to provide help when needed. This may be important for the young, but for adults the level of help provided by friends is quite low compared with that from kin. Friendship has been described as too fragile a relationship to stand the strains of giving major help, such as providing money or accommodation, looking after sick children, helping to find jobs or dealing with the police (Adams, 1967). On the other hand, people do more for friends than for strangers. Friends also provide 'social support', i.e. can help to deal with stresses by giving emotional support, acting as confidants or providing material help. The greatest benefits are obtained when the other person acts as a confidant. However, social support from friends is rather less effective than support from a spouse, and work stresses can be relieved more by support from colleagues. In an Australian study it was found that neurotics had far fewer friends than normal controls and did not belong to social networks (Henderson *et al.*, 1978).

Love Loving is not the same as liking, although it includes it. In this section we shall be concerned with 'falling in love' among the young; the equally intense but rather different attachment between the married will be discussed under Marriage.

Falling in love, having love affairs and living together occur mainly among individuals of opposite sex, between the ages of eighteen and thirty, and may or may not lead to marriage. Love usually involves sexual attraction, is more intense than liking, shows a rapid build-up and later declines rather than increasing slowly. There is a great need for the other, a caring for him or her, and a high level of intimacy and disclosure. Its presence can be measured by questionnaires like Rubin's (1973) with items such as 'I would do almost anything for . . .' and 'If I could never be with . . . I would feel miserable.'

The nature of the love relationship varies between different cultures and historical periods; young people learn how they are supposed to feel and behave. Traditionally there are two public rituals – engagement and marriage – which proclaim the stages in the relationship and result in others treating the couple in a new way. The effect of cognitive labelling is shown in a study by Rubin (op. cit.) who found that couples who accepted the love mythology fell in love more rapidly than those who didn't. He also found that married couples had a more realistic view of love. People often try to find out, for example by writing to women's magazines, if they are 'really in love'. On the labelling theory there is no difference between love and infatuation, except perhaps that infatuation is what love is called when it's over.

A number of experiments have tried to find out what makes people fall in love. Physical attractiveness is most important, particularly in the early stages (pp. 110f). Parental interference tends to strengthen attraction – the 'Romeo and Juliet' effect. Playing hard to get doesn't work very well, but those who seem to be hard for others to get are found attractive. People high in internal control are less likely to fall in love. In addition, the variables discussed for friendship affect love – similar attitudes, being liked and so on.

The best available theory of love is a version of the two-factor theory of emotions (p. 16). To be in love is the combination of a high level of arousal and labelling or interpreting it as 'being in love' as defined by the culture (Berscheid and Walster, 1974b). Several experiments show that heightened arousal of various kinds leads to sexual attraction. Dutton and Aron (1974) arranged for an attractive girl to stop young men in the middle of a high and dangerously swaying suspension bridge in Vancouver; 50 per cent of them accepted her invitation to phone her and hear more about the experiment, compared with 13 per cent of those from a very low bridge. (I have been to that bridge and noted that not everyone will go over it; perhaps those daring enough to cross are also more willing to phone strange girls.)

Many love affairs break up. Hill, Rubin and Peplau (1976) studied 105 student affairs and found that half of them broke up within two years of starting. The causes given were that the partners were bored with the relationship, had different interests or backgrounds or had different ideas about sex. Couples were more likely to break up if they differed greatly in age, education, intelligence or physical attractiveness. The males fell in love faster but the females fell out of love faster, and the break-up usually took place in the long vacation – which may itself have been one of the causes of the rift. It has also been found that young people who are low in self-esteem fall in love more often and more deeply (Dion and Dion, 1975), and that love is accompanied by distorted perceptions of the other.

Freedman (1978) compared the benefits of living together with the benefits of marriage. People who were living together were less happy than married people, but a lot happier than those who were single. They also reported that they were somewhat more satisfied with sex than marrieds, but less happy with love.

Marriage is 'a holy mystery in which man and woman become one flesh . . . that husband and wife may comfort and help one another . . . that they may have children . . . and begin a new life together in the community' (Alternative Services Book, 1980). These are some of the central features of marriage – sharing bed, food and property, producing children and caring for each other; it is a commitment to a biological partnership.

The Wish study shows that marriage is seen as *equal, cooperative* and *friendly, intense, socioemotional* and *informal*. Our satisfaction study showed that a spouse is by far the greatest source of satisfaction in all three dimensions, but especially in that of *instrumental reward*. A spouse is also the greatest source of both kinds of conflict, just as arguing is one of the most characteristic marital activities (p. 161).

Successful marriage is the most effective form of social support, relieving the effects of stress and leading to better mental and physical health. Brown and Harris (1978) found that working class women in London with husbands who acted as confidants were much less likely to become clinically depressed following stressful life events than those without such husbands. Many other studies have shown similar effects – on the chances of going to mental hospital, committing suicide and getting various forms of cancer and other illnesses (Lynch, 1977). Men seem to profit more in this way from marriage than do women. This may be because women have to adjust more to marriage, and the crises in the lives of their children, and can have a frustrating time at home, or because women usually provide more social support than men.

While many studies have shown the great importance of 'social support', it is still not clear exactly of what it consists. Being a confidant (i.e. a sympathetic listener), offering helpful advice, providing emotional support and social acceptance, giving actual or financial help, and simply doing ordinary things together, like eating and drinking, are the main possibilities. Some of these require definite social skills, such as offering necessary but unpopular advice and handling the non-verbal components of emotional support. There is some evidence that social support works best when it is a two-way affair, the recipient doing something for or with the donor rather than passively receiving help (Cohen *et al.*, 1981).

Most people get married, though in Britain a third of those who do so also get divorced. An increasing number live together without marriage over a long period. Pairs of friends may also live together, with or without sexual involvement, as may siblings, and these relationships share some of the properties of marriage.

We have found that the main activities in marriage are being in bed, watching TV, doing domestic jobs, eating, talking and arguing (p. 161). Married people live in the same house, see a great deal of each other, talk a lot together and share many activities. In the majority of marriages the wife is at home more than the husband and is in charge of most domestic activities, though dual career families are becoming more common, the domestic jobs in such cases being shared more equally.

In the traditional family there was a clear division of roles: the husband was the main provider, while the wife looked after the household and children; he was task-oriented, she was expressive. This has changed quite a lot, in that wives now earn more and husbands do more in the home. In terms of exchange theory, the partners receive somewhat different rewards, though both receive sexual satisfactions, companionship, and social support.

Marriage goes through definite stages, now often preceded by a living-together period: the honeymoon period, lasting until the arrival of the first child; the child-rearing period; the period after the last child has left home; and finally widowhood. Sexual activity declines in frequency and importance, and the nature of the relationship changes to a level of greater security and commitment. Marital satisfaction is greatest before and after the child-rearing stage. There are certain class differences, e.g. working-class spouses in Britain lead more independent social lives than upper- or middle-class spouses (Burgess, 1981).

There is a very high level of conflict in marriage, and violence is quite common. Curiously, there is no correlation between the frequency of positive and negative episodes. It has been suggested that conflicts have to be worked through if a relationship is to proceed to a deeper level; couples must expose themselves to the possibility of being changed by one another. Certain conflicts are very common in marriage – the need for very close coordination of behaviour, friction due to the different roles and spheres of interests, conflict with in-laws, and over different beliefs or values.

Marriages break up for a number of reasons. Many do so in the first five years, especially in the case of early or hasty marriages and if there are difficulties with money, accommodation or sex, the basic affective bond having never been made. During the next twenty years difficulties may arise when the wife grows to greater independence, if the two develop in different directions and as a result of trouble with the children. Some marriages break up later, after the children have gone, if there was only a social alliance to raise the children, without a strong affective attachment. Adultery, violence and alcohol are often additional sources of trouble (Dominian, 1980).

Kinship In Western Europe and North America a person's main kin are his siblings, parents and children. Parents and children make up the nuclear family, which lives together until the children leave home. Relationships with cousins, uncles, aunts and other kin outside the nuclear family may or may not be taken up in our culture. Elsewhere, e.g. in Africa and the East, kinship is more important, and relationships with a wider range of kin are maintained. Compared with purely friendly connections, kinship links are less optional and last much longer. People who are unmarried or widowed spend more time with, or actually live with, their own children or siblings. Kin do not usually share leisure activities, as friends do; they tend to meet for regular meals or visits, or at Christmas, birthdays, weddings and funerals (Adams, 1968; Firth *et al.*, 1969).

Women are more active than men in maintaining kinship links, this being especially noticeable between sisters and between mothers and daughters. Kinship among the working class in Britain has been described as a 'female trade union'. In middle-class circles the link with father and father-in-law can be important, e.g. for financial help, while the mother–daughter link may be weaker if the daughter has established herself independently before marriage

(Bell, 1968). Kinship ties last a long time, and the nature of each relationship changes greatly over time. Parents start by looking after their children, who then live away from home for years but in turn may end up looking after their parents. Siblings start by playing and quarrelling and may end up by living together in old age. They have a strong initial bond based on their shared, intimate experiences, but there is often jealousy and rivalry as well. Sisters are especially close but also quarrel a lot.

Working-class people have fewer friends but spend more time with kin, partly because they often live quite near; and they do invite them home, or rather they invite themselves. Working class husbands are often poor confidants, so sisters do the job.

Kin are especially important to old people, many of whom live with or near one of their offspring, and most of whom have seen a son, daughter or sibling during a given week and are regularly helped by their children. Telephone calls and letters are mainly to kin. Working-class old people are in closer touch with kin than the middle-class elderly, since middle-class families are more dispersed. The latter are, however, less lonely, because they have greater access to telephones and cars, write more letters, see their friends more often and in addition value privacy and can cope better with isolation (Shanas *et al.*, 1968; Atkinson, 1970). Upper-class and wealthy families are also active in maintaining kinship connections.

The nature of kinship is shown in Figure 20 (p. 198). Siblings are like friends, but *less equal* and *less intense*. In our goals study siblings are lower in the *shared interests* dimension and higher in conflict due to *criticism*. Parents are *less equal* and *more task-oriented*, and higher on the *instrumental reward* scale (material help). Adolescent children are a major source of conflict due to *criticism* and are a low source of reward.

When kin meet, they eat and drink and talk, spend time together, take an interest in each other's health and welfare, and pass on family news. They may also provide regular help, such as with baby-sitting or shopping. Kin, unlike friends, are prepared to provide major forms of help, such as money, accommodation and care for others when ill (Adams, 1967). Sociobiological, 'selfish gene' theories offer one explanation (p. 19). Hewstone, Argyle and

Furnham (in press) asked subjects how they would divide money between themselves and others; they were most generous to a spouse, followed by child, friend and work-mate, while women were more generous than men.

The bonds between kin are strong and long-lasting. Another reason for this may be the sense of shared identity with another person of the same family name (apart from mother–daughter, etc.) and some common physical features. Sharing the intimacies of family life is probably a source of bonding. Kin are part of a network of relationships which sustains links between pairs of individuals (Schneider, 1968). These bonds to a large extent survive separation by distance, or differences of age or social class. Kinship, unlike friendship, does not need to be sustained by regular and rewarding meetings.

Work-mates Most men, and many women, are at work between the ages of about twenty and sixty-five for eight hours a day. They sustain relations with peers, subordinates and superiors, and often with clients, customers, etc. In addition to the social interaction which is needed for the work, there is additional social activity – at coffee, lunch, etc. – consisting of jokes, gossip, games and so on, especially with liked co-workers.

Men are typically more involved with work relationships than women (who are more interested in friends and kin). Older people and those of higher social class, who usually have more senior and interesting jobs, are also more involved with work and the social relationships there. On the other hand, for many women, and those with monotonous jobs, the social aspects of work may be the most worthwhile part of it.

The Wish dimensional analysis shows that co-workers are quite different from family and friends in being *task-oriented, formal* and *less intense*. Our study found work-mates very poor sources of satisfaction. Relations with work superiors were seen as *unequal, task-oriented, formal* and *superficial*.

On the other hand, work superiors and associates can be an important source of social support, and are able to reduce the harmful effects of stress at work more than a spouse or friends. This is perhaps because they are in a better position actually to remove the source of stress (Payne, 1980). Furthermore, relationships with people at work are one of the main sources of job satisfaction (Argyle, 1972).

The relationship of cooperation between work-mates is found in all cultures. In ours it is probably learnt at school, but is in any case necessary for the successful performance of tasks. The leader–follower relationship is also universal, and probably learnt in the home. These relationships are different from and weaker than the others we have discussed. On the other hand, they take up a lot of the waking hours and are an important source of job satisfaction and support in dealing with work stress (Payne, 1980; Cohen and McKay, 1981).

Are work relationships superficial or not, then? In the first place, about 25 per cent of friendships arise out of work relationships, so presumably these are not. Other work relationships are confined to work, but can be very important to those concerned and include a lot of social interaction and help over and above what is required by the job; this can be seen as another kind of friendship perhaps. Many work relationships, perhaps most of them, consist of easy cooperation, but they go no further than this. And a few have to be sustained even though people dislike each other. There are often conflicts between those at work, arising out of opposing roles (e.g. management and unions), competition and rivalry, or conflicting views about policy.

The main reason for the special properties of work relationships is that they are greatly affected by the formal organization – in which people are formed into groups, directed by supervisors, placed in spatial proximity, and linked in the work-flow system. They have to interact with others in this system, whether they like them or not. However, additional 'informal' structures emerge, which are not shown on the organization chart, of people who like and help one another, form coalitions for mutual advantage, or simply act as links in the grapevine.

ACTIVITIES, RULES AND SOCIAL SKILLS
IN DIFFERENT RELATIONSHIPS

Activities Different relationships can be partly described in terms of the activities in which people engage with friends, spouses and others. Argyle and Furnham (in press,b) asked sixty people to report on the frequency with which they had taken part in twenty-six kinds of activity with others in eight different relationships. Very large variations were found; the characteristic activities for three relationships are shown in Table 7.

The numbers show the ratio of frequency for the relationship in question to the average for all eight relationships. Overall, frequencies for most situations were highest with spouses, though the most distinctive activities are those shown. Another situation is even more characteristic of spouses – being in bed together (Clarke and Smith, personal communication). It is interesting that arguing is one of the distinctive activities of spouses.

Subjects were also asked to rate typical activities for each relationship. Spouse situations were rated as frequent, long, informal and involving food and drink.

Rules We showed above that there are commonly agreed rules for social situations (p. 124). There are also rules for relationships. Argyle, Henderson and Furnham, from pilot interviews, obtained forty possible rules for each of twenty-one relationships, thirty potential universal rules being used for all of them. A larger sample were asked to indicate how strongly they felt each rule applied. A number were found to be thought applicable to all or most relationships (see Table 8).

There are additional rules for each relationship, some of which will be given later. For 'people you can't get on with' some rather interesting ones were obtained (see Table 9).

Statistical analysis shows that relationships fall into a number of clusters, sharing similar rules. One cluster contains spouse, siblings and close friends, another most work relationships, and yet another doctor, teacher and work superior.

Spouse		Work Colleague: liked, same status		Friend, similar age	
mean ratio 1·64		mean ratio 1·11		mean ratio 1·26	
situations above this ratio		*situations above this ratio*		*situations above this ratio*	
watch TV	2·61	attend lecture	2·11	dancing	2·00
do domestic jobs together	2·48	work together on joint task	1·56	tennis	1·67
play chess or other indoor game	2·31	together in a committee	1·55	sherry party	1·63
go for a walk	2·28	morning coffee or tea	1·50	joint leisure	1·63
go shopping	2·15	casual chat and telling jokes	1·35	pub	1·60
play tennis or squash	2·03	one helps the other	1·31	intimate conversation	1·52
informal meal together	1·93			walk	1·50
intimate conversation	1·92				
have argument or disagreement	1·84				

Table 7. Situations/activities *most* chosen for certain relationships (ratios to mean frequency for all relationships). (Argyle and Furnham (1982).)

1 Should respect the other's privacy
2 Should look the other person in the eye during conversation
3 Should not discuss what is said in confidence
4 Should not engage in sexual activity
5 Should seek to repay debts, favours and compliments, no matter how small
6 Should stand up for the other person in his absence
7 Should address other by his first name
8 Should be emotionally supportive
9 Should share news of success with other

Table 8. The most general rules of relationships.

1 Should respect each other's privacy
2 Should strive to be fair in relations with one another
3 Should not discuss what is said in confidence
4 Should not invite to dine at a family celebration
5 Should not engage in sexual activity
6 Should not feel free to take up as much of the other's time as one desires
7 Should not denigrate the other behind his back
8 Should not ignore the other person

Table 9. Rules for two people who don't get on with each other.

1 Should look after family when wife is unwell
2 Should show an interest in wife's daily activities
3 Should create a harmonious home atmosphere
4 Should be faithful to the wife
5 Should give birthday cards and presents
6 Should be tolerant of wife's friends
7 Should talk to wife about sex and death
8 Should disclose feelings and personal problems
9 Should not criticize wife in public

Table 10. Additional rules for husbands.

Relationship skills In order to make friends and sustain a friendship, certain skills are needed. The same applies to marriage and to all other relationships.

Marital skills These are taught in the U.S.A. in *Behavioral marital therapy* (Jacobson and Margolin, 1979). The skills taught are:

1 increasing rewardingness, verbal and non-verbal, having 'love days', keeping records of positive and negative behaviour. There is a lot of evidence that in unhappy marriages there are more negative acts than in happy ones, both verbal and non-verbal, and that these are reciprocated (Gottman, 1979);

2 *quid pro quo* contracts, e.g. he agrees to take her out two nights a week while she agrees to sex games of his choice once a week. This is derived from equity theory, which as we have seen has not been shown convincingly to apply to marriage;

3 improved communication, especially non-verbal expression of emotions and attitudes. It would probably be useful to concentrate on the husband's skills;

4 improved problem-solving, particularly the capacity to discuss relationship problems. However, nothing is known about the form such discussion or negotiation normally takes.

This kind of therapy has been shown to be quite successful (Jacobson, 1979). However, in view of the widespread failure rate of marriage, it may be worth exploring some simpler courses of action which are suggested by the research described in this chapter:

1 if attachment is based on joint activities which are important and rewarding, the range of these could be expanded, e.g. to include both leisure and domestic tasks;

2 if attachment is partly due to building a shared cognitive world, through talk and self-disclosure, it follows that spouses should talk and disclose more;

3 if environmental and social network supports are important, spouses should establish more joint social contacts;

4 they should keep the rules – those we have found for husbands appear in Table 10.

Friendship skills The most commonly reported problem here is difficulty in *making* friends. Friendships often end, but this does not seem to be nearly as traumatic as marriages breaking up. Indeed quite satisfactory friendships are often relatively short-term affairs anyway, such as those formed on holiday. Research has quite a lot to suggest about making friends:

1 frequent social contact with similar people can be achieved by joining a local club – evening class, Scottish dancing, church, etc.;

2 rewarding someone and expressing attitudes of liking for another may require social skills training, in the production of positive verbal and non-verbal messages;

3 physical attractiveness is important for friendship as well as for heterosexual affairs, and it may be easier to change appearance than behaviour;

4 self-disclosure indicates trust and is essential if a relationship is to deepen, but it should be gradual and reciprocated.

The research on activities which was reported above showed that friends usually engage in certain kinds of activity – leisure pursuits, eating, drinking and talking. To make friends it is necessary to suggest some joint activity, or to invite someone to something. Once made, friends should follow the general rules given above (Table 8), and some additional ones. Particularly important are rules of providing rewards. Friends, besides repaying debts and being emotionally supportive,

1 Should volunteer help in time of need
2 Should strive to make him/her happy while in each other's company

Rules relating to third parties are also important. In addition to keeping confidences and standing up for the other in their absence, friends

3 Should not criticise the other in public
4 Should be tolerant of each other's friends
5 Should not be jealous or critical of other relationships

We found that these third party rules were often broken by friends, and breaking them was often said to be the cause of break-up of friendships.

FURTHER READING

Duck, S., and Gilmour, R., *Personal Relationships* (4 vols), Academic Press, 1981–2.

Hinde, R. A., *Towards Understanding Relationships*, Academic Press, 1979.

CHAPTER 8

GROUPS, ORGANIZATION AND CULTURE

In the previous chapters, problems of social interaction have been simplified by concentrating on encounters between two people. In this chapter, social situations and relationships involving more than two people will be considered. First, interaction may take place between members of small social groups with three, four or more members. Second, there may be differences of power, status or role in social organizations. Third, people are steeped in a cultural and social class background, which prescribes the verbal and non-verbal means of communication, as well as the rules governing behaviour in different situations.

MEMBERSHIP OF SMALL SOCIAL GROUPS

We have seen that most animals live in groups; many human activities are also carried out in groups between three and fifteen in size. There are several rather different kinds of small group – families, work-groups and groups of friends are the most basic. There are also decision-taking and problem-solving groups, committees of various kinds and groups invented by psychologists, like T-groups and encounter groups.

Some processes of social interaction are similar in all kinds of group – all form norms and have leaders; on the other hand there are distinctive forms of social behaviour in each kind of group. Much research on small groups has taken the form of laboratory experiments; these have the advantage of being able to test hypotheses rigorously, but they tend to omit important features of real-life groups and are stripped down to those elements of group life which the experimenter knows about already.

The basic theory of groups is simple, there being two motivations for joining one – to carry out a task, play a game, etc., and to enjoy the social interaction and sustain relationships. All groups have these two sides of them – task and sociable motivations and activities, though the balance varies. People often join a group for economic or other non-social reasons in the first place; they then become involved in group activities, find these satisfying and become attached to the group. A group of friends may want to enjoy each other's company, but they have to do something, i.e. a task must be devised.

The social behaviour in groups can be divided up as follows:

	TASK	SOCIABLE
VERBAL	Information and discussion related to the task.	Gossip and chat, jokes and games, discussion of personal problems.
NON-VERBAL	Task performance, help, NV comments on performance, NV signals conveying information.	Communicating interpersonal attitudes, emotions, self-presentation.

Group formation Different kinds of group come together in different ways – friendship groups through mutual attraction, leisure groups through shared interests, work-groups under the influence of a leader and so on. Observers of groups report that they usually go through a number of developmental stages. At first members are dependent on the leader, to tell them what to do; then they often go through a stage of rebelling against him, and of conflict between sub-groups; finally a stable group structure emerges, with agreed norms, a leadership hierarchy and some degree of cohesiveness (Tuckman, 1965).

As in dyads (groups of two), it may take some time before a group is able to arrive at a pattern of interaction which is more or less acceptable to all; there may be some alternation between concern with the task and concern with interpersonal problems. As with dyads again, there are some groups of individuals for whom there is no stable pattern of interaction.

Schutz (1958) set up experimental groups whose members were incompatible in that more than one was high in dominance, thus creating a struggle for dominance and an initial failure of meshing. These groups were found to be very ineffective in the performance of cooperative tasks. There may be failure of meshing in another way. Haythorn (1956) created groups of four, where one member was designated the leader, and where different combinations of authoritarian and non-authoritarian leaders and followers were compared. The groups ran most smoothly, with least conflict between leader and followers, when both were authoritarian or both were non-authoritarian. In each case leader and followers were using social styles which fitted in a complementary way.

Once equilibrium has been established, the group may persist in this condition for some time, though changes in membership and changing external conditions will affect it. A 'cohesive' group is one in which the members are attracted to each other or to the task, and are therefore attracted towards the group. Cohesiveness can be measured by the proportion of sociometric choices which are made to members of that group, or by the frequency with which the word 'we' is used as opposed to 'I'. A group will become cohesive under the following conditions: frequent interaction between members; similar attitudes, interests and background among members; rewarding experiences in the group; a leader who can preserve harmony; absence of aggressive, schizoid or otherwise disturbing personalities; a task which requires cooperative, complementary behaviour for its completion (Lott and Lott, 1965). In cohesive groups the members cooperate and help each other more, interact more, are more satisfied and, in work groups, are absent less and happy to stay longer, and they have greater productivity at tasks which require cooperation. On the other hand, there may be too much social activity at the expense of work, and there may be hostility to other groups (Argyle, 1972).

Groups of two are of special interest since they provide the simplest instances of social interaction, and because more complex cases are explicable in terms of the principles which work here. However, dyads are unique in a number of ways – they are less stable, there is therefore more danger of interaction collapsing and there are more signs of tension, but there is less expression of agreement and disagreement (Thomas and Fink, 1963).

Groups of three also have certain unique features. The addition of a third member to a dyad, even as an observer, changes the situation entirely. Each of the original participants now has to consider how his behaviour will be seen by the new member, and his behaviour will be affected differently if this is, for example, an attractive girl, his mother or his tutor. A and B may have worked out their dominance relationships and the proportion of the time each will speak. C now has to be fitted into this hierarchy, and he may dominate both, be intermediate or be dominated by both.

In groups of three there are various kinds of internal competition and jockeying for position. With three males there is usually a straight battle for dominance, and the weakest becomes excluded. If there are two males and one female, the males will compete for the attention of the female. Females behave rather differently: if there are three females and one begins to get left out, the others will work hard to keep her in (Robson, 1966). If there is one powerful and dominating member of a triad, the others may form a coalition in which they combine together against him. The collaboration of the weak against the strong is observed in small group experiments and in real life: it has been summarized by the proposition 'in weakness there is strength'.

As group size increases from four to ten or more, the character of interaction changes. It is less easy to participate, both because others want to take the floor and because of greater audience anxiety; it is less easy to influence what the others will do; there is greater discrepancy between the amount of interaction of different members – in large groups the majority scarcely speak at all; the variety of personality and talent present is greater and there is greater differentiation of styles of behaviour; discussion is less inhibited and there is ready expression of disagreement; and if the group has work to do, there is a greater tendency to create rules and arrange for division of labour (Thomas and Fink, 1963).

Norms All small social groups develop 'norms', i.e. shared patterns of perceiving and thinking, shared kinds of communication, inter-action and appearance, common attitudes and beliefs, and shared ways of doing whatever the group does. Members will have some-thing in common from the beginning, and there is also convergence towards shared norms, particularly on the part of individual devi-ates. Such norms will govern the styles of social behaviour which are approved and admired. Anyone who fails to conform is placed under pressure to do so, and if he continues to he is rejected. Numerous experiments show that a deviate becomes the object of considerable attention, and of efforts to persuade him to change his behaviour. This is particularly likely to happen when his deviation is on some matter which is important to the group, which may affect the success of the group or which challenges deeply held beliefs. Deviates may conform for two quite different reasons – to avoid looking silly and being rejected, or because they regard the group's views as a valuable source of information. The other group members might be more expert, while consistent behaviour on the part of the group may be taken to indicate the operation of some unknown rule; this may explain why subjects in conformity experiments are prepared to go along with the group when it gives, unanimously, an apparently wrong answer. It is important that people should deviate from time to time in a constructive way and lead the group to adopt a better solution to its problems in response to a changing external situation.

It is now known that there are several different kinds of norm:

1 norms about the task, e.g. the method, rate and standard of work in work teams, deviation from which affects group goals and hence individual rewards;

2 norms regulating interaction in the group, which make the behaviour of others predictable, prevent conflicts and ensure fair distribution of rewards;

3 norms about attitudes and beliefs: the opinions of group experts are accepted, and beliefs are checked against those of the group rather than against reality, which may be more difficult;

4 norms about clothes, hair or other aspects of appearance, which project identity and thus, if not followed, may bring the group into disrepute.

Characteristic interaction sequences take place in connection with norms. A member may deviate because he does not like a norm, is conforming to another group or has thought of a better way of doing things. Deviation is often greeted with surprise, non-verbal signals of disapproval, verbal attempts at influence and finally by rejection and exclusion from the group. Sometimes it leads to laughter, sometimes the easiest thing is to ignore it and sometimes it is recognized as a possibly useful innovation. Originality and independence are especially valued in fields such as science, art and fashion, though still within certain limits. Independence is not simply a failure to conform, but rather a positive choice and one that risks disapproval by the rest of the group. It is more likely to arise if there is some positive reward for being right (Carpenter and Hollander, in press). Innovators are more likely to be successful if they are persons of high informal status, in virtue of their contributions to the group. Hollander (1958) has suggested that they earn 'idiosyncrasy credit' and that the group gives them permission to deviate, their behaviour being seen as a possibly new line of action rather than as a failure to attain the approved standard.

A persistent minority, even of two, may be able to change the norms. One deviate can be seen as an eccentric failure, but two deviates are taken more seriously. A second person disagreeing with the group casts doubt on the correctness of group norms and may open up disagreements within the majority. A minority who are unanimous, and who display conviction, offer an alternative view of things. Moscovici (1980) has found that such a minority can bring about real conversion, at first indirectly via inferences from the new ideas, and later through a change of heart after a time interval. Another view is that sub-groups exercise influence in proportion to their size, but a minority can sometimes trigger a general change in opinion if the group has lost touch with the true state of affairs outside of itself (Latané and Wolf, 1981), whereas a majority can only produce public compliance.

Hierarchies and roles All groups of animals and men form hierarchies, there being advantages in having leaders who are able to direct task activities and prevent conflict in the group. It is probably functional to have such hierarchies in that groups, especially large ones; with clear leadership structures they are more effective. During the early meetings of a group there is a struggle for status among those individuals strong in dominance motivation. Several members carry out task functions and thus become seen as potential leaders, one of these candidates finally being adopted (Stein *et al.*, 1980).

When the order has settled down, a characteristic pattern of interaction is found. The low status members at the bottom of this hierarchy talk little, they address the senior members politely and deferentially, and little notice is taken of what they have to say. A person's position in the hierarchy is primarily a function of how useful he has been in the past; thus the hierarchy is maintained in equilibrium – people are allowed to talk and are listened to if their contributions are expected to be useful. Position in the hierarchy bears little relation to personality traits, but is connected with ability at the group task. The group uses techniques of reward and punishment to maintain this system: a person who talks too much is punished, while high-status members who feel sleepy are stimulated to speak. When people at different positions in the hierarchy interact, the pattern of relationship between them is part of the total scheme of group structure (Bales, 1953).

As well as differing in power or influence, members may also differ in status; individuals may be esteemed and admired because of their past glories independently of their present power.

In addition to having different degrees of status and influence, group members adopt styles of behaviour which are differentiated in other ways. Slater (1955) first noted this effect and found that in discussion groups there was usually a popular person, or 'socio-emotional' leader, and a task leader. It is interesting that the same person did not do both these things – reflecting contrasting types of motivation among the members. Each kind of group has a characteristic set of roles which are available, though the roles of task and socio-emotional leader may occur in every kind of group. A role of 'leader of the opposition' is often found in juries, work-groups and T-groups. These roles appear for various reasons – because there are jobs to be done in groups (task leader), because groups have certain common structures (leader of the opposition), because members with different personalities want to behave differently (socio-emotional leader) and because members want to present themselves as unique individuals (joker, scapegoat).

The effect of the group on behaviour Simply being in the presence of others increases the level of physiological arousal and general activity and causes one to emit common, well-learnt responses; for example, one does better at familiar tasks, worse at unfamiliar ones (Zajonc, 1965). This is true of ants and rats as well, but for humans the effects are probably only produced by others who are evaluating or judging in some way – the presence of blindfolded people does not increase arousal (Cottrell *et al.*, 1968). (There are further complications – see Sanders, 1981.)

In some group situations, individuals behave without the usual restraints, engage in aggressive or other anti-social behaviour, and cannot remember clearly who did what. This is known as 'de-individuation', and occurs in lynch mobs, and in experiments in which subjects are made anonymous by wearing masks and white coats (Zimbardo, 1969). Groups can provide social support: people who are frightened, adolescents who can't get on with their families, and those who don't know what to think or believe, are greatly helped and comforted by belonging to close-knit social groups.

Groups are more effective than individuals in several kinds of activity. They are better at physical tasks because these often need more than one person, and because individuals can specialize in different parts of the job. They are also better at decision-taking, because different skills and knowledge can be combined, and because members can both stimulate and criticize one another. Group decision-taking has the added advantage that those concerned become committed to carrying out the decisions.

Inter-group relations The growth of positive feelings towards members of the group is often accompanied by negative feelings towards members of other groups. Sherif and colleagues (1961) divided eleven- to twelve-year-old boys at a summer camp into two groups. It was found that competitive sports, and an occasion when one group frustrated the other, led to a dangerous level of hostility. Peace was restored by getting the groups to work together for shared goals, such as restoring the deliberately interrupted water supply. Sherif's theory is that in-group and out-group attitudes are functional, in that they lead to the attainment of group goals.

Tajfel and his colleagues distinguished between inter-group and interpersonal behaviour; inter-group behaviour occurs when others are reacted to as group members rather than as individuals. Hostility to the out-group can arise without any conflict of interest, as experiments by Tajfel (1970) have shown: subjects gave preferential treatment to others who were believed to belong to the same 'group' defined vaguely in terms of similar aesthetic interests, and they were keen to give more to in-group than out-group members. The explanation put forward is that people seek self-esteem; their self-image is based partly on salient characteristics of groups to which they belong, so they emphasize features of their groups in which they are superior to others. Mann (1963) found that South African Hindus accept their economic inferiority but believe they are superior in spiritual, social and practical fields. According to this line of thought, the best way to reduce inter-group conflict is to eliminate in-group–out-group differences and to emphasize the common characteristics of groups (Turner and Giles, 1981). Sherif thinks the best method is to create or emphasize common goals.

Different kinds of group So far we have been concerned with the properties of groups in general; we shall now look at some of the special features of particular kinds of group – families, work-groups and groups of friends (see also pp. 150f).

Families differ from many other kinds of group in having a distinctive role-structure of father, mother, sons and daughters. In every culture there is a culturally prescribed relationship between husband and wife with some differentiation of the roles, and between mother–son, older–younger daughter, etc. There is variation between families, as a result of the personalities and abilities of the members. Family life takes place in the home and centres round eating, sleeping, child-rearing, other domestic jobs, watching TV and further leisure activities. The pursuits of the different members have to be coordinated within the space and with the facilities available. Members share the same financial fortunes and position in society. Interaction inside the family has a special quality of great informality – there is almost no self-presentation and little restraint of affection or aggression. In other kinds of groups the members do not usually take their clothes off, laugh uproariously, cry, attack or kiss each other or crawl all over each other, as family members often do – nor do they quarrel so violently. The links between family members also have a unique quality: the parents are tied together by a long history of love and life together and see their children, who are very dependent on them, as part of themselves, while the death of a close relation is a deeply distressing experience from which people may never fully recover (Gorer, 1965).

Groups of friends are different in many ways; they have no formal structure and no task, but consist of people of similar age, background, values and interests, who come together primarily for affiliative purposes. Members also obtain social support, advice and help with common problems. For young people between fifteen and twenty-five the peer group is of great importance; it gives them a social milieu, where they can be independent of the home, meet members of the opposite sex and develop new social skills and an ego-identity (Muuss, 1962). Friendship groups have no 'task' in the usual sense, but they devise activities which generate the desired forms of social interaction – eating and drinking, dancing, playing games and just talking. The character of the interaction varies between different cultures and age-groups, but usually has a warm and relaxed character. On the other hand self-presentation is important: members want to be accepted and thought well of, dress being of importance in this connection.

The sociometric structure is important – who likes whom, who is in and who is out. Acceptance depends on conforming to the group norms and realizing the group values, as well as being kind and helpful. However, friends usually form networks rather than closed groups, containing some very popular people, some tight-knit cliques, and chains of communication. The hierarchical structure is not important, though informal leaders appear from time to time to deal with particular jobs, and there are several opinion leaders whose advice is taken on clothes, books, politics, etc. The group norms are important and distinguish the group from other groups; the in-group who conform are greatly valued, the out-group who do not conform are not.

Work-groups exist primarily on account of the particular tasks they are to tackle. A task affects the relations between people. A may inspect B's work, may be B's assistant, may cooperate with B in a joint task or may be next to him on an assembly line – a distinctive kind of relationship is likely to result in each case. Work-groups meet in a complex environmental setting and sub-culture, which limits and defines social behaviour. They are also part of a social organization, and have a leader and other kinds of role-differentiation. However, work groups have a life of their own which affects what happens and how much work is done. If cohesiveness is very low there will be little cooperation and output will fall; in addition there will be a lot of absenteeism and labour turnover. The group may have a different pattern of communication, incentives, leadership, or division of work from that officially laid down, because it suits the members better. In addition to their work behaviour work-groups engage in purely sociable behaviour such as jokes, games and gossip. The social relations formed involve only part of the personality and members may know little of one another's life outside. However, an important part of the personality is involved, in that livelihood, career and identity depend on work, and there can be considerable intensity of feeling over both cooperative and competitive relationships. There can be relaxed intimacy over the purely sociable activities at work, but physical violence may be used against those who deviate from work norms.

We now have a fairly clear idea how work-groups should be designed to ensure maximum productivity and maximum job satisfaction. They should be fairly small – not more than fifteen members; cohesiveness should be high; they should work as a cooperative team for shared rewards; status differences should be small; and there should be the optimum style of supervision (pp. 262f), with participation in decision-taking (Argyle, 1972).

SOCIAL ORGANIZATIONS

A great deal of social behaviour takes place against a background of social organization – in schools, industry, hospitals and elsewhere. 'Social organization' means the existence of a series of ranks, positions or offices – such as teacher, foreman, hospital sister, etc. – which persist regardless of particular occupants. Behaviour in organizations is to a considerable extent *pre-programmed*, having been worked out by previous members. The roles interlock – doctor–nurse, patient–nurse and so on.

The growth of organization As groups become bigger and their tasks more complex, a formal structure gradually develops, with a leadership hierarchy and divisions of function. Social organization is an essential part of modern life, because it would be impossible to coordinate the activities of the numbers of people involved in large-scale enterprises without extensive division of labour and a hierarchy of leadership. As a small workshop expands to become a factory, or when a guerrilla band becomes an army, the paraphernalia of social organization become necessary. To manufacture motor cars, for example, thousands of different parts must be made by a large number of different people and fitted together. There is thus a great deal of labour division, several levels of leadership, lines of communication and committees for decision-taking. Since it is difficult for one person to supervise more than ten to fifteen others, as soon as the group is larger than this a second level of management is needed.

Even crowds have a rudimentary social organization. Marsh has found that football fans have an age-graded hierarchy of 'novices', 'rowdies' and 'town boys', and also several kinds of leader – 'chant leaders', 'aggro leaders' and 'organizers' (the last for booking coaches, etc.) (Marsh *et al.*, 1978).

Social organization is essential, but the precise forms which we have are not necessarily the best, and are in fact found to be dissatisfying by many who serve in them. They have developed slowly. Industrial organizations as we know them today, for example, have been derived from the first small factories established during the industrial revolution, by trial and error methods. Factories have developed both in response to changing technology and to changing ideas about organization – classical organization theory and the human relations movement in particular.

There are several different kinds of social organization. Etzioni (1961) distinguished between:

coercive organizations, e.g. prisons and mental hospitals, in which people do what they are told because they have to, through fear of punishment, and are unable to leave;

utilitarian organizations, e.g. industries, in which members work in exchange for rewards;

moral organizations, e.g. churches, hospitals and universities, members of which are committed to the values and goals of the organization.

The senior members have quite different kinds of power in the three cases – by punishment, reward or appeal to shared goals respectively. Power can also be based on a leader's expertise, or on the desire of subordinates to identify with him ('referent power'). By power is meant the capacity to influence the behaviour of others, and those low in a hierarchy also have this – they can act collectively, as in strikes, and they can withdraw cooperation or other rewards from their superiors.

Behaviour in organizations differs from that in small social groups in a number of ways. Interaction patterns are not so much a product of particular groups of personalities, but are part of the organizational structure. People come to occupy positions of influence or leadership not through the spontaneous choice of their subordinates, but because they are placed there by higher authority.

Not all doctors or nurses behave in exactly the same way – there are variations due to personality and past experience. However, deviation from official practices goes a lot further than this. It has long been known that industrial workers engage in a wide range of unofficial practices, including ingenious forms of scrounging and time-wasting, in order to make life tolerable. The same has been reported of life in the army and in mental hospitals. Elizabeth Rosser has recently studied the underworld of English schools. She found that the pupils have their own procedural ideas and 'rules' for teachers derived from these: if a teacher breaks these rules – for example, by being unfair, too strict or boring – she is punished. What appears to be uncontrollable chaos from the point of view of the authorities turns out to be the operation of another set of rules (Marsh, Rosser and Harré, 1978).

Positions and roles Organizations consist of a set of related positions, whose occupants play interlocking roles. A role is the pattern of behaviour shared by most occupants of a position, and which comes to be expected of them. In a hospital, for example, there are obvious differences between the behaviour of patients, doctors, nurses, visitors, etc. Roles include a variety of aspects of behaviour – the work done, ways of interacting with other members of the organization (e.g. foreman–manager, foreman–worker), attitudes and beliefs, and clothes worn.

The pressures to conform to a role can be very strong. Zimbardo (1973) paid a number of normal, middle-class student volunteers to play the roles of prison guards and prisoners, assigned arbitrarily, with appropriate uniforms in an imitation prison. Many of the guards became brutal, sadistic and tyrannical, and many of the prisoners became servile, selfish and hostile, and suffered from hysterical crying and severe depression. The experiment had to be stopped after six days and nights.

Why do people conform so strongly to roles? There are various pressures to do so, not the least being that someone who deviates will be regarded as eccentric, mad, or not 'right' in some way. In addition roles are *interlocking*, so that if doctors and nurses play their roles, patients have no choice but to play theirs. In any case, a role may provide the most effective means of doing a job; teachers, for example, traditionally have a loud, clear and didactic voice, and adopting the same may save someone new to the profession much trial and error. Furthermore, only certain kinds of people want, or are able, to become, say, bishops or barmen, so only particular types of person are found occupying these positions. Newcomers learn a role by imitating senior members, and may be given special practice in role-playing during training courses.

Many members of organizations experience *role conflict*, which can take various forms. A person may be under conflicting pressures from different groups of people in the organization. For example, different demands may be made on foremen by managers and by workers, and female students may be expected to be hard-working and intellectual by their teachers but not by the male students. In such cases there may be withdrawal from those exerting the pressure.

Role conflict often leads to anxiety, tension, illness and reduced levels of work. There may also be ambiguity about what a role entails, when a job is not clearly defined or when a new role is created. There can be conflict between role and personality; for example, if an authoritarian personality is a member of a democratic organization. A person may also find himself playing two incompatible roles, e.g., a military chaplain, or a teacher whose own child is in the school.

Interaction in organizations Social organization introduces a totally new element which has not so far been considered. To predict how A and B will behave towards one another it may be much more useful to know their positions in the organization than to know about their personalities or preferred styles of interaction. In the extreme cases of church services and drill parades the whole course of interaction can be 'predicted' by knowing the formal procedure. Even a person's popularity may be more a function of his position than of his personality – it depends whether he has a rewarding role like awarding bonuses and giving out free buns, or has a punitive role.

It is impossible to understand why the members of an organization interact as they do without knowing their organization chart. There have been many studies of the communication between the members of industrial management hierarchies, like that shown in Figure 21 (reviewed in Argyle, 1972). The main findings are as follows:

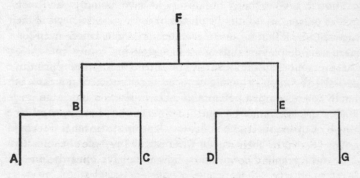

Figure 21. Organization chart.

A and B Relations with the immediate superior are often rather strained and formal. A may ask B for help, information or advice; he may also have to report progress, possibly delaying and distorting the news if it is bad; and he may want to make suggestions or complaints, which B might not be very eager to hear. B may give orders, advice, expert information or comments on A's performance.

A and C Relations with immediate colleagues can vary from close cooperation in a team, through carefully reciprocated helpfulness, to cut-throat competition.

A and D Lateral relations with equal status people outside the group are often friendly and relaxed. They are useful in stimulating rapid information-flow and cooperation, and are the basis of the 'grapevine'. Friendship choices are often in A–D relationships.

A and E Relations with those of different status, but outside the line of command, are easier than direct superior–subordinate links and can act like an A–D relationship.

 A and F It is difficult for F to communicate with persons two or more steps below him in the hierarchy. If he goes through B, four encounters have to take place before some delayed and distorted feedback reaches him, yet if B is left out he will be upset. If notices or other mass media are used there is no feedback.

Since a person's behaviour varies with the rank or position of those with whom he comes into contact, it is important to be able to categorize people; many organizations have uniforms, and members of others can usually be placed by more subtle aspects of their appearance. When an outsider enters an organization, even for a short visit, there is great pressure to find out his 'equivalent rank' so that everyone shall know exactly how to treat him. In many primitive societies the main principle of social organization is not rank but family relationship; a potential mother-in-law is avoided, an uncle is played jokes on, and so forth. It is reported of one savage tribe which operated such a classificatory kinship system that if it could not be discovered how a visitor was related to everyone he was eaten – because people did not know how to behave towards him. In Western society, when people of different social status meet, at conferences, office parties and the like, there is a characteristic type of interaction:

note the keen interest, the total absorption of the lesser members . . . the greater member is looking past the ear of the lesser, scanning the throng for an acquaintance whose status is greater than his own from whom enhancement may be drawn [Brown, 1965].

Permanent relationships in the organization have a similar quality. Less important people are much concerned about what their superiors think of them; their superiors, however, are more concerned with what *their* superiors are thinking.

Nearly all organizations have a hierarchical structure and this seems to be necessary to provide the necessary administration and coordination. However there are a number of difficulties about hierarchies. As we showed above, there are difficulties of communication up and down hierarchies; these become more acute when there are many levels in the hierarchy or if relationships are authoritarian. It is often found that those in the lowest ranks are discontented, alienated and inefficient. There are several ways of changing organizations to minimize these effects:

1 the style of leadership can be changed so that it is more democratic, leaders delegating and encouraging participation in decisions (cf. pp. 264f);

2 the number of levels can be reduced by increasing the span of control and decentralizing the organization into small units;

3 formal arrangements can be made for consultation as in 'industrial democracy' and student representation.

As regards the last point, research has found that such consultation works better if all levels are represented (especially first-line supervisors), if the joint committees are not just advisory but have real power, and if management take it seriously and don't simply push through their own plans. It has been shown to lead to increased productivity, less absenteeism and labour turnover, better decision-taking and better relations between management and workers (Argyle, 1972).

Another aspect of social organization is the work-flow system. Workers may, for example, be on an assembly line, which means that they interact only with their neighbours but are dependent on the whole group for their pay. They may be in a group under a foreman on individual piece-work, or may be isolated at control points in an automated system. These arrangements have definite effects on the relations between people – they may make them love or hate each other, depending on whether they are helping or hindering one another, and they may make communications easy or impossible. The Tavistock Institute of Human Relations has shown that it is possible to devise improved social arrangements with exactly the same technology. For example, Trist and colleagues (1963) found that the Longwall method of coal-mining could be employed with greater productivity and less absenteeism if the three main jobs were done on all of the three shifts; previously the jobs of cutting, filling and stonework were done by different shifts, who never met, resulting in a lack of cooperation.

CULTURE

Social interaction takes place within a cultural setting. By the culture of a group of people is meant their whole way of life – their language, ways of perceiving, categorizing and thinking about the world, forms of non-verbal communication and social interaction, rules and conventions about behaviour, moral values and ideals, technology and material culture, art, science, literature and history. All these aspects of culture affect social behaviour, directly or indirectly.

Human infants are born with basic biological needs and a certain amount of intrinsic equipment. However, human beings have greater powers of learning than animals, as well as a longer period of dependence on their parents, so that different solutions to life's problems can be learnt. As a result of the development of language humans can communicate their solutions to these problems to one another, and there is continuous modification of the cultural store.

There is a culture that is shared by the inhabitants of Great Britain, and there are sub-cultures for particular geographical areas, social classes and organizations, and even for particular small social groups. Several aspects of culture affect the processes of interaction, notably the conventions governing social behaviour, moral rules covering interpersonal behaviour, verbal and non-verbal means of communication and other social techniques.

Language This instances one of the most obvious differences between cultures. However, when a new language has been learnt there are still problems about its use. In several cultures there is polite usage, words being designed to please rather than inform. Americans often give instructions or orders as if they are questions – 'Would you like to . . . ?' Cultures vary in the use of exaggeration: 'If an Arab says what he means without the expected exaggeration, other Arabs may still think that he means the opposite' (Shouby, 1951). English upper-middle-class speech includes considerable understatement; a person who fails to follow this convention is regarded as boastful. In Asian countries people are reluctant to give the answer 'no', for it leads to a loss of face by the other: there are differences in the range of personal pronouns available: the British have only 'you', the French have 'tu' and 'vous', and in Sri Lanka there are about twenty alternatives communicating degrees of intimacy and deference.

The language also carries the categories of thought which are important in a culture. For example, the colours of the rainbow are divided up differently in different cultures; Zuni Indians have difficulty in recognizing an orange stimulus shown them previously, because they have no word for orange. The Eskimos have three words for snow, where we would need several words to describe each variety (Brown and Lenneberg, 1954). Special styles of social behaviour are labelled, such as *machismo* (Mexico – flamboyant bravery), *chutzpah* (Yiddish – outrageous cheek). When a concept or distinction is important in a culture, this becomes reflected in the language, which in turn helps people to deal with situations common in the culture, and in the production of relevant behaviour. Old concepts and words disappear and are replaced by new ones. A long time ago, an uncle of mine advised me about tipping, saying, 'A half-crown is a gentleman's coin.' Since then, however, both concepts in this statement have disappeared.

Non-verbal communication The non-verbal accompaniments of speech vary in different cultures. For example, Italians make great use of gestures when talking, while Arabs and others touch one another a lot during conversation. Tone of voice is very important for Arabs too, since their words tend to be ambiguous and stereotyped. Japanese speech includes a number of hissing sounds, which indicate deference, and the word 'Hai', which means understanding.

As we saw in Chapter 2, there are cultural differences in the use and meaning of non-verbal signals for interpersonal attitudes and emotions.

Facial expression Much the same facial expressions are used in all cultures, but there are different rules about when they can be used; for example, the Japanese rarely show sadness or other negative emotions, and may smile or giggle instead.

Bodily contact is used more in some countries than others and takes very diverse forms – various kinds of embracing, stroking, buffeting or kissing to greet people, and various kinds of hand-holding or leg-entwining during encounters.

Distance Arabs and others stand much closer than Europeans or Americans, and at a more directly facing angle.

Gaze In the 'contact' cultures where people touch each other and stand close together, they also look a lot at one another.

Gesture shows the greatest cultural diversity, since there are almost no innate gestures. The same one may have a variety of meanings the world over.

Other aspects of social interaction

Greetings have similar components in most cultures – touching, mutual gaze, bowing, head-nods, smiling. The Indians and Japanese do not touch, and a variety of exotic greetings are found in primitive societies – smelling cheeks and rubbing noses, taking off some or all clothes, kissing beards and so on (Argyle, 1975).

Establishing rapport Americans are able to establish a certain, rather superficial contact very quickly, whereas the British are experienced as more 'stand-offish', 'closed' or simply difficult to get to know. This may be due to differences in affiliative motivation, or to differences in the social techniques which are acquired.

Self-presentation occurs in all cultures. However, in Britain there is a taboo on direct, verbal self-presentation (pp. 205f), while in India and Japan it is quite normal to speak highly of oneself. In most of the East, 'face' is of great importance and must not be lost.

Etiquette All cultures have their social rules; when these are elaborate and rigid they are referred to as 'etiquette'. In Western countries, it is only in old-fashioned upper-class circles that these rules are made into explicit codes of conduct. In the Far East, especially in Japan, formal etiquette is more widely followed, but this only applies to certain traditional social situations, and not apparently to getting on buses and trains.

Rules and conventions We have seen that rules are necessary to enable people to attain goals and satisfy needs (pp. 123f). However, it is possible to operate with quite different rules, such as driving on the right or on the left. There may be contrasting sets of rules for such matters as bribery, nepotism, gifts, buying and selling, eating and drinking, punctuality and seating guests at table. One may encounter totally new situations, with their rules; for example, visitors to Oxford University may have to cope with the procedures surrounding dessert, vivas, collections and other strange events. In developing countries there are often two sets of rules corresponding to traditional and modern attitudes – about time, gifts, parental authority and the position of women, for example (Dawson *et al.*, 1971).

Goffman (1963) has shown how these rules penetrate to the key processes of social interaction and govern, for example, the detailed sequences of eye and other bodily movements. Kissing one's wife goodbye is done quite differently at a bus-stop and at an air terminal, for example. Such rules are usually unverbalized, and we are only dimly aware of them until someone breaks them.

Social relationships The kinds of relationships which we described in the last chapter take somewhat different forms in different cultures. In developing countries families are very important: kin relationships are closer, greater familial demands are made on individuals and a wider range of kin is recognized than in developed countries. Among Arab peoples more than one wife is allowed, while in China a concubine may be added and great respect is paid to elderly parents. The role of women varies a good deal: traditionally in Arab cultures women could not work but spent most of their time at home, while in Israel, China and Russia women do nearly the same jobs as men. Sexual mores vary from widespread promiscuity to tight control over unmarried women, the latter especially where women can inherit land, so that marriages need to be carefully watched. There are similar variations in the acceptance of homosexuality. In most of the world outside North America and Europe, working relationships involve greater distance between the ranks and more authoritarian supervisors than in those two areas, while groups of all kinds are tighter, with more power over their members.

Motivation The goals pursued in different cultures vary, and sometimes we can see how this has come about. For example, tribes which are constantly at war with their neighbours encourage aggressiveness in young males (Zigler and Child, 1969).

Achievement motivation is created by strong independence training of children, and results in hard work and risk-taking in order to make money, increase status and build up large enterprises. McClelland and Winter (1969) succeeded in improving achievement behaviour in Indian managers, with the result that they increased the size and turnover of their firms.

Assertiveness training is much in demand in the U.S.A., particularly from women. In Britain people want to learn how to make friends, while in Indonesia submissiveness is valued more than assertiveness. Extraversion scores are higher in the U.S.A., Australia and Canada than in Britain, and in the East great value is placed on maintaining good relationships and not losing face (Noesjirwan, 1978).

Ideals and values Cultures vary in their moral rules governing sexual behaviour, use of drugs and other matters. Even within modern societies there are great variations between different groups of people in the extent to which alternative moral values and ideals are accepted. They are taught by parents, teachers, clergymen, politicians and others, and are learnt by children brought up in the culture. Values and ideals function as restraints which control and inhibit certain spontaneous patterns of behaviour. While aggressive and sexual behaviour are among the main targets of these controls, the whole style and strategy of social behaviour may also be affected.

Telling the truth is valued in most cultures, but the truth is often not told. In our own culture it is also thought important not to hurt people's feelings, and in some cultures there is a great desire to please the hearer.

It has been found by Triandis (1972) that there are great cultural variations in what is most valued. In parts of India, for example, wealth is not desired because it can lead to arrogance and fear of thieves. In Greece, punishment is valued because it leads to justice. In Japan, serenity and aesthetic satisfaction are most valued. Wealth and health are greatly valued in the West, but not in parts of the East.

Moral codes may be learnt as simple sets of rules – 'It is wrong to tell a lie', or as rather high-level principles such as 'Do unto others as you would they do unto you.' They may be expressed as attitudes which should be adopted – 'Love your neighbour.' Most moral codes in fact recommend behaviour which is more affiliative, less dominating and less aggressive than social behaviour often is.

Social class In every society there are distinctive relationships between men and women, the old and the young, and other such divisions. Most societies, and all modern industrial ones, are stratified into classes. These are groups of people who regard members of the other groups as inferior or superior, and who share a common culture. The higher groups have more money, property and power. Members of each social class mix freely and can form intimate relationships with other members, but are much less likely to do so with people from other classes. Class is really a continuous variable, and boundaries are hard to define, though groupings and barriers appear from time to time. A development in the British class system during the 1950s was the emergence of an upper working class, whose members shared much of the material culture of the middle class, but did not mix socially with that class or have the same pattern of social behaviour (Goldthorpe *et al.*, 1969). Social class is shared by families, and depends mainly on the husband's occupation, income and education, and on the size and location of the home. Class systems vary in different countries. While class is mainly a function of occupation and education in Britain, it depends almost entirely on money in the U.S.A. The social distance between classes, i.e. the difficulties of communication and interaction and the difficulty of moving from one class to another, are greatest in caste and feudal societies and very low in the U.S.A.; Britain is intermediate in this respect.

Classes have different cultures, so what has been said about these applies here too. Instead of individual languages there are varying accents, and in Britain these provide of course one of the main clues to class.

There are also class differences in the way language is used. Bernstein (1959) suggested that working-class people used a 'restricted code', consisting of short and simple sentences, often uncompleted, with a lot of slang and idiom, many personal pronouns, and recurring rhetorical questions of the type 'didn't I?' Middle-class people use a restricted code, but they can also use an 'elaborated' one which is more impersonal, more complex and more grammatical. Bernstein suggests that the restricted code is suited to maintaining relationships in face-to-face groups, while the elaborated code is better for decision-taking and administration. There has been extensive research into these ideas, which shows that there are class differences of the kinds suggested in Britain, the U.S.A. and Australia. Middle-class people do use more complex syntax and a larger vocabulary, and are more effective at communicating impersonal information. However, these class differences occur as matters of degree, and working-class people can use the elaborated code if necessary, though they find it more difficult. One explanation for this difference might be that working-class children are bored by school and cannot be bothered to acquire the more educated style of speech (Robinson, 1978).

It has sometimes been suggested that middle-class people are more socially skilled than working-class people. However, their goals are probably different: middle-class behaviour is directed more to the accurate communication of information, working-class behaviour to the maintenance of social ties, if Bernstein is right.

When individuals from different social classes meet, the kinds of problem arise that are discussed below in connection with people from different cultures. The results are the same – there is misunderstanding and mutual rejection. There is the additional problem that social classes are ranked in a social prestige hierarchy, so that people react to those from other social classes as superiors and inferiors. For many people the social class of others is as important as sex and age, and is recognized fairly easily from their speech and clothes or from their social behaviour. This leads to the adoption of the appropriate style of interaction, which may be culturally prescribed. Such encounters are often a source of discomfort and tension to both parties, the more so the greater the difference in class and the more feudal the society. People who are found formal, dull or remote by outsiders can be genial, gay and relaxed when with members of their own group.

On the other hand, there may be a perfectly easy exchange between members of different social classes when they are in some established role-relationship. It is in public places, on purely social occasions and between strangers that inter-class difficulties appear. Mary Sissons arranged for an actor to stop eighty people in Paddington Station and ask them the way to Hyde Park. For half of them he was dressed and behaved as if upper-middle-class, for half he appeared to be working-class. The interviews were filmed and tape-recorded, and the social class of the respondents was obtained by subsequent interview. It was found that the middle-class/middle-class encounters went most smoothly compared with the other three combinations of social class; there was instant rapport, the encounters lasted longer, respondents smiled more and there was a definite ending (Sissons, 1971).

Social mobility upwards is widely desired, and in industrialized societies is very common, but it has its drawbacks. Like the immigrant, the mobile person has to learn a new language, a new set of conventions and values, and has to unlearn the ones he had before. Unless he does so he will not be accepted by the new group.

Intercultural encounters When people from two different cultures meet, there is infinite scope for misunderstanding and confusion. This may be a matter of misinterpreting the other's communications, verbal or non-verbal. There is the Englishman who depreciates his own abilities in what turns out to be a highly misleading way; there is the Arab who starves at a banquet because he is only offered the dishes once; there is the African who puts his hand on a Western knee. There may be difficulties in setting up a stable pattern of interaction – Americans and Europeans have been seen retreating backwards or gyrating in circles at international conferences, pursued by Latin Americans trying to establish their habitual degree of proximity (Hall, 1955). Westerners are perplexed by Japanese who giggle when hearing or delivering bad news. American businessmen find it difficult to adjust to the more hierarchical pattern of relationships in their overseas branches, where subordinates do not speak their mind to their superiors.

The result of these cross-cultural misunderstandings is likely to be that each person rejects the other as one who has failed to conform to the standards of civilized society, and looks on him as impossible to get on with. There are several solutions to this problem: one is to find out the cultural patterns of the other, and either conform oneself, or at least use them to interpret the other's behaviour properly. The difficulty here is that many of these patterns of behaviour are very subtle, and it takes a long familiarity with the culture to know them all. Another approach is to be far more flexible and tolerant when dealing with people from other cultures, and to make a real effort to understand and to control one's reactions to the unusual aspects of their behaviour. Several research groups have been engaged in developing methods of training people to function effectively in alien cultures.

Language learning is most valuable, especially for those who are going to stay some time and if they can learn the polite and colloquial usages.

Educational methods This is an area of social skills training where there is a lot to learn, and where lectures and reading can be very valuable. A special method is the use of Culture Assimilators: a critical incident survey discovers the forty to sixty main problem situations in the culture in question, which leads to the construction of a do-it-yourself tutor text. The Arab Culture Assimilator developed at the University of Illinois consists of fifty-five problem episodes for trainees to solve, which are intended to teach them about such matters as the role of women, dealing with subordinates, entertaining guests and the importance of religion. It has been found that this kind of training produces some improvement in interaction with Arabs and Thais (Fiedler *et al.*, 1971).

Role playing and simulations Another approach has been used by Peter Collett at Oxford. Englishmen were taught the interaction styles known to be used by Arabs – standing closer, touching, etc. These trainees got on better with Arabs and were liked better than untrained subjects (Collett, 1971). Where new social skills need to be learnt such techniques are very desirable.

Interaction with members of the other culture is used on a number of inter-cultural training courses.

Training for inter-cultural communication is now given regularly in Britain, the U.S.A. and elsewhere, for diplomats, businessmen and members of the forces and Peace Corps. Follow-up studies have shown that courses using some of the components described above, and lasting three to ten days or longer, are quite successful, in that those who have been trained are more likely to complete their stay, are rated by their hosts as more effective or more likeable and enjoy themselves more in the country visited (Brislin and Pedersen, 1976).

FURTHER READING

Baron, R. A., and Byrne, D., *Social Psychology: Understanding Human Interaction,* 3rd edn, Allyn and Bacon, Boston, 1981, chs. 6 and 10.

Bochner, S. (ed.), *Intercultural Communication*, Pergamon, 1982.

Argyle, M., *The Social Psychology of Work*, Penguin Books, 1972.

CHAPTER 9

SELF-IMAGE AND SELF-PRESENTATION

We showed in Chapter 5 how people categorize each other in order to know how to behave towards them. When a person is constantly categorized and treated in a particular way, he acquires a *self-image*. Depending on how far others treat him with approval and respect he will acquire some degree of *self-esteem*. The self affects behaviour in a number of ways, of which the most important is *self-presentation*; that is, behaviour intended to create certain impressions for others.

It was postulated in Chapter 1 that people have a need for a distinct and consistent self-image and a need for self-esteem. This may result in attempts to elicit responses from others which provide confirmation of these images and attitudes towards the self. The self-image is one of the central and stable features of personality, and a person cannot be fully understood unless the contents and structure of his self-image are known.

THE DIMENSIONS OF SELF AND THEIR MEASUREMENT

The self-image This term, like 'ego-identity', refers to how a person consciously perceives himself. The central core usually consists of his name, bodily feelings, body-image, sex and age. For a man the job will also be central, unless he is suffering from job alienation. For a woman her family and husband's job may also be central. The core will contain other qualities that may be particularly salient, such as social class, religion, particular achievements of note or anything that makes a person different from others. The self-image contains some enduring aspects, and others which vary with the situation and the role being played.

The same person occupies a number of roles; he may be a lecturer, a father and a member of various committees and clubs. He plays these roles in a characteristic style; the way he sees himself in those roles is a part of his ego-identity. He may perceive himself vaguely or clearly. The more he has discussed his personal problems with others the more clearly he is likely to see himself. During psychotherapy, the therapist may provide the concepts which the patient can use to talk about himself. Some aspects of the self-image are more important to a person than others: it is more upsetting if these are challenged or lost, people are keenest to play the roles involved (e.g. scientist, orator), they will try hard to develop the necessary skills and the performance spreads to other roles (Rosenberg, 1981).

One method of finding the contents of a person's self-image is the Twenty Statements Test: subjects are asked to give twenty answers to the question 'Who am I?'. The first answers are usually roles – sex, social class, job, etc., and the rest consist of personality traits or evaluations – happy, good, intelligent, etc. (Kuhn and McPartland, 1954). This test gives some measure of the importance of each item to the subject, but has not yet been shown to be particularly reliable or valid.

Another method of assessing the self-image is by seven-point scales such as the Semantic Differential; subjects are asked to describe 'the kind of person I actually am' along a series of seven-point scales such as:

cold   warm;
attractive   – unattractive;
stupid   – clever;
strong   – weak;
kind   – cruel.
        (Osgood *et al.*, 1957)

However, the original scales of the Semantic Differential need to be modified for measuring the self-image.

The Adjective Check List consists of 300 adjectives; subjects can be asked which ones apply to themselves, and the results can be converted into scores on factors such as self-favourability, self-confidence and self-control (Gough and Heilbrun, 1965). There are also a number of indirect, 'unconscious' ways of assessing the self-image – projective tests, story completion and the like. Wylie (1974) gives an extensive account of methods of assessing the self-image.

The body image is an important part of the self-image, especially for girls and young women. Males are most pleased with their bodies when they are large, females are most pleased when their bodies are small but with large busts (Jourard and Secord, 1955). This, at any rate, was the situation in the U.S.A. in the 1950s; the most desired male and female physiques vary quite a lot between cultures and historical periods.

How far does a person's self-image correspond with the way he is seen by others? As will be seen, people present a somewhat improved, idealized and censored version of themselves for public inspection, and may come to believe it themselves. On the other hand, reality in the form of others' reactions prevents the self-image from getting too far out of line. It is no good thinking you are the King of France if no one else shares this view. However, some people succeed in insulating themselves from the views of others so that they are simply unaware of how they are regarded.

Self-esteem. A person's self-esteem is a measure of the extent to which he approves of and accepts himself, and regards himself as praiseworthy, either absolutely or in comparison with others. Like ego-identity, self-esteem has a stable core, together with a series of peripheral esteems based on different role-relationships, and it varies quite a lot between situations (Gergen and Morse, 1967). One complication about self-esteem is that some people develop an exaggerated self-regard in compensation for basic feelings of inferiority. In these cases it is difficult to decide whether they 'really' have high or low self-esteem – it depends on whether this is measured by direct or indirect means.

One of the best measures is the Index of Adjustment and Values (IAV), which consists of forty-nine adjectives, forty good and nine bad, on which the self is rated on five-point scales (Bills, Vance and McLean, 1951). Another way is to measure the overall discrepancy between self and ideal self, or ego-ideal.

The ego-ideal This term refers to the kind of person one would most like to be; it is a personal goal to be striven for, and it may also be the image that is presented to others. It may be based on particular individuals who are taken as admired models, and who may be parents, teachers, film stars, or characters from literature. It may consist of a fusion of desired characteristics drawn from various sources. The ego-ideal may be remote and unattainable, or it may be just a little better than the self-image in certain respects. The gap between the two can be assessed by means of the measures described already. The Semantic Differential can be filled in to describe 'the kind of person I actually am', and 'the kind of person I would most like to be'. The average discrepancy between scale scores is then worked out thus:

$$(\text{ego-ideal}) \ (\text{self})$$

$$\text{attractive} - - \overset{\text{x}}{-} - - - \overset{\text{x}}{-} \text{ unattractive}$$

A number of studies have found that neurotics have greater self/ego-ideal conflict than normals, and that the discrepancy gets smaller during psychotherapy – and this is mainly because of changes in self-ratings. However, there are some groups of people, by no means well-adjusted, who show very little conflict because they perceive themselves so inaccurately (Wylie, 1979).

When there is much conflict, it contributes to low self-esteem. It may also lead to efforts to attain the ego-ideal: when there is actually movement in this direction there is said to be 'self-realization'. There may be efforts to actually change the personality, i.e., some aspects of behaviour, in some way; or there may be efforts to persuade others to categorize one differently, by better self-presentation. A curious feature of the ideal self is that a person who attains it does not necessarily rest on his laurels enjoying the self-esteem, but may revise his goals upwards – like a high-jumper who moves the bar up a notch.

Integration of the self (achievement of identity) A child may admire saints and soldiers, poets and financiers, but eventually he has to decide which is the direction in which he really wants to go. The degree of integration or diffusion of ego-identity is an important aspect of personality. At one extreme are the completely dedicated, single-minded fanatics, at the other are those adolescents who do not yet know 'who they are or where they are going'. The more integrated the self-image, the more consistent a person's behaviour will be: one effect of the self-image on behaviour is the suppression of behaviour that is out of line. This 'consistency' may take various forms, depending on whether the self-image is based on the attributes of some person, on a set of ethical or ideological rules of conduct, or on an occupational or social-class role.

THE ORIGINS OF THE SELF

The reactions of others The main origin of self-image and self-esteem is probably the reactions of others – we come to see ourselves as others categorize us. This has been called the theory of the 'looking-glass self' – to see ourselves we look to see how we are reflected in the reactions of others. There is experimental evidence that others' reactions affect self-ratings. In one experiment subjects were asked to read poems: some were evaluated favourably, others unfavourably, by a supposed speech expert, and self-ratings on ability to read poems and on related activities shifted accordingly (Videbeck, 1960). If parents tell a child he is clever, or treat him as if he is untrustworthy, these attributes may become part of the ego-identity. The whole pattern of reactions is important here, the spoken and the unspoken.

Parents and teachers do not hesitate to give full descriptive feedback to children, but amongst older people there is something of a taboo on such direct verbal feedback, especially in its negative aspects, and it has been suggested that it would be helpful to provide people with rather more of such information than is currently regarded as polite. On the other hand, this can be a very traumatic way of finding out about oneself, and information should be delivered with tact, or indirectly by the use of subtle hints and non-verbal reactions.

The impact of the reactions of others is greatest when we care about their opinions and respect their judgement, when they are expert on the field in question, when we think they are sincere and unbiased, when there is a consensus of such views, and on individuals who have not yet crystallized their self-image (Rosenberg, 1981).

Comparison with others Self-perception may include concepts such as 'tall' or 'clever'; however, these only have meaning in comparison with the height or cleverness of others. An important source of the self-image is the comparison of oneself with brothers, sisters, friends or others who are constantly present and are sufficiently similar to invite comparison. If other families in the neighbourhood are wealthier than his own, a child will regard himself as poor; if his brothers and sisters, or those in the same school form, are more intelligent, he will come to see himself as not clever, and so on. People compare their abilities or fortunes with others who are similar: a tennis-player does not compare himself either with Wimbledon champions or with hopeless beginners, manual workers do not compare their wages with those of the managing director or of Indian peasants. Subjects in experiments are most interested to know about those who are slightly better than themselves (Latané, 1966), as if they were trying to do better by small instalments. In a study of a large number of adolescents in New York State, Rosenberg (1965) found that those with the highest self-esteem tended to be of higher social class, to have done better at school and to have been leaders in clubs – all of which could be bases for favourable comparisons of self with others.

Social roles These include sex, age, social class, occupation, religion, race, marital status and other categories and their labels. People see themselves as doctors, criminals, etc., ascribe to themselves the properties of such roles and evaluate themselves accordingly. This is partly a result of actually playing the roles. Medical students come to look upon themselves as doctors during their training – 31 per cent in the first year, 83 per cent in the fourth year and nearly all when dealing with patients (Merton *et al.*, 1957). An important source of the self-image is simply the roles a person has played in the past or is playing in the present. Adults often see themselves primarily in terms of the job they do, although roles of particular importance or excitement in their past may be even more salient (e.g. 'When I was in the Navy . . .').

There are individual differences in role performance, and a person may come to see himself as an *intelligent* juvenile delinquent, i.e. as combining a role and a trait. Goffman (1956a) suggested that in order to perform a role effectively, the newcomer has to put on a mask to act the part; however, when he has acted the part for long enough and others have accepted the performance this becomes a real part of his personality and is no longer a mask.

Identification with models Children identify with a succession of people – parents, teachers and others – that is, they admire and want to be like them. The ego-ideal is mainly based on a fusion of these models. However, it has been found in a number of experiments that identification also modifies the self-image, i.e. people feel that they *already* resemble the model.

The adolescent identity crisis Children play at roles, adolescents experiment with them. During student life it is possible to try out a number of roles and identities without commitment, such as being an actor, journalist or revolutionary. However, pressures to commit oneself build up, and somewhere between the ages of sixteen and twenty-four there is often an identity crisis, when a person is forced to make up his mind about which of all these bits and pieces of identity to hang on to and which to suppress (Erikson, 1956). The basis of this is partly the need to choose one job rather than another, a marital partner, a political and religious outlook, and a lifestyle. In addition, the development of greater powers of abstract thought probably makes it more important than before to be *consistently* vegetarian, radical, intellectual or whatever it may be.

The state of an individual's identity can be established by an interview assessing whether he has gone through a crisis period and how far he is committed in two main spheres – occupation and ideology. Four main kinds of identity are found among students in the U.S.A. and Canada (Marcia, 1966). In the most highly developed, an integrated identity has been achieved, which is to have 'a feeling of being at home in one's body, a sense of knowing where one is going, and an inner assuredness of anticipated recognition from those who count' (Erikson, op. cit.).

1 *Identity achievement* Here the individual has been through a decision making period, or crisis, and has made occupational, religious and political commitments.

2 *Moratorium* The individual is in a period of crisis, trying to make up his mind between alternative careers, having religious doubts and feeling confused about politics.

3 *Foreclosure* Although occupationally and ideologically committed, the individual did not go through a period of crisis, rebellion or exploration of alternatives; he has accepted parental guidance on his occupation and typically shares his parents' views on religion and politics.

4 *Identity diffusion* Here a person may or may not have passed through a crisis, but in either case he has not decided upon, nor is he much concerned about, his occupational, religious and political orientation.

An additional type of individual, identified by the term *alienated achievement*, is characterized as being 'committed to not being committed'. This kind of person, though well integrated in the Eriksonian sense, rejects the social value of commitment itself, which may be the basis for his desire to learn handicrafts or join a commune. This is regarded as belonging to a transient historical period and is reported to be on the decline in North America.

The identity statuses correlate with a number of other aspects of personality. For example, identity achievers reach the highest levels of attainment in college (though their IQ is no higher than others'), perform well under stress and are the least affected by failure; they and the moratoriums have the most satisfactory interpersonal relationships with both sexes. Moratoriums, however, suffer the greatest anxiety and are rebellious and competitive. Foreclosures are authoritarian and value obedience and loyalty. Diffusions are more influenced by peers, but tend to be withdrawn and have low levels of intimacy. The statuses also correspond to patterns of child-rearing: foreclosures had very close relations with their parents, while the parents of diffusions were unconcerned and detached. During the college years many students move towards identity achievement.

Because of varying social expectations, the story for women is a bit different. Their career is often of less importance, and because they are expected to absorb more readily their parents' and then their husband's identity their own crisis usually comes much later in life. Female foreclosures are quite similar to identity achievers, perhaps because this is an acceptable style for young women, or was before the women's movement.

It is recognized that things are different in other cultures; for example, foreclosure is probably the most common form in those societies and social classes where young people are not able to spend several years finding out who they are. In North America foreclosures are found to be rigid, authoritarian, insecure and morally immature; it is not known whether this is the case in other cultures (Bourne, 1978).

The need for self-esteem We have seen that there are forces in the personality acting to achieve a *unified* identity, and that this is controlled by outside forces acting to keep it *realistic*. There is another force acting to produce a *favourable* self-image, which provides sufficient self-esteem. We have seen that self-ratings are usually somewhat more generous than ratings given by others. However, the self-image depends on the reactions of others; this is why such a lot of effort is put into self-presentation and the manipulation of others' perceptions. What happens if others' evaluations are *more* favourable than self-evaluation? Experiments show that such evaluations are neither believed nor remembered (Shrauger, 1975).

The need for self-esteem is usually limited by reality; if this is not the case behaviour becomes absurd and preposterous, and there is continual lack of confirmation by others. This happens in the instance of paranoia (pp. 217f). In fact people differ widely in their feelings of esteem, from conceit to inferiority. Both extremes usually reflect failure to perceive accurately the present responses of others, and can be regarded as failures of adjustment. A mythical psychotherapist is said to have told a patient who suffered from feelings of inferiority, 'But you really *are* inferior.' The real reason that people feel inferior is usually that they have been unduly rejected by their parents, or have chosen too elevated a comparison group.

It is quite possible to select prestigeful items out of the long list of self-attributes and roles once played, and such items often become a favourite item of conservation. However, total self-esteem is greatly affected by the ego-ideal. Thus self-esteem depends jointly on a person's position on a series of evaluative dimensions, and upon the value placed on each of these dimensions. Values depend on the group, so self-esteem depends on whether the group values a person's attributes – but a group will have been joined because it does value them.

It is interesting that self-esteem is *not* any lower among members of racial or other minority groups subjected to discrimination, probably because it depends on the evaluation of, and comparisons with, individuals in the same group (Wylie, 1979). However, the self-esteem of such people is reduced if they live in mixed communities.

CONDITIONS UNDER WHICH THE SELF IS ACTIVATED

The self is not at work all the time – people are not continually trying to discover, sustain or present a self-image. For example, when at home rather than at work, in the audience rather than on the stage, the self-system is not very active.

Most people feel self-conscious when appearing in front of an audience, and some feel very anxious. It has been found that these effects are greater when the audience is large and of high status, (Fig. 22, Latané, 1981). The performer is the centre of attention for a number of people and his performance will be assessed, so there is the danger that he will receive disapproving reactions, and self-esteem may be damaged.

When someone addresses any kind of audience it is no good his speaking in the informal 'familial' style – he won't be heard properly. It is inevitable that he must put on some kind of 'performance'. Once he does so he is accepting a certain definition of the situation and presenting a certain face: he is someone who is able to perform before this audience and is worth attending to. It is this implicit claim which creates the risk of loss of face. We shall discuss later the social skills of dealing with audiences, including how stage fright can be reduced (pp. 258f).

There are many social situations where other people can be regarded as a kind of audience and where one's performance may be assessed. Argyle and Williams (1969) asked subjects, 'To what extent did you feel mainly the observer or the observed?' after they had been in a variety of situations. It was found that they felt more observed (a) when being interviewed, rather than

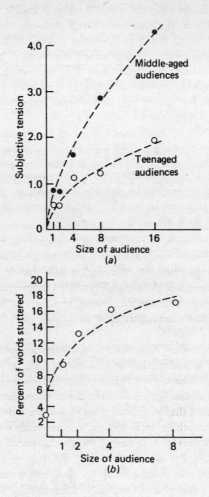

Figure 22. Social tension as a function of size and age of audience (from Latané, 1981).

interviewing, (b) when with an older person, especially in the case of seventeen-year-old subjects, and (c) when a female with males. Individuals differ in the extent to which they see themselves as observers of others or being observed by others. It is found that some people consistently see themselves as observed, particularly males who are insecure and dependent. It is interesting to find that females feel observed, especially by males; they tend to wear more colourful and interesting clothes and to take more trouble about their appearance than males.

The self can be activated in other ways. Duval and Wicklund (1972) called this 'objective self-awareness' – the awareness of oneself as an object, as seen from outside. They produced this state simply by placing people in front of mirrors. An individual will be more self-conscious if he or she is different in some obvious way from everyone else in the room; for example, by wearing distinctive clothes or by being the only female or black present. Conversely 'de-individuation' can be brought about by dressing everyone up in white lab coats or other uniforms; this produces a loss of individual responsibility, and people even forget who said what. Self-awareness is produced by 'penetration' of territory or privacy – being discovered with too few clothes on, or when one has not been able to arrange one's appearance, or when awkward private facts are disclosed.

There are individual differences in self-consciousness. Some people suffer from *audience anxiety*, that is they feel nervous when appearing in public or when made the centre of attention. Another variable is *exhibitionism*, which is the desire to appear in public and be seen. It is found that these two dimensions are independent, so that some people both desire to be seen and are made anxious by it; such people are found to make a large number of speech errors when speaking in public (Paivio, 1965).

Those who have low self-esteem are shy, easily embarrassed, eager to be approved of and are easily influenced by social pressures; they are clearly taking the observed role. Insecure people, i.e. those who have not formed a stable self-image, are very sensitive to the reactions of others, since they are still seeking information which will affect their self-image. Those who have achieved an integrated identity are no longer so bothered about the reactions of others, and are not upset if others mistake their identity or react negatively towards them (Marcia, 1966).

THE EFFECTS OF THE SELF-IMAGE ON BEHAVIOUR

What happens when the self is activated, by audiences, mirrors or in other ways? In the first place there is a heightened level of physiological arousal, which results in greater effort, greater productivity if some task is being performed, as well as disruption of that performance if arousal is too great. Secondly, attention is directed towards the self rather than to others, and the self is seen as from outside. Duval and Wicklund suggest that this makes people aware of the discrepancies between self and ideal self, and self-image and the perception by others. They found that subjects who had been made aware of such discrepancies and were placed in front of a mirror, left the mirror as soon as they could; in other experiments it was found that subjects gave lower self-ratings when in front of a mirror (Wickland, 1975). On the other hand, Carver (1979) suggests that while self-awareness leads to a comparison between aspects of the self and certain external standards, the outcome is not always negative.

The motivation for self-presentation People want to project a self-image for several reasons. To begin with, for interaction to occur at all it is necessary for the participants to be able to categorize one another – they need guidance on how to respond to each other. It was shown before that different styles of behaviour are used depending on the social class, occupation, nationality, etc. of those present. If it is not clear where a person falls on such dimensions, or if the important things about him are concealed, people do not know how to interact with him and will be very perplexed. It is essential that all interactors should present themselves clearly in *some* way. It is necessary to arrive at a working agreement about identities with those present.

An individual may be concerned about his face for professional purposes. There is a good reason for this: clients are more likely to respond in the desired way if they have confidence in the expertise of the practitioner. There is widespread evidence that pupils learn more if they think their teachers are good, and that patients in psychotherapy recover faster if they believe that the therapist can cure them. Another reason a person may need confirmation of his self-image or self-esteem is that he may be 'insecure' – i.e. be in constant need of reassurance from others that he is what he hopes he is. If the self-image has not been firmly established in the past, more time has to be spent looking in the mirror of others' reactions in the present.

Goffman (1956a) observed that undertakers, salesmen, waiters and other professional and service workers engage in a lot of deception and impression manipulation (see p. 208). The stage is set in the 'front regions' of premises, and may involve collusion between team-members; members of the public are kept out of the back regions, which are dirtier and less impressive, and where behaviour is more vulgar and informal. Goffman maintains that a similar degree of deception occurs in many other non-professional situations, such as a family receiving guests. Part of this theory has been confirmed by Canter's finding (in press) that the main division seen in the spaces of houses is between the public and private rooms.

Verbal and non-verbal self-presentation How do people project an identity? The easiest way would be simply to tell other people how nice, important or clever we are. It is fairly obvious why this doesn't work – everyone would like to make such claims, but are they true? Verbal self-presentation appears to be acceptable only if it is very indirect; if such messages are too direct they can easily become ridiculous, as in name-dropping. Stephen Potter has given a satirical account of indirect ways of claiming a prestigeful identity in his book *One-Upmanship* (1952). For example:

LAYMAN: Thank you, Doctor. I was coming home rather late last night from the House of Commons . . .

M.D.–MAN: Thank you . . . now if you'll just let me put these . . . hair brushes and things off the bed for you . . . that's right . . .

LAYMAN: I was coming home rather late. Army Act, really . . .

M.D.–MAN: Now just undo the top button of your shirt or whatever it is you're wearing . . .

LAYMAN: I say I was coming . . .

M.D.–MAN: Now if you've got some hot water – really hot – and a clean towel.
LAYMAN: Yes, just outside. The Postmaster-General . . .
M.D.–MAN: Open your mouth, please.

E. E. Jones has carried out a series of experiments on ingratiation, in which subjects were motivated to give a good impression, for some purpose (1964). He found that people were very careful over their self-presentation; for example, mentioning their good points in unimportant areas only, subjects in a high status role being particularly modest. Gove *et al.* (1980), in a large American survey, found that as many as 26·5 per cent of people admitted to having pretended to be less intelligent or knowledgeable than they really were – men more than women, though wives had often played dumb in this way with husbands. This is almost the reverse of self-presentation, and evidently it too can be advantageous.

Self-presentation is done most efficiently by non-verbal communication. Signals like clothes, hair, voice and general style of behaviour have more impact than words. Sometimes these non-verbal signs are actually part of what is symbolized – like upper-class speech or football-fan clothes. Sometimes they symbolize aspects of the self which cannot be easily displayed in the course of interaction, like being honest or intelligent.

The main non-verbal signals here are clothes. Social class is easily signalled and recognized in this way. Accents are equally effective, and professional people may impress their clients by their offices and cars. Clothes can also send information about personality. Gibbins (1969) found that English grammar-school girls were agreed as to what kind of girl would wear various sorts of clothes, whether she would be promiscuous, go to church, drink, etc.; the clothes they themselves preferred had images which resembled both their actual and ideal self.

Hair is used in a similar way. In many times and places long hair has been worn by male outcasts, intellectuals, dropouts and ascetics; having it cut represents re-entering society or living under a disciplined regime, like monks and soldiers do. On the other hand, some rebellious groups wear very short hair (e.g. skinheads), and long hair for males has sometimes been socially acceptable. Perhaps hair has no constant meaning at all, but is simply an important area for expressing opposition to prevailing norms.

Clothes, hair and other aspects of appearance differ from other non-verbal signals in that there are changes in fashion. The explanation is probably that élite fashions are copied by those of lower social status, so the higher-status groups have to adopt newer fashions to show that they are different. This doctrine was confirmed in an American survey by Hurlock (1929) in which 40 per cent of women and 20 per cent of men admitted that they would follow a fashion in order to appear equal to those of higher status, and about 50 per cent said they changed their styles when their social inferiors adopted them.

Whole styles of behaviour may be due to self-presentation. Aggression is more likely to occur when there is an audience, and non-aggressive responses to insults are concealed (Felson, 1978).

Deception and concealment Another feature of self-presentation is concealment: people are careful not to reveal aspects of themselves which are likely to lead to disapproval. Jourard (1964) surveyed large numbers of students, using a questionnaire asking how much they had revealed about themselves to other people. This varied greatly with content: more was revealed about opinions and attitudes than about sexual behaviour or money, for instance. People will reveal more to those they can trust not to reject them – to their mothers, close friends, people who are similar to themselves and (we may add) to psychiatrists and clergymen. Another case of concealment is the cautious, ritualized and conventional behaviour which people display on first meeting strangers. Disclosure is a risk, as there is a danger of the other person disapproving. There is extensive evidence that self-disclosure is reciprocated – a principle which is used by some psychotherapists and interviewers. People who disclose more are liked, provided that what they disclose is acceptable (Chaikin and Derlega, 1976).

Deception and concealment are quite common, as Goffman (1956a) has shown. For example, discreditable episodes or features of the self are concealed. In any group of people who know each other well, there is collaboration in the process of forgetting unfortunate events. Similarly, if someone has a low opinion of a colleague it is probable that the most constructive line of action involves some concealment of these opinions. Some people are 'stigmatized', in that they would be socially rejected if the truth were known – homosexuals, ex-convicts, mental patients, members of disreputable professions. They conceal these facts from outsiders, but can often recognize one another. Deception by undertakers and waiters is not so much about the self as about other features of the professional performance. Sometimes this is to the performer's advantage – as with salesmen and waiters – sometimes it is to the client's advantage – as with undertakers and doctors.

Jourard and others, however, have argued that behaviour *ought* to be authentic and sincere. Instead of treating the deception versus authenticity debate as a moral issue, it can be seen as a difference between two kinds of personalities. Snyder (1979) devised the Self-Monitoring (SM) scale, with items like: 'When I am uncertain how to act in social situations, I look to the behavior of others for cues' and 'In different situations and with different people I often act like very different persons.' A series of experiments have shown that people high on the SM scale are sensitive to situations and try to present themselves in a suitable way; they see themselves as flexible and adaptable. Those low on the scale have a clear and enduring self-image and want to be true to themselves. High SMs are able to control their emotional expression, give the impression of being friendly and extraverted, not anxious or nervous, whether they really are or not (Lippa, 1978), are less shy, commonly take the initiative and talk more with strangers. In these ways high SMs are more socially skilled, but low SMs are more sincere and their behaviour is a truer reflection of their attitudes. The two types of people even have different kinds of self: low SMs have a stable self-image, seeing themselves as principled and consistent, while high SMs see themselves as the sum of a series of different situational role performances.

Embarrassment Embarrassment is contagious, spreading rapidly to all present. Once a person has lost control this makes the situation worse, as he is now ashamed also of his lack of poise. He is temporarily incapable of interacting.

Goffman (1956b) offered a theory of embarrassment: people commonly present a self which is partly bogus; if this image is discredited in the course of interaction, embarrassment ensues. For example, a person's job, qualifications or social origins may turn out to be less impressive than had been suggested. This theory can be checked against the 1,000 instances of embarrassment collected by Gross and Stone (1964). About a third of these cases involved discrediting of self-presentation, but the rest could not really be classified in this way, and other sources of embarrassment need to be considered.

Another theory is that embarrassment is due to a failure by an individual to meet certain social expectations, leading to his receiving a fall in public esteem, and hence experiencing a fall in his self-esteem (Modigliani, 1971). This has been confirmed in a study in which subjects judged that people who, for example, knocked over piles of cans or choked on their food, were perceived as more clumsy, incompetent, immature and unintelligent if they did it in public, and that the actors' subjective ratings on such scales were thought to be lower than the way they were actually perceived by others (Semin and Manstead, 1981).

Embarrassment can be produced by forgetfulness, such as not remembering someone's name. Take the case of a man who met Princess Margaret at a party:

Man: The old firm still flourishes, eh?
Princess: You could say that.
Man: Your sister still well, I hope, still flourishing?
Princess: Still Queen.

It can also be caused unwittingly, by ignorance, e.g. of the fact that a person is divorced, is a Jew or has just lost his wife. Accidents can be very embarrassing: Gross and Stone report an extraordinary case of a man at a banquet who got the tablecloth caught in his trouser zip-fastener and pulled everything off the table when he rose to speak. Such episodes are more embarrassing at formal occasions since one is to some extent putting on a performance and implicitly making claims of competence. Rule-breaking can be embarrassing, whether through ignorance or the effects of drink, fatigue or insanity. Rule-breaking causes consternation because it is unexpected, breaking the smooth flow of interaction, and because others may not know how to deal with it.

Can embarrassment be avoided? Some people are able to remain poised when embarrassing incidents occur; they 'keep their cool' and prevent the situation from disintegrating. Adolescents often tease and insult one another, perhaps as a kind of training in dealing with embarrassment. Some of the possible causes of embarrassment can be avoided by presenting a face which cannot be invalidated, and it is less likely to happen to those who are not dependent on external confirmation of their self-image and self-esteem. Breakdown of interaction may still occur, however, as a result of accidental errors, as in social gaffes. Rules of etiquette and skills of tact help to avoid such instances. An example of etiquette is the rule not to send invitations too long before the event, when it is difficult to refuse them. An example of tact is knocking on a door or coughing when a couple may be making love on the other side of it. Embarrassment can perhaps be controlled by understanding its causes. There is really no need to be disturbed by accidents committed in good faith and without hostile intention – it is more useful to put things right.

When a person is embarrassed, the others present usually want to prevent the collapse of social interaction, and will help in various ways. To begin with, they will try to prevent loss of face by being tactful in the ways described. They may pretend that nothing has happened, make excuses for the offender – he was only joking, was off form etc., or in some other way 'rescue the situation'. Finally, if face is irrevocably lost they may help the injured party to rehabilitate himself in the group in a new guise (Goffman, 1956b; Gross and Stone, 1964).

Disconfirmation of self-image When A's face has been disbelieved or discredited there are various strategies open to him. One is simply to ignore what has happened or to laugh it off as unimportant. It would be expected from the analysis given in earlier chapters that a person who had failed to project an image would try alternative ways of doing so. If he is rattled he may fall back on less subtle techniques of the kind 'Look here, young man, I've written more books about this subject than you've read', 'Do you realize that I . . .', etc.

What very often happens is that A forms a lower opinion of a person or group that does not treat him properly, and he goes off to present himself to someone else. It has been found that salesgirls in shops preserve their image of competence in the face of customers whom they can't please by categorizing them as 'nasty', or in some similar way (Lombard, 1955). If a low opinion is formed of B, it doesn't matter whether B confirms the girl's self-image of competence or not. A number of experiments show that people withdraw from groups who do not react to them in the desired way, and that they prefer the company and friendship of those who confirm their self-image (Secord and Backman, 1974).

Sometimes a person is still keen to belong to a group even though it does not accept his self-image or does not treat him with enough respect. When it is mainly esteem which has been withheld by the group, it is possible to alter behaviour in a way that will produce the desired response from others. It is found that insecure people are more affected by social influences and pressures of all kinds. In small social groups, for example, one of the main causes of conformity is the avoidance of being rejected, as deviates tend to be. Those who conform most are those who feel inferior, lack self-confidence, and are dependent on others (Krech, Crutchfield and Ballachey, 1962). People may embark on all kinds of self-improvement, either apparent or real, in response to negative reactions from others, including the modification of styles of interaction as in operant verbal conditioning.

The remaining responses can really be regarded as 'defence mechanisms', whose main object is the avoidance of anxiety, while no realistic adjustment of self-image or behaviour is involved. One of these is self-deception in its various forms. A person may distort the reactions of others in a favourable direction or simply not perceive them at all. The extreme of this is psychotic withdrawal from the difficulties of interpersonal relations into a private world of fantasies which cannot be disturbed by outside events.

FURTHER READING

Goffman, E., *The Presentation of Self in Everyday Life*, Edinburgh University Press, 1956.
Rosenberg, M., 'The self-concept; social product and social force', in

Rosenberg, M., and Turner, R. H. (eds), *Social Psychology: Sociological Perspective*, Basic Books, New York, 1981.

Wicklund, R. A., 'Objective self awareness', *Advances in Experimental Social Psychology*, 1975, pp. 233–75.

Wylie, R., *The Self-Concept* (2 vols), University of Nebraska Press, Lincoln, 1974 and 1979.

CHAPTER 10

SOCIAL BEHAVIOUR AND MENTAL DISORDER

THIS topic is of importance for two reasons. Firstly, we can learn a lot about normal social performance by studying the ways in which it goes wrong; each kind of failure in social performance shows us a feature of normal social behaviour which has to be managed properly. Secondly, the study of the social behaviour of mental patients may throw light on the nature of mental disorders and have implications for new forms of treatment. In fact it has already done so: social skills training for mental patients is one of the main practical applications of the research described in this book.

We shall not attempt in this chapter to give a complete or balanced account of mental disorders, and shall only be concerned with the *social* behaviour of mental patients. Freud maintained that mental disorders were primarily disturbances of the sexual instinct. Sullivan suggested that they were disturbances of social behaviour. In fact the social behaviour of patients is inadequate in a variety of ways. There are several views about how the failure of social behaviour may be related to the other aspects of disorders. One theory is that failure to learn the right social skills in childhood results in later social rejection and failure to cope with life events; this in turn causes anxiety, depression or other symptoms. Another theory is that basic disturbances in the personality disrupt social behaviour; for example, intense anxiety may prevent a person from using his social skills, or these may be disrupted by cognitive or physiological factors. Another possibility is that a person is deliberately producing certain social signals in a bid for help or sympathy. In both of the last cases the inadequate behaviour may lead to rejection, a source of further difficulty.

There is evidence from twin studies that mental disorders are partly inherited, and this is particularly true of the psychoses, such as schizophrenia, rather than of the neuroses; this would lend support to the second theory. On the other hand, the psychoses are affected by childhood experiences, are often precipitated by rejection or other social stresses, and some of the main symptoms are in the sphere of social performance, so that the first process may also be operating, and this is even more likely with the neuroses.

The bid-for-help theory, we shall find, is applicable to depression. According to each of these theories, however, it would be valuable to retrain patients in social skills, and according to the first this would be the most useful treatment.

SOCIAL BEHAVIOUR OBSERVED IN THE MAIN MENTAL DISORDERS

In this section a descriptive account will be given of the social behaviour which is observed in the main types of mental disorder. Some of this is commonly reported by clinicians and can be seen in any mental hospital. The more subtle aspects require the use of some of the research methods described earlier, such as the analysis of voice quality, direction of gaze, synchronizing of speech, person perception and so on.

The categories into which patients are classified vary between countries and historical periods; American psychiatrists label five times as many patients 'schizophrenic' as British psychiatrists (Cooper *et al.*, 1972). I shall use the current British classification.

Schizophrenia This term is used to cover a wide variety of conditions, but the basic syndrome consists of withdrawal from social relationships, disturbance of thought and speech, hearing voices, a failure of persistent, goal-directed behaviour and a flat emotional state. The disturbance of social behaviour is only one of the symptoms, but is one of the most characteristic and is a principal reason for patients' inability to deal with everyday life. They simply cannot communicate properly or take part in ordinary social encounters. They are of great interest to social psychologists, since the failure of social behaviour is more basic than for other patients – there is no meeting of minds, no collaboration to send and receive messages. Many schizophrenics engage in very little social behaviour; they remain isolated and detached from other people and are engaged with private fantasies and daydreams. When they are in a group or interview they appear not to be attending to the situation at all, and may make irrelevant remarks, giving a clue to the fantasies with which they are preoccupied.

Considering first the details of social performance, schizophrenics look odd and untidy, and do not wear their clothes well; they adopt unsuitable proximities – either too near or too far; they orient themselves away from other people – often against a wall; postures and gestures may be weird – they symbolize private fantasies and may not be intended to communicate anything; facial expression is blank, though there can be grimaces; there is very little speech, and this is rambling and incoherent, is not synchronized with the speech of others, and is often on totally irrelevant topics. Schizophrenics are often found to avert gaze; however, Rutter has found that they do not do so if they are talking about impersonal topics (p. 94).

Turning to more general patterns of social behaviour, there is no cooperation or formation of social groups; schizophrenics do not form relationships with one another, though they may be on the receiving end of relationships with hospital staff; they are made anxious by social situations, are upset by criticism, and do not like being supervised; they are very unresponsive to non-verbal signals, though to some extent they can receive verbal messages such as simple instructions. There is evidence that schizophrenics avoid people more than other stimuli; Williams (1974), working at Oxford, found in one test that schizophrenics spent more time looking at a TV film about fish than attending to a second person in the room.

The causes of schizophrenia are not yet known, nor is there any known cure, although tranquillizing drugs suppress the symptoms while they are being taken. Since about 0·8 per cent of the world's population suffer from schizophrenia, this is an extremely pressing scientific and social problem. One possibility is that the primary cause is biochemical – it may be due to some substance in the brain, like mescaline or LSD, which produce symptoms similar to schizophrenia. This had been likened to the effects of spraying a computer with water; however, the quest for this substance has so far been unsuccessful. Twin studies show that schizophrenia is partly inherited, but it need not be transmitted biochemically, any more than is intelligence. It is worth exploring hypotheses about possible social origins of schizophrenia. Schizophrenics are found to come from families which are disturbed in certain characteristic ways, such as having dominant and rejecting mothers and various kinds of failure of communication – e.g. one person's remarks are not acknowledged by another, members of the family fail to come to an agreement but then act as if they had, together with a lot of conflict and hostility (Jacob, 1975). Schizophrenia is often triggered by stressful life events, such as death, ill-health or other disasters in the family, or sudden disturbances to the patient's way of life, during the three weeks before onset (Brown *et al.*, 1973).

There are several very interesting lines of thought and research which between them provide a possible social psychological explanation of most features of schizophrenia. We shall describe three of the main approaches briefly.

1 *Failures of non-verbal communication* It has been suggested that the failure to communicate properly is due to verbal signals being accompanied by meta-signals (usually non-verbal) which deny the original message, or deny that anything sensible was said, or which create a paradoxical communication, such as 'I am a liar' – a so-called 'double-bind'. It is suggested that schizophrenics behave in this way in order to escape from intolerable social situations. Clinical studies have suggested that the parents of schizophrenics use such paradoxical communication, as in 'Why don't you love me?' (said crossly), and it is argued that the behaviour is learnt (Watzlawick *et al.*, 1967). The evidence for this general theory is weak, though schizophrenics report that their parents used double-binds (Berger, 1965).

An alternative formulation in this area might be to assert that schizophrenics simply have a deficiency in the perception and emission of non-verbal signals. There is clear evidence that this is so. A number of studies have shown that they are less responsive to non-verbal cues than are normal people.

2 *Failures of thought processes needed for social behaviour* The two main symptoms of schizophrenia are thought disturbance and failure of social behaviour; are they related? It has been found that schizo-

phrenics find it more difficult to rank photographs of people consistently than to rank photographs of physical objects, and that they make no inferences from one dimension to another (Bannister and Salmon, 1966). It looks as if schizophrenics may have a specific cognitive deficiency – of not being able to conceptualize persons or emotions – though it is not known what the cause is.

3 *Persistent rule-breaking* It has been suggested by some sociologists that the only common feature of the diverse symptoms produced by schizophrenics is rule-breaking. This could be because they come from weird families which broke rules, or because they found that some advantage came from behaving thus. It has been found that schizophrenics report considerably worse symptoms if they are interviewed to see if they should be discharged, than if interviewed to see if they should be placed in a closed ward (Braginsky *et al.*, 1969). It seems that they want to stay in hospital, but on an open ward, and can manipulate their symptoms in order to bring this about. It is found that schizophrenics adjust to the hospital in diverse ways, including avoiding the staff and making full use of the leisure facilities. Such behaviour may best suit those social misfits and failures who have found life outside stressful and frustrating, and seek a pleasant refuge which is undemanding, comfortable, and requires little work and contact with other people.

Paranoid reactions These consist of delusions about the self and others. In cases of personality disintegration accompanied by strongly held delusions the condition is termed paranoid schizophrenia. When the personality is more intact it is called paranoia. Paranoid reactions are commonest in the middle-aged and elderly, while other kinds of schizophrenia occur in the young. Paranoids, it is found, are secretive and seclusive, not trusting or confiding in people, but are generally able to communicate and develop rapport better than schizophrenics. They are always found to be suffering from thought disturbance, but this is invariably focused on relations with other people. Paranoids feel that they are being plotted against, spied upon or otherwise victimized, and that this is the explanation of their other failures. They may believe that their behaviour is being controlled from a distance, by TV, laser beams or whatever is the latest technology, the Brazilian railways or the secret police. Their perception of the world is disturbed in that they think the behaviour of others is oriented primarily towards themselves. They may also have delusions of grandeur, believing that they have an important mission or that they carry a special message or discovery.

While perfectly capable of normal interaction, they are extremely sensitive to minor slights, insults and rejections, and are quite unable to receive or profit by feedback from others concerning their ideas or self-image. At the first hint of negative feedback, their defences become rigid, and other people are blamed instead. Paranoids often cause annoyance by their touchy, hostile, arrogant and dominating behaviour, in which they constantly want to demonstrate their superiority. They think that there is a conspiracy against them and that people are talking about them behind their back; as they become gradually excluded from the community this becomes the case (Lemmert, 1962).

Paranoia can be regarded as mainly a disturbance of the self-image, made possible by the tendency to form false beliefs in order to reduce anxiety. For example, a child may explain his failure in an examination by saying that the teacher was not fair; if the parents support this view they could be encouraging paranoid thinking. This is more likely to happen to children who are isolated from the healthy ridicule of the peer group. Paranoia is precipitated by social stresses such as failure, competition or loss of a supporting social relationship.

Manic and depressive states These are mainly disturbances of mood, but there are also characteristic styles of social behaviour. Some patients are manic or depressive at different times, and some alternate between the two, indicating that the states are probably closely related. Manics are euphoric, self-confident and full of energy; depressives are overwhelmed by feelings of misery, guilt and inadequacy, and are lacking in motivation.

Manics wear smart, striking but rather loud clothes, look extremely well and very pleased with themselves, are smiling and alert, and have a loud confident voice of robust, resonant quality. They talk incessantly and tend to monopolize the conversation with their hilarious jokes and outrageous stories, but are easily distracted and move rapidly from topic to topic. Their excitement and jollity are infectious, and they are good at being the life and soul of the party. Manics have a self-confidence and self-esteem for which there is no adequate basis, and they will not take criticism from others. They enjoy making speeches and writing letters to important people. On the other hand they are quite good at handling people. This, together with their energy and self-confidence, often leads to a successful career in one of the more colourful occupations such as politics or show business. Their chief failings in social competence are an inability to perceive themselves accurately and in annoying others by their dominance and unsuitable jokes. Their delusional self-importance, their constant talking and a tendency to bizarre behaviour may lead to their becoming a public nuisance.

The social behaviour of depressives has been studied by Libet and Lewinsohn (1973), who found that they speak and initiate very little, are slow to respond and have a low level of rewardingness. They are drab and sombre in appearance, look miserable, have a drooping posture, and their voices are flat, low-pitched and monotonous. They have little energy and will sit and brood by themselves. They have a lower opinion of themselves than is warranted, are obsessed with feelings of failure and guilt, and may contemplate suicide; they are completely lacking in self-confidence. Their self-image is as inaccurate as is that of manics.

Lewinsohn (1975) suggested that depressives' lack of social skill leads to their receiving very few rewards from others, which produces their depressed state. Howes and Hokanson (1979) found that subjects who met role-played depressives for seven minutes at a time spoke to them rather little, i.e. rejected them, while giving expressions of support, as they did to role-players of physical illness. Thus depressed social signals do elicit sympathy, but also rejection.

Seligman (1975) has suggested an interpretation of depression in terms of 'learned helplessness'. Dogs that had experience of uncontrollable electric shocks made little attempt in a later situation to escape them – they had been trained to give up. Human beings, however, are more complicated. When they lose control of a situation, they engage at first in vigorous positive efforts to regain command, known as 'reactance'; it is only if the loss of control continues that learned helplessness sets in (Wortman and Brehm, 1975). Patients who experience both manic and depressive phases presumably cannot be accounted for in this way, other processes, biochemical or psychological, presumably being involved.

Manic and depressive conditions are partly genetic in origin. They are also affected by childhood experience, a lot of pressure from within the family to be respectable and successful, and competition from siblings. A great deal of depression is 'reactive', i.e. precipitated by recent events.

The effect of stressful life events Depression and other forms of mental disorder are precipitated by stressful life events, these being mainly social in character. Scales are constructed by asking samples of people to give relative weights to different events. Some of the items and weights found by Paykel, McGuiness and Gomez (1976) with a British sample appear in Table 12. It can be seen that bereavement, divorce and other losses of relationship score very highly, as does loss of job, which includes the loss of a whole set of social attachments.

death of child	19·53
death of spouse	19·14
being sent to gaol	17·76
serious financial difficulties	17·58
spouse unfaithful	17·28
divorced	16·29
fired	15·93
unemployed for one month	15·43
serious physical illness (in hospital or one month off work)	14·67
fail important exam or course	14·38
begin extramarital affair	13·70
increased arguments with resident family member (e.g. children)	13·97
increased arguments with boss and co-workers	12·28
move to another country	11·14
retirement	10·05
child leaves home (e.g. college)	7·85
wanted pregnancy	3·70

Table 12. Ratings of the seriousness of life events (from Paykel *et al.*, 1976).

A number of studies have shown that those people who have a high score for such events during the past six months are more likely to become ill, mentally or physically. In the case of schizophrenia, it is happenings during the past three weeks which count. Some people are more upset by such occurrences than others, especially working-class people and those without social support from spouses or friends. Brown and Harris (1978) found that among working-class women in London who had experienced stressful life events in the previous six months, 41 per cent of those who did not have a supportive husband were clinically depressed, compared with 10 per cent of those who did. Depression was more likely to afflict them if they had lost their mother in childhood, had several young children at home and did not have a job.

These studies show that depression and other forms of mental and physical illness are greatly affected by the lack or loss of supportive relationships, combined with other sources of stress, including a difficult childhood (Cochrane, 1980).

Neurosis – general Neuroticism occurs as a matter of degree, everyone experiencing anxiety and stress at some time. However, between five and eight per cent of the population are unduly anxious, can stand very little stress, have reduced energy, function below their true capacity, have headaches or other aches and pains, can't sleep and find other people difficult to deal with. People with anxiety neurosis may have a general 'free-floating' worry about nothing in particular, phobias for height, travel or other situations, and obsessions, such as a concern with dirt and cleanliness. If they suffer from social anxiety, they can be seen to be in a state of tension in social situations, from their strained faces, trembling hands and tense postures. Such people talk very fast, nervously and rather indistinctly, and they tend to speak first in an encounter. However, their utterances are short, they make many speech errors, and they may lose control of the quality of their speech. They may be competent at social interaction, and are often very sensitive to the responses of others, but they get into difficulties as a result of their other symptoms. An obsessional who is worried about the smell of bad breath, and a person with a phobia of closed or open spaces, will have difficulties in taking part in many encounters. Like other neurotics, people with anxiety neurosis tend to be self-centred, demanding and more concerned with their own needs and problems than with those of others. In addition, anxiety neurotics are tense, irritable and easily upset; they are often found annoying and unrewarding by others, and so can become gradually isolated.

Not all neurotics are socially inadequate. Bryant *et al.* (1976) observed the social behaviour of out-patients diagnosed as neurotic. It was found that of ninety-two patients studied, 27 per cent were judged to be socially inadequate, 46 per cent of the males (mostly unmarried) and 16 per cent of the females; 21 per cent were thought to be suitable for social skills training. This is a minority of the whole population of neurotics, though one which is of particular interest to social psychologists. In this study, the socially inadequate were significantly less extraverted, sociable, dominant and confident, and they reported more difficulty in social situations. They appeared colder, less assertive, less happy, less controlling, less rewarding and more anxious than the socially adequate group. They were also significantly more likely to have had in adolescence a history of solitariness and difficulty in making friends, and of unsuccessful attempts at 'dating'. In terms of elements of behaviour, they tended towards the 'inactive' or unassertive side, being on the whole rather silent, showing little interest in others, speaking very briefly and in a slow and rather monotonous voice, rarely handing over the conversation, sitting very still and rigid, and assuming a dull, fixed expression. Trower (1980) found the behaviour which best distinguished the socially inadequate was their reduced amount of speech, looking, smiling, gesturing and posture shifting.

Neurotics are often socially isolated. Henderson *et al.* (1978) found that they had far fewer friends than comparable non-neurotics. Lack of friends is one of the commonest complaints on the part of those seeking social skills training (SST). Neurotics may engage in queer, destructive social techniques, whose effects are highly disturbing. The motivation may be aggression, or relief of inner tensions in complex ways, as described by Berne (1966). For example, a fraudulent contract may be offered, as in 'Rapo': a female leads a male on until he makes an advance, whereupon she indignantly rejects him. In 'Why don't you – Yes, but' someone appears to be seeking advice about a problem; whatever solution is offered he is able to point out the obvious objections to it.

It may be useful to distinguish between those who are socially inadequate – i.e., do not possess certain social skills – and social phobics – who have the skills but are too anxious to use them – although the two groups overlap. Since SST produces considerable improvement in neurotics, social deficits may be a basic cause of other symptoms for some of them. On the other hand, the fact that relaxation and desensitization also improve social behaviour suggests that anxiety is simply suppressing skills which are already there. Trower *et al.* (1978) found that socially unskilled patients were helped more by SST than by desensitization; phobics were helped equally by both methods of treatment.

Hysteria This is a form of neurotic breakdown which is more common among extraverts, whereas anxiety neurosis is more common among introverts (Eysenck, 1957). There are also hysterical personalities among normal people, who share some of the same behaviour. Hysteria consists mainly of apparent bodily complaints, which are based on blockages at higher levels of the central nervous system. These include motor blockages (paralyses), sensory blockages (anaesthesias) and failures of memory. The characteristic social behaviour of hysterics also has a quality of role playing: they over-dramatize themselves, exaggerate their emotional states and pretend to be more interesting and exciting than they really are. They are very anxious for their self-image to be reinforced and very sensitive to feedback concerning it. They like to be the centre of attention, need to be admired and are often successful as actresses, politicians and public speakers. They are competent interactors, more active than normal people, although not as active as manics.

Hysterics are often females who have been over-protected by their mothers. One theory is that they have been rewarded for minor illnesses, both by avoiding events and by receiving extra maternal care, so that feeling ill becomes the automatic reaction to stress. This can be regarded as a special kind of non-verbal communication, used when verbal utterances have failed. The message may be a demand for attention, love, sympathy or help, or it may signal guilt and self-punishment. The hysteric uses these signals to control people in the same way that she was able to control her mother (Szasz, 1961).

Delinquents and psychopaths These people are found to be lacking in various aspects of social skills. They cannot cope with some everyday situations and react in a more aggressive and inappropriately assertive manner than controls (Freedman *et al.*, 1978). Among some subjects there is evidence of lack of perceptual sensitivity (McDavid and Schroder, 1957); this can lead them into trouble if they fail to realize how they are annoying other people, so that they get into fights.

There are several different types of delinquent. 'Pseudo-social' delinquents are not abnormal in any clinical sense and are quite different from the impulsive and affectionless psychopaths. They reject adults and others in authority, but behave perfectly well towards members of their group or gang, and indeed may be loyally devoted. Their most interesting feature for present purposes is the total barrier which exists between them and adults – a one-sided barrier in that it is extremely difficult for adults to establish a relationship with them. Various techniques have been suggested for application in institutions, such as the use of young adults who can be seen as suitable models and who work hard to establish rapport.

Groups of football hooligans, drug addicts, violent revolutionaries and others are similar. The behaviour of these and other delinquent groups can partly be explained in terms of learning to be members of an alternative social world, with its own rules, values and beliefs, which gives gratifications which cannot be obtained elsewhere. They are labelled by the outside world as 'football hooligans', for example, and this label becomes part of their self-image, helping to separate them from society, in a process of 'deviance amplification'. There appears to be a failure of social behaviour in dealing with 'straight' society. Sarason and Ganzer (1971), however, have had some success in training delinquents to go for job interviews, for example.

Psychopaths are a very interesting group from the present point of view, since they show none of the usual symptoms of neurosis (e.g. anxiety) or of psychosis (e.g. disturbances of thought or mood), but are disturbed primarily in the social sphere. The main symptoms are impulsiveness, unrestrained aggression or sexuality, lack of conscience, and lack of sympathy, affection or consideration for others. Examples are aggressive young males and nymphomaniac young females. While they appear to have no interest in affiliative relations with people, they often join groups and organizations and become a very disturbing influence. When a psychopath is a member of a small group there is little hope of the group being cohesive or cooperative. It is as if they are sensitive to sources of conflict or tension, either in individuals or between different group members, and succeed in making things worse.

Psychopaths sometimes behave with charm and spontaneity. They are thus able to manipulate other people to their own ends, but their relations with others are always a means to ends and never ends in themselves. Psychopaths are rather like some salesmen – they want to interact with people so that they can get their bonus, but have no further interest in the people concerned. They cannot form relationships of friendship, love or permanent attachment with other people. They are not concerned about the welfare or sufferings of others, are basically indifferent to them and quite lacking in remorse for their own past acts: it is as if they are unable to understand how other people are feeling.

There is some genetic basis to psychopathy. More important is a childhood history of lack of love, ill-treatment, neglect, lack of discipline and lack of a stable home, combined with certain social conditions – social and economic deprivation, juvenile gangs in the area and absence of satisfying work opportunities.

TYPES OF BREAKDOWN OF SOCIAL PERFORMANCE IN MENTAL DISORDER

Our immediate interest in this chapter is finding out the different ways in which social behaviour may break down, since this will throw light on the mechanisms of social skill. Study of breakdown of social behaviour in mental patients may be of practical importance too. If mental disorders are either caused or exacerbated by a failure of social performance, this information may be valuable in suggesting methods of prevention and cure. It is a matter of extreme urgency at the present time to discover more effective ways of treating mental patients, so these ideas are worth pursuing.

Failures of social competence can be of a number of different types, as has been seen in the last section. These will be classified and related to different parts of the social-skill mechanism. These forms of failure occur in extreme forms in mental patients, but they are widely found in 'normal' members of the community.

Skills and plans During social interaction, many patients are passive and dependent, fail to take the initiative and appear to be pursuing no persistent goals. Alternatively they may pursue inappropriate goals, like Berne's patients, or be completely unaware of the effect their behaviour is having on others. Schizophrenics are grossly deficient in social skills. Many neurotics and many socially isolated people have inadequate social skills of some kind. They may be unable to deal with everyday encounters without great awkwardness; they may have difficulty in sustaining an ordinary conversation; they may be unable to deal with whole groups of people – the opposite sex, older persons, different social classes, dominant people, etc.

Rewardingness Nearly all mental patients are very unrewarding to be with, which leads to their isolation and makes life difficult for hospital staff. Different kinds of patient are unrewarding in different ways – schizophrenics have been described as 'socially bankrupt' since they are so unresponsive; depressives are depressing; neurotics are preoccupied with themselves; and psychopaths are only interested in other people as means to ends.

Verbal communication Schizophrenics are particularly inadequate in this sphere, but many other patients are deficient in the skilled use of speech. The commonest problems are the inability to speak much and being unable to sustain a conversation. Patients may simply reply to questions without expanding or produce boring bits of information about themselves, fail to respond with a relevant utterance, interrupt or produce long pauses.

Non-verbal communication Many patients have low rates of smiling, looking and gesturing, are either very inexpressive, in face or voice, or express negative emotions and attitudes, such as sarcasm, suspicion or hostility, and may fail to produce feedback signals while others are speaking.

Perception of other people Many patients demonstrate inaccuracy in this sphere. Schizophrenics are very unreceptive to non-verbal signals and are not able to interpret the behaviour of others in terms of emotions or other psychological constructs. Paranoids fail to receive messages which contain any criticism of themselves and are thus unable to modify their behaviour or their self-image. Patients with anxiety neurosis, on the other hand, are *too* sensitive to signs of criticism or displeasure on the part of others.

Taking the role of the other Many mental patients are unable to take the role of the other. In general they are found to be egocentric and to talk about themselves more than other people do (Meldman, 1967); this is very marked in hysterics. They are often totally unable to see anyone else's point of view, as in schizophrenia and psychopathy; or they are mistaken about the reactions of others, as in paranoia and to a lesser extent in anxiety neurosis.

Self-presentation There are disturbances of self-image in most disorders. Hysterics are perpetually trying to get others to accept their own over-dramatized self-image. This is seen most clearly in impostors and pretenders who half-believe in the parts they are playing. Paranoids are rather different: they are in no doubt about their self-image, but they are annoyed that other people will not accept it. Some people get into trouble through adopting an inappropriate appearance or manner, e.g. of the wrong sex, age or class.

Situational skills Some patients have difficulties with particular situations – parties, dates, telephoning, committee meetings, etc. – and need to learn their special features and the skills involved.

THE EFFECTS OF TREATMENT ON SOCIAL BEHAVIOUR

We must distinguish at this point between the neuroses, such as anxiety and hysteria, and the psychoses, such as schizophrenia and the manic and depressive states. The neuroses have traditionally been treated by psychotherapy, though the recovery rate is very slow, not much faster than the spontaneous rate of recovery for untreated patients. The psychoses have traditionally been treated by physical methods, though the value of psychological and social techniques is being increasingly recognized. The present position is that schizophrenics can be temporarily improved by means of drugs, but that they deteriorate as soon as they stop taking the drug: some success is claimed for social therapy while the patients are sedated.

The outlook for depressives is rather better, since electro-convulsive therapy and anti-depressant drugs are often successful. For both the neuroses and the psychoses there is an urgent need to find better methods of treatment. If the breakdown of social performance is an important element for any of these conditions it is important to know how far it is affected by existing methods of treatment. We may also be able to deduce something about the pattern of causation by seeing whether the social behaviour or the other symptoms are affected first.

Individual psychotherapy Many patients who embark upon psychotherapy suffer from interpersonal difficulties, either over specific problems at work or in the home, or over more general social matters. Some come to the therapist since they have no one else to talk to; he provides a kind of friendship, but may be able to use it to teach them how to get on with other people (Lennard and Bernstein, 1960). Although therapists vary in what they do, certain procedures are common to all (pp. 250f).

- Some psychotherapists believe that interpersonal problems lie at the root of mental disorder, and they direct their therapy towards the patient's social behaviour and relationships. For example, Berne (1966) analysed his patients' behaviour in terms of the game-like techniques which they were using (pp. 222f), and whether they were assuming child, adult or parent roles. Rogers (1942) directed his treatment primarily towards the self-system of his patients, to bring about greater self-acceptance, less conflict between self and ideal self, and more commitment to persistent courses of action.

There has been a lot of disagreement over whether psychotherapy actually cures people any faster than they would recover spontaneously – up to 70 per cent recover after two years without treatment. However, a number of carefully controlled studies show that there is more improvement both in social behaviour and in other respects (see p. 252).

Behaviour therapy This consists of a number of training techniques based on learning theory. The most widely used form of behaviour therapy is 'desensitization' for phobias: the patient is lightly hypnotized, relaxes deeply and imagines the least frightening of a hierarchy of fearful stimuli, e.g. connected with heights, flying or spiders, relaxes again and imagines the next stimulus in the hierarchy. A recent development is 'flooding', in which the patient confronts the most frightening stimulus either in reality or imagination for twenty minutes or so. These methods are very successful with specific phobias, and it is claimed that more general personality disturbance can be helped by dealing with central areas of anxiety. For discussion of the numerous follow-up studies see Kazdin and Wilcoxon (1976).

It is recognized by some behaviour therapists that further training in social behaviour may be needed. For example, homosexuals may need to be taught how to deal with women as well as not to feel attracted towards men. We now turn to such methods of training.

Social skills training (SST) for neurotic patients This is now a widely used method of treatment for a great variety of patients. The methods used are described in Chapter 12 (pp. 276f). Here I shall discuss how well it has been found to work in follow-up studies (see Twentyman and Zimering, 1979).

Psychotic in-patients The early studies showed that these patients could be trained to be more assertive and better at NVC, but they nevertheless remained in hospital. Recently more intensive studies, working on one area of behaviour at a time (the 'multiple base-line' method), with one to four patients for thirty hours or more, has succeeded in bringing about enough improvement for them to go home (Hersen, 1979). Other studies have found a similar degree of improvement in severely depressed patients (Zeiss *et al.*, 1979).

Out-patient neurotics have shown improvement or complete recovery after SST, which has been found to be more effective than psychotherapy but not much better, if at all, than desensitization. The main difference is that the SST patients improve more in the area of specifically social skills and anxieties. A number of our patients have improved markedly, not only in social performance but in other aspects of their behaviour as well, including in one case apparently physiological symptoms such as anorexia (not eating) and amenorrhœa (stoppage of periods).

Our methods have been closely based on social psychological research into specific deficits and how these can be corrected. In some cases this has led to very rapid recovery, as in the case of a young woman whose difficulties were entirely due to inappropriate self-presentation, her clothes and voice being those of someone of a much older generation.

Other patients Alcoholics and drug addicts have been helped by SST, though the effects have not always lasted. SST is now included as part of a more comprehensive treatment package. Delinquents and prisoners have been treated with some success, especially in the case of aggressive and sexual offenders, and pre-release training has been given in how to get a job and deal with other problems in the world outside. Disturbed children have been helped, particularly those who are socially isolated or aggressive.

Therapeutic community treatment The previous methods described are mainly applicable to neurotic patients. Schizophrenics and other psychotic patients are usually treated in hospitals, and the therapeutic community is a way of organizing mental hospitals. Mental hospitals have come under severe criticism in recent years: it has been argued that they treat patients as if they were irresponsible and naughty children, and force them into the role of lunatics. It was found by Wing (1967) that the longer patients are inside, the more 'institutionalized' they become – i.e. they get adjusted to their dependent position in the hospital and lose all contact with the outside world. Szasz (1961) has argued that mental hospitals actually make people worse, by classifying harmless eccentrics as lunatics and teaching them the appropriate role behaviour.

In hospitals organized as therapeutic communities efforts are made to train patients in more desirable social skills. The staff are trained to treat the patients less autocratically and to conduct group therapy on the wards. The patients do manual work for regular hours each day and are paid for it. Patients are given various other jobs and responsibilities such as helping to run clubs, and social contacts with other patients are encouraged, as are trips outside the hospital. In these ways patients are given practice in various aspects of social behaviour and relationships.

Experiments have been made with new kinds of therapeutic community, in which small groups of patients are made less dependent on the staff, take more responsibility for themselves and work in the community. Fairweather and colleagues (1969) compared the effects of a 'small-group ward' and a traditional ward in a mental hospital. In the first, small groups were made responsible for getting jobs done, recommending patients for increased privileges and other matters. Behaviour on the ward was greatly improved, patients left hospital sooner, more were employed later and they spent more time with friends.

Other studies have found that such milieu therapy alone is not very effective: the best outcomes for schizophrenics and other severely disturbed patients are obtained with a combination of a therapeutic milieu, tranquillizing drugs and individual or group therapy (May, 1968).

CONCLUSIONS

There is some disturbance of social performance in nearly all mental patients, both neurotic and psychotic. In other words some of the symptoms are in the sphere of social behaviour, and for certain patients these are the main or only symptoms. The causes of mental disorders are partly in the social sphere – peculiar childhood experiences and more recent life events. It is interesting that the most troublesome of these are largely social in character, involving especially loss of a close relationship.

The evidence is not clear as to whether the failure of social behaviour is primary or secondary. If we can speculate, it looks as if the disturbance of social behaviour may be primary for the neuroses. In other cases it is not so clear what the sequence of causation may be. In the case of schizophrenia, for example, it looks as if the failure of social performance may be the result of more basic, genetic factors – affecting non-verbal signalling or cognitive processes, or both – and that this then leads to withdrawal and hospitalization.

SST for mental patients has become widely used, although it requires intensive treatment in the case of psychotics and is not much better than behaviour therapy in the case of neurotics. However, this form of treatment is quite new and the techniques are still being developed, as will be shown in Chapter 12.

FURTHER READING

Argyle, M., 'Social competence and mental health', in Argyle, M. (ed.), *Social Skills and Health*, Methuen, 1981.

Feldman, M. P., and Orford, J. F. (eds), *Psychological Problems: The Social Context*, Wiley, 1980.

Phillips, E. L., *The Social Skills Basis of Psychopathology*, Grune and Stratton, New York, 1978.

Trower, P., Bryant, B., and Argyle, M., *Social Skills and Mental Health*, Methuen, 1978.

CHAPTER II

SOME PROFESSIONAL SOCIAL SKILLS

SOCIAL behaviour has been looked at as a skilled performance which is used to elicit certain desired responses from other people. This approach can be used to give an account of professional social skills; in each of these the performer carries out a task which consists mainly of handling other people in order to get them to react in certain ways. The criteria for success at such professional tasks were discussed earlier (pp. 76f), and are clearer in some cases (such as selling) than in others (such as teaching). For some of these tasks there has been a good deal of research into which social techniques, or which kinds of people, are most effective. It is found that there are fairly large individual differences – for example, a ratio of five to one in average takings is not uncommon among salesgirls in the same department, and there are similar variations between the absenteeism and labour turnover rates under different supervisors.

Some social skills for which there is a substantial body of research have been selected for discussion here. Others which might have been included are the skills of the barrister, the negotiator and the social worker. However, the skills discussed are relevant to some of these – barristers use the skills of public speaking, and social workers use therapeutic skills, for example. The social skills of everyday life have been covered to some extent in previous chapters. The professional skills which are described below involve rather special techniques which are not necessarily acquired as a result of everyday experience. They also require a certain amount of knowledge – for example, teachers need to know their subject as well as how to teach – and this side of social skills will not be considered here.

We shall start with skills in which one person is handled at a time.

INTERVIEWING

The selection interview Millions of interviews take place each year to assess the suitability of applicants for jobs. The main purpose is to find out information from the candidate (C), from which the interviewer (Int) can predict how well C would do in the job. In addition Int may provide C with information about the organization, improve its public image and persuade C to take the job – here the situation becomes one of bargaining or negotiation. In fact this often happens at the end of the interviews after one C has been offered the job.

Although interviewing is universally used as at least a part of selection schemes, there has been some criticism of its validity by psychologists. Part of the problem is that Int has other information about C – biographical, examination and test results, etc. – from which it is possible to make a prediction without any interview at all. However, the results of a number of studies show that the predictions made following the interview are better than those made from background data alone (Ulrich and Trumbo, 1965). It has also been found that some Ints are very much better than others – and that some are unable to predict job success better than chance; we shall discuss later which kinds of Int are best. Further it has been found that certain areas of information can be assessed more accurately by interview than others. C's style of interpersonal behaviour, and his likelihood of adjusting to the social aspects of the job situation is one such area; another is C's motivation to work, which can probably be more accurately assessed by interview than in any other way.

There are certain conventions about selection interviews. It is usually expected that these should last between ten and forty minutes, with longer interviews for more important jobs, that Int will ask most of the questions and take notes, though C will be able to ask questions later, and that it is a formal occasion where Int and C will face each other across a desk, though this convention is changing in favour of a 90° orientation with a low coffee table or no table at all. If any of these rules is broken some explanation should be given to C.

The selection interview can be given by one Int or by a whole panel of them. As will be seen, one of the major problems with this kind of interview is overcoming the anxiety of C, especially with young or inexperienced Cs. This is far worse with a board interview: Cs have been known to collapse physically, and this method gives an advantage to the most self-confident and self-assured Cs, who may not be the best-equipped in other ways. It is far easier to establish a good relationship and to get C talking freely in a one-to-one interview. It is nevertheless valuable for C to be interviewed by several Ints with different personalities and different points of view and areas of expertise, so it is probably best for C to have a series of individual interviews.

Some of the social techniques which have been found useful by experienced interviewers will now be described. It is unfortunate that it cannot be claimed that there is any more rigorous research backing for all of these.

Before interviews take place it is necessary to draw up a job description, giving details of the qualifications needed for the position. Prior to each interview, C's dossier should be studied – his curriculum vitae, reports from referees, etc. – and the main points to be settled should be decided upon, such as whether or not he is intelligent enough, his reasons for taking a year off from college and so on.

The selection interview has four main phases:

1 welcome, in which the procedure is explained, and C is put at ease and encouraged to talk freely;

2 gathering information, in which Int goes over C's records, with the aid of the dossier, and tries to assess C on a number of traits;

3 supplying information, in which C is invited to ask any questions he may have;

4 conclusion, in which it is explained what happens next.

There may also be a phase of negotiation (in which C is offered the job) for which the interviewer requires further social skills.

In phase 1, Int establishes rapport with C and reduces C's anxiety. This can be done by a period of a few minutes' relaxed small talk, discovering common friends or interests, or by asking C questions about interesting or successful things he is known to have done recently, accompanied by positive non-verbal signals. In phase 2, Int goes over C's biographical record, asking questions which help in C's assessment. Int should have a definite list of topics to be covered in a certain order: research shows that the interview is more effective when it has a definite plan such as going through the biographical record. These topics will often include C's family and home background, his education at school and later, his past jobs and present employment, his interests and leisure activities, his attitudes and beliefs, his health and adjustment.

There are special skills in asking questions. Each topic is usually introduced with an open-ended question, followed by a series of follow-up questions. Int's questions should be responsive to what C has just said, so that there is a proper dialogue or flow of conversation. The questions on a given topic can be designed to obtain information about different aspects of C's abilities or personality. For example, leisure activities can be pursued to find out about social skills, creativity or emotional stability. Some areas need carefully-phrased questions to elicit relevant answers; for example, *judgement* can be assessed from questions about C's opinions about complex and controversial social issues with which he is acquainted. Int will have some ideas about C from biographical and other data, which he may have in front of him – in fact the more such data he can have before the interview the better. He can then test various hypotheses about C, e.g. that C is lazy, neurotic, and so on. It is found that much more notice is taken by Ints of adverse information, and the interview can be regarded to some extent as a search for such information. This is partly justified by C's use of the complementary strategy, i.e. of covering up his weak points. Nevertheless, it is useful for Ints to be on the look-out for strong points in Cs as well.

It is important for Int to be able to extract negative information, and he may need to find out, for example, why C left a certain job so quickly or why he was sent down from college. The putting of such questions requires considerable skill. It is partly a matter of careful phrasing of the question; for example, the latter question could be put, 'I gather you had some difficulties with the college authorities – could you tell me about that?' Such questions need to be delivered in a friendly, perhaps slightly humorous manner, and C's face should be saved afterwards by a sympathetic comment.

Ints often use techniques which will increase C's amount of speech – open-ended questions, agreement and encouragement, and the use of silence (see p. 61). Int should listen carefully to the emotional undertones and implications of C's speech, and respond in a way that shows he understands, accepts and sympathizes.

However, he should not take the role of C to the extent of trying to get C the job, because there are other Cs to be considered; Int should remain somewhat detached while at the same time being genuinely sympathetic. While Int's role is to carry out selection rather than vocational guidance, he may give some vocational advice if it is asked for. The interview should be a rewarding experience for C, and he should feel that he has been properly and fairly assessed.

Int should try to assess a number of abilities and personality traits that are thought to be most relevant to the job, such as creativity, ability to cope with stress and attitudes to authority. Each of these dimensions can be assessed from the answers to suitable questions. For example, attitudes to authority can be assessed by asking about past relationships with others of higher or lower status, and attitudes towards traditionally respected groups and institutions and commonly despised social groups. In each area several different questions should be asked, in order to sample the dimension under consideration.

The behaviour of C during an interview cannot be regarded as a typical sample of his performance from which a prediction can be made; Int should concentrate on eliciting verbal reports of behaviour in situations resembling the future work situation. Thus an estimate of a C's creativity can be obtained by asking him to describe situations in which he might have displayed originality.

Part of the skill of interviewing consists of being able to deal with awkward Cs. General experience suggests that there are a number of types of awkward C most commonly encountered:

talks too much;
talks too little;
very nervous;
bombastic;
wrong role (e.g. seeks vocational guidance or tries to ask all the
    questions);
over-smooth presentation;
unrewarding;
not interested in job;
neurotic;
different class or culture.

There are special ways of dealing with each of these problems. For example, the C who talks too much can be dealt with by (a) asking more closed questions, (b) using less reinforcement, or (c) indicating that a short answer is wanted.

Research into the accuracy of the selection interview shows that there are considerable differences between Ints. The most accurate are those who are similar to the Cs in age and social background, intelligent and well-adjusted, not easily shocked, quiet, serious, introverted, unexcitable and giving an impression of sincerity and sympathy. There are a number of common sources of error in selection interviews and these were described earlier under person perception (p. 114) – being too influenced by first impressions and physical appearance, preferring Cs from certain backgrounds, forming a global favourable or unfavourable impression, and placing more emphasis on negative than positive points. Early impressions about C should be checked by asking further questions.

What social skills should be used by C to make Int more likely to give him the job? It has been found that C stands a higher chance of being accepted when Int does most of the talking, when the interview flows smoothly, with few disagreements being expressed (Sydiaha, 1961), and when C smiles, looks and nods more (Forbes and Jackson, 1980). Ints seem to prefer Cs who are well-washed, quietly dressed, politely attentive, submissive and keen, and they are likely to reject Cs who are rude, over-dominant, not interested or irritating in other ways. There seems to be a definite 'role of the candidate' – he is expected to be nicely behaved and acquiescent – although he may not be expected to be quite like this if he gets the job. There are certain subtleties about being a good C – it is necessary for C to draw attention to his good qualities while remaining modest and submissive. He may need to show what a decisive and forceful person he is, but without using these powers on the selection board.

The social survey interview The aims of the survey interviewer (Int) are to obtain accurate replies from the respondent (R) about his opinions, attitudes, behaviour or whatever the survey happens to be about. The reliability of survey interviews is not very high: in a number of studies Rs were asked the same questions a second time after a short interval, and it was found that about eighty per cent repeated their previous answers if the same Int was used, and about sixty per cent did if a different Int was used (Hyman *et al.*, 1955). It is possible to assess the adequacy of Int's performance by analysing tape-recordings of his interviews, in order to check for errors and biases, though this does not measure validity directly. In several studies, as many as twenty mistakes of various kinds per interview have been found (Brenner, 1981).

The procedure begins with Int asking R to take part in the survey as a favour, since R gets nothing material out of it. This suggests the first main problem of the survey interviewer – that of establishing contact with and motivating R. Int is typically of rather higher social class and more education than R, which leads to problems of communication. Male and female Ints are liable to be given different answers on certain topics; so are Ints from different racial or social-class groups. The best results are obtained when Int is similar to R in these respects. Rs are generally unused to the interview situation and often give the wrong kind of answer, which is a further problem for Int. It is found that R's willingness to cooperate and the content of his answers both vary with the role of Int. If Int appears to be connected with income tax, for example, Rs will be unwilling to talk about their income and will distort their replies. Industrial workers will give different answers to representatives of management or of the unions; the most accurate replies would probably be given to an independent investigator from outside, and the author usually wears a 'neutral suit' for such interviewing. This is a good example of the importance of a social-skill performer establishing the right identity from the outset. It is becoming increasingly easy to handle this situation as people become more familiar with the role and the survey interview becomes an accepted type of social situation. The expectations concerning it are that Int will ask a number of personal questions, that R will do most of the talking and that the whole thing will last not longer than five to fifteen minutes. When psychological research interviews or motivation research interviews are given, R has to be taught a new tradition.

We now come to the social skills used by the survey interviewer. Firstly he must establish contact with R and persuade him to take part. If rapport is not established, R will refuse to cooperate; some Ints have a high rate of failure of this kind, and it leads to error in the results. By rapport is meant a smooth pattern of interaction in which both feel comfortable and there are few pauses and interruptions, together with some degree of mutual trust and acceptance. Int should treat the other as an equal and eliminate social barriers. He should show a keen and sympathetic interest, listen carefully, be accepting and uncritical of what is said and indicate that there is plenty of time. For different purposes different degrees of rapport may be needed: to ask intimate questions about income or sex requires more rapport than asking questions about interests or attitudes.

There are two general methods of motivating R. One is to interest him in the survey, suggesting that it may accomplish results that R would like. The other is to make the interview satisfying in itself by the provision of a friendly and sympathetic listener to R's opinions. It is usually recommended that Int should not pretend to be a 'friend' of R, since this would lead to R distorting his replies to please Int; rather Int should be helpful and sympathetic towards R's point of view, while remaining somewhat detached and retaining the 'stranger value' of a person who will not be seen again.

There are a number of rules in which Ints are trained, e.g. read each question slowly and exactly as it is written, record answers verbatim, and make sure each answer is correctly understood and adequate. It is most important that questions should not be leading or in any way invite the answer 'yes'. For this reason 'yes–no' questions should be avoided, and other alternatives offered instead. It is important that one answer should not seem to be more socially desirable than another; if alternative choices are offered, each should appear equally respectable. Int should not bias questions by putting vocal emphasis on particular words and should not bias the recorded replies by imputing the usual views of people of the age or social class of R. Int should conceal his own views from R and should not argue with him, no matter how absurd the opinions expressed by the latter. Particular skill is needed with potentially embarrassing issues, such as income or sexual behaviour: Int should adopt a relaxed matter-of-fact manner, or he can present R with a list of alternatives to check. He can explain to R that he is not concerned with assessing R, and that all answers are equally acceptable, perhaps indicating that a wide range of different answers is commonly obtained. A number of special methods are used in motivation research interviews to get at genuine feelings. R is more likely to be cooperative if he sees how each question is relevant to the main purpose of the interview, and it may be useful to explain the point of certain questions.

There are two main types of question which are used in surveys. One is closed, in which R is invited to choose between 'yes', 'no' and 'don't know', or between some other series of alternatives. The other is the open-ended, in which R is invited to talk freely about his behaviour, opinions or experiences in some area. In most surveys both kinds of question are used, though the proportions vary considerably: public opinion polls use more closed questions, research surveys make more use of open-ended ones. The latter are useful if R's attitudes are being explored in detail, if he has not formulated his views or if it is not known what the main alternative answers will be.

When open-ended questions are used, a series of follow-up questions is needed, and this provides an excellent example of reactions to feedback. When Int has asked an open-ended question on some topic, R will often give a reply that is inadequate in one way or another:

1 R refuses to answer the question: Int can explain the purpose of the survey or the particular question;

2 R partly misunderstands the question and talks about the wrong things: Int can then repeat and clarify the question, stressing what is wanted;

3 R doesn't produce enough information: Int can ask him to 'tell me more about this';

4 R is confused about the issue: Int invites him to talk the topic out to clarify his ideas;

5 R deals only with certain aspects of the problem: Int can ask more specifically about the areas omitted, possibly putting a series of increasingly direct questions in a 'funnel' structure (Kahn and Cannell, 1957).

A definite sequence of topic areas is also adopted. The easiest and least threatening are taken first, and more difficult ones later, when more confidence has been established. There should also be some sequence of topics so that the interview makes sense to R. Care is taken with the very first questions, and also with the last, so that the interview can end on a pleasant note.

It is important that Int should communicate clearly with R, and this may be difficult because of their different backgrounds. Each question should be clear, unambiguous, and concerned with a single idea. The questions should be appropriate to the level of sophistication of R. If R simply lacks the necessary words or concepts, explanation or examples may be necessary. It is sometimes the practice to alter the wording of questions for use with cultural minority groups so as to make them of 'equivalent meaning'.

Finally, Int should listen very carefully to what R has to say. He should not be concerned about whether what R says is true or false, but should see it as the expression of his attitudes and of his way of looking at the world: this is what the interview is trying to find out.

SELLING

Selling is done all over the world, though in very different ways and at different times and places: compare the endless bargaining with vendors in the markets of the Middle East, the mechanical rigidity of encyclopedia salesmen, the high-pressure methods once common in the U.S.A. and the passive role of supermarket attendants. I shall discuss three kinds of selling – retail sales in shops, salesman-initiated selling of commodities such as insurance, and industrial sales. There are certain principles which are common to all three.

The aim in each case is to sell as much as possible, but in addition the salesperson (S) wants to satisfy the customer (C), partly for altruistic motives, but also so that C will come again and tell friends about the shop or firm, thus enhancing long-term sales. Ss are often given a bonus, related to the number of sales made. Sales are easier when initiated by C, much more difficult when the contact has to be made by S, as in most insurance sales.

The order of moves varies somewhat between different kinds of selling, but often includes:

S finding out C's needs;
S offering one or more items;
C asking questions;
C making objections;
S showing advantages of items and dealing with objections;
S clinching the sale.

Retail sales It is common to find that some Ss are selling only twenty to forty per cent of what others in the same department are selling: this is an excellent example of the effects of different degrees of social skills shown in objective and quantitative terms. The use of individual bonus schemes may tempt Ss to use more persuasive methods and to go for the more prosperous-looking Cs; it also causes conflicts among the sales staff. A better scheme is probably to pay a group bonus that is shared between members of a department or counter, though this is inconvenient to administer and many shops manage without a bonus at all. The Ss in a department are supervised by the buyer for that department. Ostensibly C has power over S, and may indeed treat S as a kind of servant; this is particularly true of some upper-middle-class Cs, and is much resented by Ss.

According to studies of department stores by myself and Mary Lydall, most sales do not involve a complex sequence of steps: persuasion by S is rare, and Cs spend a lot of time looking by themselves at the goods on display. Some of the briefer sales encounters which we have observed include the following: C selects stockings from the stand, hands them to S, who takes the money and wraps them; C asks for a particular object, naming make, size, price, etc.; C looks through dresses on the rack, selects those she is interested in, and S shows C to a changing room where she tries them on and decides which to have. What happens is totally different in other departments in the same store – in some C can help herself, in others she has to be served.

We will now try to give an account of the complete possible sequence of events involved in a sale.

1 Categorization of C by S. This is sometimes in terms of how much money C is likely to spend or what style of clothes C is wearing, the latter being a useful guide to her tastes. It has been found in some shops, however, that Ss categorize Cs in terms of a kind of local mythology – 'peppery colonels', 'elderly frustrated females', etc. (Woodward, 1960).

2 Establishing contact with C. C may ask for help, ask specific questions, ask to see particular objects or stand expectantly at the counter. If C is wandering about or looking at goods on display, S may approach her, but this requires skill and judgement about whether C is ready to be helped.

3 S finds out C's needs. C may approach S directly, or may respond to S's opening by saying, 'I would like to buy a tie', though she may at this point specify her needs in greater detail, 'I would like something fairly bright'. S should listen carefully to whatever C has to say and try to understand what C is really after. Often C's wishes are vague, and S now needs to find out which of a thousand possible ties C would be most interested in. S needs to ask questions, to narrow down the field of choice. The strategies which can be used are similar to those in 'Twenty Questions' (except that direct questions can be asked, e.g. 'Which colour would you prefer?'). However, C may be thinking in terms of all manner of private classification schemes, as indicated by describing ties as 'bright', 'blue', 'terylene', 'with it', etc., and S must attune herself rapidly to C's conceptual structure.

4 S shows C a variety of items, if necessary demonstrating them or letting C try them on. There are several different strategies here. In the matter of price, for example, some Ss show the middle-range item first, others show the most expensive. In either case it is important to make use of feedback, C's reaction providing a hint as to what should be shown next. Similarly, a clearer idea of C's needs can be obtained by studying her reactions to the objects shown. Again it is important to show the right number of objects: if too many are shown C feels confused and can't decide, if too few C feels coerced. The way S handles the goods can convey a message: in some shops the more expensive goods are handled more reverently.

5 S gives information and advice. C may ask questions about the

goods at this stage, or raise objections. The experienced S will know the answers to questions and the replies to criticisms, and can point to particular advantages of each object. If S has found out C's needs, she can point out how various objects would meet her needs. If S really believes in the goods, and wants to help C, this will be a quite genuine argument.

6 Clinching the sale. This can be done in a variety of ways, different ones probably being suitable for different Cs. Some Cs can be left to decide for themselves, others can be persuaded that a particular object would be the best one for them; for others it can be assumed that they have decided already – 'Will you take it now, or shall we deliver it, Madam?'

7 After the sale S can increase C's feelings of satisfaction by providing further information about the object chosen and discussing after-sales service. She attends to payment and delivery, and suggests further related purchases to C.

It is necessary for S to be able to adapt to C's style of interaction, and to be able to handle a variety of Cs. This will affect whether C should be approached or not, whether C should be offered advice and information or not, and what kind of goods should be offered – in terms of price and style. Special techniques are needed with awkward customers – they may be handed over to another, preferably older, S or they may be left with a large assortment of goods to choose for themselves.

S will be more persuasive if she really knows the goods and projects an image of competence. C will be more likely to attend to S if S is friendly and easy to get on with. Observational studies by myself and Mary Lydall found that high-selling salesgirls established good rapport and had a smoother pattern of interaction than others. Chapple and Donald (1947) gave the standard interview to 154 Ss. The best Ss were very active and talked a lot, but were flexible and could adjust well to different styles of interaction. Those who oversold and had goods returned were dominant and made a lot of interruptions.

Industrial sales The relationship between S and C is rather different here: C has usually initiated the contact, S has considerable expertise and is in some ways like a consultant, and the problems under discussion are complex. Research by Rackham and colleagues has found that the most successful industrial salesmen use the following skills:

    1 S must be acceptable – this depends on his apparent expertise and the reputation of his firm;

    2 S asks about C's requirements, and puts 'need–payoff' questions like 'How much would you save if . . . ?' C asks about the probable benefits of different features in the solution – 'feature–benefit' analysis;

    3 S provides the right level of technical details for C;

    4 S takes C's objections seriously and is able to deal with them without getting into arguments;

    5 closing the sale techniques are not successful with expensive products.

                             (Poppleton, 1981)

Creative selling (e.g. of insurance) In this kind of sale it is S who initiates the encounter. Most Cs don't buy, perhaps 90 per cent, so it is a very unfavourable situation for S, and can be very stressful. One method is for Ss to select people similar to themselves as prospects; another is the use of 'referred leads', one C suggesting others.

    Poppleton (op. cit.) found that most Ss do not use standard openings or techniques, and that the use of stories and anecdotes was often successful. One of the main divisions is between the 'hard' and 'soft' sell. There is some evidence that the hard sell is more successful with Cs who are less well educated and informed, the soft sell with the better educated and informed.

SOCIAL SKILLS OF DOCTORS AND NURSES

Doctors The long-term goals of doctors (Ds) are to cure patients (Ps) when they are ill, to alleviate suffering when this is not possible, to prevent people becoming ill and to educate Ps in a better understanding of health and illness. These goals are reached via a number of intermediate ones; for example, curing P involves D first diagnosing the problem, then planning the treatment and finally increasing

P's compliance. More immediate goals still include reducing P's concern and increasing his or her satisfaction with the treatment. Some aspects of Ds' effectiveness could in principle be measured from the health or recovery rates of their Ps, though this does not entirely include their health education activities. In practice Ds are assessed by observation of their performance in the surgery, or videotapes of it, dealing with genuine or role-played Ps. The aspects of Ds' behaviour which are assessed are those which have been found to contribute to the long-term goals, and which are listed below.

General practitioners (G.P.s) see Ps on average for six minutes each, hospital doctors for longer. An interview consists of a number of fairly distinct episodes:

1 relating to P;
2 discussing the reason for P's attendance;
3 conducting a verbal or physical examination or both;
4 consideration of P's condition;
5 detailing treatment or further investigation;
6 terminating.

Byrne and Long (1976) found that all six phases occurred in 63 per cent of interviews, and that sometimes part of the sequence was repeated.

It has been found that quite a lot of Ps are not satisfied with consultations, do not remember what they are told and fail to carry out D's instructions. G.P.s in turn experience communication difficulties in 21 per cent of consultations, especially with working class Ps and Ps who have often been before with the same problem (Pendleton, 1981). There are certain social skills of Ds which have been found to be related to P satisfaction: when D is warm and friendly, gives reassurance, expresses sympathy and understanding, and discovers and deals with P's concerns and expectations, P generally comes away happy. We will now look at the more detailed skills needed for the specific goals or tasks of the consultation.

Collecting information, history-taking, diagnosis Ps are more satisfied when they feel that they have been examined thoroughly; however, G.P.s often stop at the first symptom, and P may not reveal his real worries. Quite a number of Ds fail in this way to spot psychiatric illness, though this can be improved by training. Most important, both G.P.s and hospital doctors often fail to deal with obvious signs of emotional distress. Giving reassurance is an important source of satisfaction for P.

Some SST for doctors has concentrated on history-taking skills, and produced favourable results in that more information is obtained, more accurate diagnoses made and psychiatric symptoms recognized more often (Maguire, 1981); but it has not so far dealt with D's educational role, e.g. in giving explanations.

Explanation P is more satisfied if D explains what is the matter simply and clearly. In one study only 6 per cent of working-class Ps and 18 per cent of class I Ps said that their Ds were good at explaining (Ley, 1977). In fact, Ds give less explanation to working-class Ps than anyone else – the very people who know least about health and whose need for information is greatest. Ps are often given inadequate information before undergoing operations, and Ds sometimes conceal the true situation in cases of serious illness, though this may be the best course of action in some cases.

Memory and compliance It is well established that Ps often forget what they are told and fail to comply with D's instructions. However, Pendleton (op. cit.) has found that Ps do remember 84 per cent of instructions about medication and 76 per cent of what they were told to do. It is, of course, still worth using techniques to increase compliance with instructions, such as emphasis, repetition and the use of clear and simple language.

There are a number of particular social skill problems for Ds:

1 *Dealing with working-class Ps* Ds see working-class Ps for a shorter time than they do middle- and upper-class Ps, and give them less explanation; subsequently these Ps do not feel Ds explain things well. The same is probably true of members of ethnic minority groups.

2 *Dealing with emotions* Ds often treat Ps as bodies rather than as persons; the effects of emotional states, social relationships and stressful life events on health are very great, so this is a serious omission. It is interesting that Ds are actually quite good at

recognizing Ps' emotions (Pendleton, op. cit.), but unfortunate that they often fail to make full use of this information.

Nurses The official goals of nurses (Ns) are to look after Ps' bodies and to administer, or help to administer, treatment. The Ps, however, regard Ns also as sources of information and social support. The effectiveness of Ns can be assessed in terms of P satisfaction, length of recovery time or ratings by sisters.

While there is not much research on relative effectiveness of different social skills used by nurses, numerous schemes of skill training for nurses have been developed. The aims of these courses are to encourage:

1 self-confidence and personal growth;
2 kindness, compassion and courtesy;
3 communication skills, including interviewing ability and assertiveness;
4 enhanced non-verbal communication;
5 perception of Ps' emotional and information needs.

(Davis, 1981)

Conversation and providing information Ps often complain that they do not receive enough information about their illness, treatment, progress and tests; 70 per cent said they received no information from nurses (Cartwright, 1964). There appears to be some uncertainty about N's role here, and how far it is her job to reveal such facts. Several studies have shown that when Ps are given more of an explanation before an operation they recover faster and need fewer drugs afterwards. It is also unclear whether or not talking to Ps is part of a nurse's job; some Ns think that it isn't, but Ps have a great desire for it. However, Ns appear to be rather poor conversationalists, their chats with Ps lasting on average forty-five seconds. These exchanges are usually ended by Ns, and although conversation tends to be disease-orientated, Ns often avoid answering questions and frequently change the topic (Davis, op. cit.). Student nurses in particular are very hesitant to give information, especially to those who are dying.

Social support and reassurance Ns do think that it is part of their job to give hope and support, if not information. This is done by verbal reassurance and appropriate non-verbal communication. (Touching Ps before an operation reduces subsequent recovery time for females but not for males (Whitcher and Fisher, 1979).) Ps certainly need this support: in one study 66 per cent were upset by emotional aspects of their stay, including discourteous staff and communication problems (Anderson, 1973). In other studies most Ps have thought that Ns were sympathetic, efficient and thoughtful. Ns need social support too, from their colleagues; where this is available the rate of accidents and errors is reduced (Sheehan *et al.*, 1981).

However, Ns get fed up with Ps who complain or express too much suffering, and they react by ignoring them or addressing them sarcastically, and by enforcing the rules strictly. Ns like some Ps more than others, and do more for them. Most Ns prefer male wards to female – there being a jollier atmosphere – and surgical wards to medical – since Ps recover faster in the former (Parkes, 1980).

There are a number of special social skills problems for nurses:

1 the uncertainty about how much information to pass on, and the difficulties of exercising discretion here;

2 the difficulty of dealing with unrewarding Ps and the temptation to ignore or punish them;

3 the dangers of over-involvement, especially with dying Ps.

PSYCHOTHERAPY AND COUNSELLING

These terms will be used fairly broadly to include any situation in which one person tries to solve another's psychological problems by means of conversation. There are many different techniques of psychotherapy, but some of the main varieties can be indicated briefly.

1 *Freudian psychoanalysis* Patients recall dreams and early childhood events, and the psychoanalyst interprets the patient's condition in terms of psychoanalytic theory. The full treatment involves about three sessions a week up to a total of three to six hundred, though many fail to complete the course.

2 *Rogers's non-directive therapy* Here the therapist (T) helps the patient (P) to understand his emotional reactions by verbally labelling or 'reflecting' what has been expressed, and by giving non-directive encouragement for further revelations. Treatment requires thirty to fifty sessions

3 *Counselling and brief psychotherapy* This consists of discussion about P's here-and-now problems, and what can be done about them. T may use one of a variety of psychological theories or an 'eclectic' combination of them; the number of sessions is typically five to ten. This is the most widely practised kind of psychotherapy – it is given by National Health Service psychiatrists in England, by numerous American non-medical psychotherapists and counsellors, and of course by even more numerous clergymen, general practitioners and sympathetic friends.

4 *Cognitive–rational therapy* This form of psychotherapy, which owes its existence to Ellis and Beck, consists of showing the patient that his emotional problems are due to irrational thinking. The therapist acts as a kind of teacher and shows the patient how to think differently about things.

The goals of psychotherapy vary somewhat according to the theories held by T They usually include:

the removal of feelings of psychological distress or discomfort, such as anxiety and depression;
improving P's functioning in work and inter-personal relations;
the removal of other symptoms of mental disorder.

The relationship between P and T is affected by the following factors:

P comes voluntarily because he wants to be cured (unless sent by the legal authorities);
traditionally P pays a fee, though this is not the case in the National Health Service;
T has power and prestige based on his medical or other professional standing, his psychological expertise and often his social class. Since P can terminate treatment whenever he wishes,

T has no formal power over him, but P may come to see T as the means to the much desired goal of recovery.

The recovery rate for neurotic patients is something like 66–70 per cent in two years, while some get worse. However, neurotic patients also recover 'spontaneously', i.e. without any formal treatment. There is considerable controversy as to what the rate of spontaneous recovery is. One view is that the neurotic condition simply waxes and wanes in response to external stresses, so that patients may appear to get either better or worse while being treated (Subotnik, 1972). There have been a number of studies comparing recovery rates of Ps receiving psychotherapy with those of control groups of similar Ps who had no treatment. Smith and Glass (1977) re-analysed the results of 375 such studies, involving over 25,000 patients, and showed that the treated patients improved on average somewhat more than the untreated controls in terms of reduced anxiety, increased self-esteem, and adjustment and achievement at work. The behaviour-oriented therapies did a little better than other forms, but there are no differences between the various types of psychotherapy.

It has been found, however, that some Ts have higher success rates than others, as do certain types of P – so it is evident that under the right conditions psychotherapy can do some good. A lot of therapy is with more than one person – husband and wife, or parents and an adolescent child – and here there is usually no alternative form of treatment. It is clear that some Ts actually make some Ps worse, and that there are considerable variations in social skill here. We will discuss later which Ts are the best, but first we will describe some of the social techniques which are widely used in psychotherapy. The following are common to all forms of treatment:

1 T expresses a warm, accepting and uncritical attitude of interested concern towards P, and creates a strong interpersonal relationship; it is a kind of ideal friendship, in which T participates emotionally, though it is restricted to the therapeutic hour;

2 P is encouraged to talk about his anxieties, conflicts and other bottled-up emotions; the cathartic expression of these feelings, and sharing them with another person who does not react critically,

helps to relieve them, and enables P to think about painful problems;

3 T tries to explore P's subjective world of feeling and thinking, to understand P's point of view and to open up communication with him;

4 T tries to give P insight into why he reacts as he does, and thus to change him. This is done by the verbal labelling of P's behaviour; psychoanalysts and others will offer a theoretical interpretation as well, e.g. obsessional hand-washing may be explained as the symbolic cleansing of guilt;

5 T helps P to make plans and positive decisions – to try out new ways of dealing with people and situations and to make positive efforts, thus becoming committed, rather than remaining indifferent and passive.

(Sundberg and Tyler, 1962)

Different therapists place different emphasis on these common elements, and they vary particularly in their handling of number 4, bringing about emotional or cognitive changes. Much psychotherapy is given in groups, and it is possible that group therapy is beneficial for patients with interpersonal problems. Lastly, T must terminate the treatment, at the end of each session and at the end of the series. This is anticipated by previous remarks; T summarizes what has been accomplished and refers to possible future meetings.

We have seen that there is no difference in success rate between psychotherapists of different schools, and a number of studies have shown that it is the general social skills of the therapist which are important. There is quite good evidence that empathy, warmth and genuineness are valuable. In addition, positive non-verbal signals, expressive voice quality and accurate perception are important. Bad habits include confrontation, anger, disapproval, dealing with emotional issues too soon and failing to provide support (Trower and Dryden, 1981).

In several studies it has been found that briefly trained students and non-graduate housewives have been as successful as highly trained therapists. It has been argued by Schofield (1964) that everyone experiences unhappiness and distress at times, and is in need of help, but not so much through any specialized techniques of psychotherapy as through sympathy, listening ability and friendship. It is clear that minor degrees of psychological distress are very widespread, and that qualified psychotherapists are in short supply. The solution may be for the basic techniques of psychotherapy to be more widely practised on a non-professional and semi-professional basis by members of the social network.

Ts prefer and can establish a better relationship with certain kinds of P – those who are middle-class, keen to recover, intelligent, submissive, friendly and only moderately maladjusted: it is the other Ps who do not recover and are found difficult by Ts, especially by the inexperienced (Luborsky *et al.*, 1971).

TEACHING

This section will deal with the teaching of children and adults in classes, i.e. in groups between five and forty in number. Teaching seems to have one primary goal and two subsidiary ones. The primary goal is to increase the knowledge, understanding or skills of the pupils (Ps). The subsidiary ones are for the teacher (T) to increase the motivation and interest of Ps, and to maintain order and discipline. They are subsidiary in the sense that the primary goal cannot be attained without them. Further goals could be listed, e.g. that Ps should enjoy the classes, and that they should develop in mental health, self-control or other aspects of personality. The commonest source of failure in teaching is in difficulties with discipline: there is evidence that young Ts, especially girls, find this the hardest problem, and this is probably the main reason for their abandoning the profession.

The problems of teaching vary according to the age of the Ps. Younger Ps are usually a captive audience, but are eager to please T; older Ps are less anxious to please, but may be highly motivated for other reasons, especially if they have been successful pupils in the past. In between these groups motivation may be lower, and it is with pupils of fourteen or fifteen that keeping order is most difficult. T usually has some formal power, both disciplinary and in controlling the future progress of Ps. T may also have power based on his or her expertise and position to help Ps realize their ambitions.

Some of the social techniques used in teaching will now be discussed in relation to the three main goals.

Maintaining discipline This has become a major problem in British and American city schools in recent years. The main solution is probably to get Ps interested in what is being taught, so that any disturbance is felt to be holding up progress, and group support for T can be obtained. Opportunities for disturbance should be avoided – as when there are unfilled pauses, equipment goes wrong or Ps have unclear instructions about what to do. Part of the trouble is that pupils have ideas about what teachers should and should not do. If teachers do not adhere to these 'rules' they are punished (p. 177). To avoid trouble, therefore, T should be absolutely fair in dealing with different Ps and not have favourites – a very common source of annoyance. She should not make unreasonable demands, so there must be a certain amount of consultation and negotiation. The warm-and-dominant style of supervision should be used (p. 264); she should use firmness and persuasion, in a spirit of support and friendliness, rather than of hostility, and in a confident manner. This is partly done by non-verbal communication – indicating clearly her attitude and her intention to control the situation. Discipline can be maintained by punitive and threatening methods, but this creates an anxious and unpleasant atmosphere and makes Ps dislike T, thus hampering the learning process, and discourages a creative, problem-solving approach to the subject under consideration. A study of Canadian university students found the teaching habits which were most disliked were 'ignoring, discouraging and restricting questions; reacting to students' contributions with ridicule, sarcasm, belittlement, hostility, anger and arrogance; squelching students; interrupting students' contributions, or failing to promote discussion or questions' (Crawford and Signori, 1962).

Arousing motivation This is more of a problem in teaching than in most other professions. Ultimately it is a matter of arousing some drive which most Ps have. The need for achievement can be stimulated if Ps think there is some probability of success, either in terms of marks, competing against peers or other forms of recognition. If Ps can have some experience of success and receive regular knowledge of results, or if other academic goals depend on the standard reached, this form of motivation will be aroused. Some Ps may be motivated by the need to be approved by T, a person in authority; some may identify with T and assimilate T's enthusiasm for the subject. If Ps like T they will like the subject (Oeser, 1955). The curiosity drive, to find out new things and to solve puzzles, may be aroused by presenting the material as a set of intriguing and challenging problems. Similarly T can use material or examples that are dramatic, unusual, funny or striking in some other way. Activity methods are one way of doing this, as are film-strips and other visual aids. Finally, T can show how the subject-matter is relevant to the needs and interests of the group.

Conveying information, knowledge or skill Much of educational psychology is concerned with the social techniques which are most effective for this purpose. There are several different types of activity which can be used: T tells Ps about the material, as in a lecture; T questions Ps to see how much they have understood; T leads a general discussion of the subject; T gives Ps work to do, and goes round to check on progress; T uses visual aids, demonstrations or visits, together with discussion.

The detailed techniques of teaching, of course, vary with the subject, and special methods are used for science, languages, English, etc. There are, however, several basic principles of learning which should be observed. T should get Ps actively involved in the material – by discussing it, writing about it, doing projects or experiments, and so on. T should give feedback, both in the form of praise for success and of correction for errors. T should try to give Ps insight and understanding of basic principles.

A lot of research has been done comparing the amount learnt, or the exam results obtained, with different teaching skills (Rosenshine, 1971). Those which have been found to be most effective are as follows:

1 introducing (structuring) topics or activities clearly;
2 explaining clearly, with examples and illustrative materials;
3 systematic and businesslike organization of lessons;

4 variety of teaching materials and methods;
5 use of questions, especially higher-order questions;
6 use of praise and other reinforcement, verbal and non-verbal;
7 encouraging pupil-participation;
8 making use of Ps' ideas, clarifying and developing them further;
9 warmth, rapport and enthusiasm, mainly shown non-verbally.

The teaching of these skills has been built into microteaching programmes (p. 281), one of the best examples of social skills training founded on research into which techniques produce the best results.

Teaching consists of repeated cycles of interaction. Flanders (1970) has found cycles such as those shown in Figure 23. For example:

T: teaches, explains
T: asks question (to which she knows the answer)
P: replies

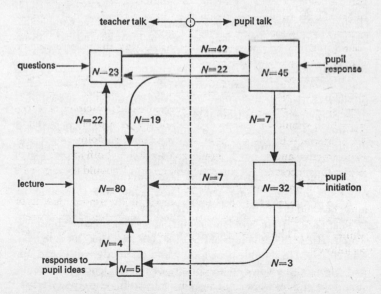

Figure 23. Cycles of interaction in the classroom (Flanders, 1970).

Flanders suggests that a lot of the skill of teaching consists of the ability to control such cycles and to move from one to another.

Teaching can also be looked at in terms of episodes. A lesson, or part of a lesson, will have a definite goal and topic; the repeated cycles will be directed towards getting across a particular set of information or skills. These teaching episodes may take a number of different forms.

PUBLIC SPEAKING AND LECTURING

There are many kinds of public speaking – e.g. political speeches, sermons, lectures, after-dinner speeches. The main goal of a public speaker (PS) is to change the attitudes or behaviour of members of the audience (A), or to increase their knowledge and understanding. Often these two aims are combined, but political and religious PSs and other propagandists emphasize the first, while lecturers in educational establishments emphasize the second. The same person may have different goals on different occasions, for example if he gives both sermons and lectures on theology. There is no doubt that PSs can be very effective in attaining these goals. For example, Billy Graham converted 100,000 people during his first three campaigns in Great Britain – about four per cent of those attending; half of these people were still church attenders a year later (Argyle and Beit-Hallahmi, 1975). Graham was exceptionally successful, but many other evangelists are much less effective. In some colleges the public lecture is the main form of instruction, and students acquire most of their education from this source. On the other hand many lecturers are regarded by their students as quite hopeless; if the lectures are not compulsory, few students go, and these often learn very little. The main sources of failure in a PS are being inaudible, boring, unconvincing, talking too fast, walking about or having other mannerisms, being nervous, not being able to handle an audience and presenting the material badly.

There are certain problems requiring special social techniques, which arise with both kinds of PS. First, it is necessary for A to hear him clearly. He should speak loudly and distinctly, with head up, and 'project' his voice to all corners of the audience. He should sound the ends of words, not drop his voice at the ends of sentences, avoid saying 'er', and keep pitch, voice quality, and breathing under control. Elocution teachers can provide help with difficulties in this sphere.

Secondly, it is necessary for PS to have sufficient prestige for A to take him seriously and accept what he has to say. He will have more effect on A if they believe that he is an expert on his subject and is well-intentioned towards them. Such prestige may have been earned by PS's past achievements, built up by the chairman's introduction, helped by PS's appearance or created by PS adopting a confident manner and demonstrating his expertise by the excellence of his presentation.

Thirdly, many PSs are anxious when in front of an audience. It makes them feel 'observed' and increases their level of arousal, because their esteem and image are exposed to the risk of being damaged. The arousal will be greater the larger and the more important the audience, and up to a point PS's performance is enhanced by this; beyond that, however, it becomes disrupted by anxiety (see p. 22). Although stage fright usually becomes less with experience, it declines very slowly.

How can audience anxiety be reduced?

1 It is worth remembering that anxiety is usually greatest before the performance starts; once it has begun the performer has to concentrate on the task rather than on himself.

2 The performer should prepare his materials very carefully so that he has confidence in them. He should also have decided on his precise relationship with the audience – is he trying to entertain them, to persuade them to do something, to tell them about some new research? Has he the right, and is he in a position, to do this?

3 His self-presentation should be carefully managed and as genuine as possible (pp. 208f). In most cases he is primarily presenting the materials rather than himself, as we argue below.

4 If all else fails, desensitization treatment is very successful (Paul, 1966).

PS must start by establishing rapport with A, and getting its attention and confidence. This may include explaining how he comes to be there, what he is going to talk about and why, and indicating his previous contacts with A or the organization in question. PS should also make certain that he can be clearly heard and that he is not speaking too fast or too softly: for this he can usually rely on visual feedback.

PS should keep his A under control. He should study its reactions carefully and be on the lookout for people not being able to hear, falling asleep, looking bored, puzzled or cross, or not taking it seriously enough. He should take rapid corrective action, for example, speaking louder, explaining points that are not clear, arousing more interest or quietening them down. However, PS should not be dependent on continual positive reactions from A; he is often more concerned with the overall, long-term impact of his presentation.

Persuasion and propaganda The successful political or religious speaker does not behave when on the platform in a relaxed, informal and 'familial' style; on the contrary he has 'presence' and dramatizes himself and his message by a certain amount of showmanship. Schizophrenics and hysterics have often been successful in the past as religious leaders, probably because their intense conviction or dramatic self-presentation carried authority with their As. This kind of PS should not allow his A to relax, but should stir it up into a state of emotional arousal. Many studies show that attitude change takes place more easily when the A is emotionally aroused (Sargant, 1957). Some PSs are adept at arousing the emotions of their As. This is done by the dramatic description of emotively arousing events – such as the horrors of hell, the outrages of the enemy or the sufferings of the poor. This is combined with an intense manner, conveyed by facial expression and tone of voice, so that A is unable to treat the matter lightly. The experienced PS discovers which examples or stories are the most effective with particular kinds of audience. Having aroused such an emotional state, the classical social technique used by propagandists is then to show that the A can relieve its anxiety, or satisfy its anger, by acting in certain ways. The nineteenth-century revivalists would make their As terrified of going to hell, and then tell them what they must do to be saved; many modern advertisements follow a similar strategy.

Research has shown how persuasive messages should be organized to have the maximum effect. One-sided messages are best, unless the A is initially opposed or educated, in which case objections should be stated and dealt with. If the message is simple and straightforward, the A should be left to draw the conclusions itself, otherwise PS should do this. Overt behaviour is affected most if specific actions are recommended. Earlier arguments have most effect, so the most appealing part of the argument should come first. It is useful to start with statements with which A will agree, in order to win its confidence.

Lecturing The social techniques used by a lecturer to convey knowledge and understanding are rather different. He should not adopt the intense manner of the propagandist, which tends to suppress the thinking process. However, successful lecturers have a variety of styles, and it is not possible to prescribe which one is most effective. While lecturers should not arouse the emotions in the same way as propagandists, they should arouse interest, intellectual excitement and curiosity. They should not simply produce a lot of information that nobody wants, so a lecturer should start by stating what problems he is going to deal with, and getting A's attention from the outset. He should follow an intelligible plan, which may be built up on the blackboard or shown in a handout, and he should come to clear conclusions. It is important to accompany the statement of principles by concrete examples.

One of the main problems with a lecture is that A can't remember it all. Possible solutions are: not including too much, not making it too long, relating it to A's experience and encouraging A to take notes. Furthermore, a lecture should be made enjoyable and memorable by the use of materials which are of special interest to the audience, dramatic or simply funny. Particular skill is needed when introducing A to novel ideas or ways of looking at things; it may be necessary to use striking and carefully chosen examples, to jolt A out of its previous ways of thinking. Visual aids such as slides, overhead projector, films and charts can help with the presentation and make it more varied and interesting. The lecturer can keep A's interest by adopting a manner which keeps it involved in the situation – use of eye-contact, and a striking and pleasant style of behaviour. He should spend as little time as possible looking at notes, writing on the blackboard or otherwise interrupting contact with A. He should show his own enthusiasm for the materials, and a positive attitude towards A, by facial expression and tone of voice. Spatial arrangements are important, especially when visual aids are used: the best room available should be chosen and arranged to best advantage, so that everyone is comfortable and can see and hear. The lecturer should be as near as possible, and able to see A. During the discussion the contributions of the audience should be taken seriously and sympathetically, and an effort made to see the points of view expressed. The lecturer should not merely 'deal with' the points made, but use them as an opportunity to explain himself further. He should avoid any confrontation with the audience.

There are self-presentation problems here too. Not only is a lecture more than the transmission of a text, it is also more than a performance by PS. As Goffman (1981) says:

> The lecturer and the audience join in affirming a single proposition. They join in affirming that organized talking can reflect, express, delineate, portray – if not come to grips with – the real world, and that, finally, there is a real, structured, somewhat unitary world out there to comprehend . . . Whatever his substantive domain, whatever his school of thought, and whatever his inclination to piety or impiety, he signs the same agreement and he serves the same cause: to protect us from the wind, to stand up and seriously project the assumption that through lecturing, a meaningful picture of some part of the world can be conveyed, and that the talker can have access to a picture worth conveying [pp. 194–5].

SUPERVISION OF GROUPS

We include here not only industrial foremen, but directors of research groups and leaders of other groups that have a task to do. The primary goal of the supervisor (S) is to get the work done, but an important secondary goal is to keep the team satisfied – otherwise there will be absenteeism, labour turnover and a general lack of cooperation. Ss may fail in a number of ways of which the most common are:

relying too much on formal power;
being too authoritative;
not giving enough direction, so that other members of the group assume leadership;

producing high output but low job satisfaction;
producing high job satisfaction but low output.

In studies of groups of manual workers it is found that groups under certain supervisors may produce 50 per cent more work than under other supervisors; if the work is machine-paced or under wage-incentives these differences are smaller, though with very bad supervision the difference can be greater (Argyle, 1972). The effects on rates of absenteeism and labour turnover are rather greater – ratios of 4 or even 8:1 have been found; again the worst supervisors produce the most marked effects (Fleishman and Harris, 1962).

A great deal of research has been carried out into the social techniques which are most effective, mainly by comparing the behaviour of Ss in charge of high-output and low-output teams. Similar results have been obtained from research which has been done in a variety of American industries (Likert, 1961), in British electrical engineering factories (Argyle *et al.*, 1958), in Japanese industry, in clerical organizations, in sports teams and in the armed forces. The main findings will now be discussed.

Initiating structure It is essential that the supervisor should really supervise, and in the following ways:

1 planning and scheduling the work to be done, and making sure supplies are available;
2 instructing and training subordinates in how to do their work;
3 checking and correcting the work that has been done;
4 giving subordinates feedback on how well they are doing;
5 motivating subordinates to work effectively.

If he fails to do these things, it is likely that the group or some of its members will take over these functions. On the other hand, S should do all this with a light hand, since men do not like him breathing down their necks and constantly interfering. He should see them frequently, showing interest, giving help where it is needed, but giving as little direction and criticism as possible. In 'job enrichment' schemes some of S's jobs, such as checking, are delegated to members of the group.

Consideration Ss are more effective when they look after the needs, interests and welfare of their men. This is particularly true when they are powerful enough to be really able to do something for them. In matters of discipline they should be persuasive rather than punitive, and try to find out the causes of the offending behaviour. It is interesting that foremen who are more concerned with the welfare of the men than with production usually succeed in getting higher rates of output. On the other hand, a number of studies show that S should be somewhat detached and independent: he should do his own job rather than theirs, and not be afraid of exerting influence over them.

Neither of these dimensions is much good alone, however, the *combination* of initiating structure and consideration being necessary (Hunt and Larson, 1977). This is found difficult to attain – we have seen that informal groups often have two leaders, one for each of these jobs. Part of the difficulty is that directing the task tends to put a leader at a distance from the group, while getting on well with members means he may lose his authority as a task leader. The solution may lie in a further aspect of supervisory skill.

Democratic–persuasive style A democratic leader is usually more effective than an autocratic one. He does not just rely on his formal powers, but on:

  1 motivating people by explanation and persuasion, rather than just giving orders;
  2 allowing subordinates to participate in decisions that affect them;
  3 using techniques of group discussion and group decision.

By means of these skills the supervisor succeeds in getting the group to set high targets and to internalize the motivation to reach them, without exerting pressure himself. There are of course limits to what the group can decide. It can usually decide about details of administration – who shall work where, how training or holiday schemes shall be implemented. The group can also make suggestions on more far-reaching matters which S can relay to his superiors. He exerts direction and influence but in a way that does not arouse resentment and antagonism. He can still be a real leader, rather than just a chairman for the group.

Another aspect of supervisory style is the exchange of rewards. S offers recognition, bonus payments, etc. in exchange for good work, and perhaps negotiates different bargains with each member, whereby some receive more approval but also have to work harder.

Ss must have enough power, and formal power must be 'legitimated'; this happens when S is seen to possess expertise at his job, when he is seen to be a committed member of the team and when the group is successful.

The optimum style of leadership varies with the situation. Fiedler (1978) has found that an emphasis on relationships rather than task (consideration versus initiating structure) is most effective under moderately favourable conditions only, e.g. when there is a fairly good relation with the group. It may be necessary to use different techniques at different times with the same group: a research group in the planning stage needs permissive handling so that all ideas can come forward, but once the design has been decided a stricter style is better. Similarly there are advantages in a more autocratic style when the group is large, or when the members are themselves authoritarian in personality and accustomed to a strict pattern of leadership.

Another range of problems arises in connection with difficult group members. Sometimes such people are more amenable to group influence than to leaders, e.g. those who are hostile to authority – they should be left to the other group members to control. Another type is more responsive to people in authority – they should be dealt with by the leader privately. The most difficult to deal with are psychopaths, who care neither for leaders nor groups. The only solution is to isolate them as far as possible from the main group activities, to prevent them disrupting the group.

MANAGEMENT SKILLS

Committee chairmanship The task of committees and other discussion groups is to solve problems and take decisions in a way that is acceptable to those present, and to those they represent. In some cases the emphasis is on problem-solving and creativity, in others the emphasis is on obtaining consensus. The main value of taking decisions in committee is to find widely acceptable decisions; those present will then be committed to carrying them out. Groups are better than individuals for solving problems if individuals with different skills and knowledge can be combined. Thus, they produce more brain power than any one person. There is also interaction between members, so that one suggests new thoughts to another, and one member's bright ideas are criticized and evaluated by others. These groups usually have a chairman, unless there are only three or four people present. The chairman has a generally accepted social role of controlling discussion and helping the group make decisions. His position is often more temporary than that of other group leaders, and the chairmanship may be rotated so that other committee members take it in turns. Being chairman carries a certain amount of power, but it has to be used with skill. A chairman should see that all members are able to express their views, and that the decisions arrived at are agreeable to as many of them as possible. He should be able to keep control with a light touch, and keep people in order without upsetting them.

A certain amount of research has been done by Maier and Solem (1952) and Hoffman (1965) into which skills of chairmanship produce the best effects. They found, for example, that better and more widely accepted solutions are obtained if minority views can be expressed. Sometimes groups arrive at a solution rather quickly; if the chairman asks them to think of an alternative solution, this is often preferred in the end. The chairman can help the group by focusing on disagreements and searching for a creative solution.

The chairman should study the agenda carefully beforehand, and prepare his introduction to the different items. He should be able to anticipate the items which may cause difficulty; he may speak to some members beforehand if he wants to call on their expertise, or needs their support.

At the beginning of the meeting the chairman should create the right atmosphere, by the use of appropriate non-verbal signals. There are several phases to the discussion of each item on the agenda. First, the chairman introduces the item by outlining the problem to be discussed, summarizing briefly the main background factors, the arguments on each side, and so on. Then the committee is invited to discuss the problem; enough time should be allowed for different views to be expressed, and the chairman should try to keep the discussion orderly, so that different points are dealt with in turn. Now the chairman can help the group to come to a decision, by focusing on disagreements among them and trying to arrive at a creative solution, evaluating different solutions in relation to criteria if these can be agreed, considering sub-problems in turn, or asking the committee to consider two possible solutions. Finally, an attempt is made to secure the group's support for a particular solution. If this is impossible it may be necessary to take a vote; this is unsatisfactory, since it means that some members are not happy about the decision, and will not support it very enthusiastically.

The moves which are made by a chairman are listed by Rackham and Morgan – building, supporting, etc. (see p. 282) – and are used by them for training in chairmanship skills.

A chairman should be aware of the main processes of behaviour in groups, and be able to prevent these processes interfering with the effective working of the committee. The formation of a status hierarchy will inhibit low-status members from contributing: they should be encouraged to speak. The reason that groups often take riskier decisions than individuals is that, in most situations, such behaviour is valued in the culture, and it is flattering to the self-image to believe that one is more daring than the other members of the group. As a result, those who discover that they have been making less risky decisions than others shift in the risky direction after group discussion.

Another danger of committees is that in a crisis a 'kitchen cabinet' can become isolated from outsiders and ignore their views, suppress deviation and have an illusion of unanimity and a belief in its own morality; as a result the committee may take disastrously wrong decisions (Janis and Mann, 1977).

Negotiation Managers have to negotiate with trade unions, firms other than their own and Government. Negotiation is a kind of joint decision-making between representatives of two sides who are in conflict, though there is joint interest in reaching a settlement. The goal of a negotiator (N) is to reach an agreement quickly which gives his side the best deal obtainable and will be accepted by all concerned. The success of N can be assessed by ratings from both sides concerning his effectiveness, his record for reaching agreements and the extent to which his agreements stick.

The social situation of negotiation is a complex one. Both sides are representatives; it is easier for them if they are 'leaders' rather than 'delegates', since then they are in a better position to sell the agreement reached. There are usually several Ns on each side, and the two sides are in conflict with one another. On the other hand, they must cooperate over the process of negotiation and may know each other well. In the second phase of negotiation (see below) they shift away from their roles as representatives in conflict to one of more interpersonal cooperation. McGrath (1966) observed that N was influenced by three forces – the party he represents, the opposing N and the broader community. When the first force is too strong, it is difficult to reach agreement. There are also power differences between the two sides, depending on the nature of the negotiation. This of course affects the outcome, especially when proceedings are conducted in a formal manner (Morley and Stephenson, 1977).

Sometimes a professional mediator or chairman is appointed. He may be able to steer Ns towards a more problem-solving approach after a deadlock, and arrive at a solution which is face-saving for both sides. Sometimes informal discussion between junior representatives of the two sides can find a solution when their superiors have failed, since they are freer to explore possible concessions – though their solution may not be accepted in the end by their own sides.

The basic procedure is for each party to start by stating its case and its preferred solution. This is followed by exchange of information, for example about each side's problems and payoffs, and a series of concessions, which are usually reciprocated until agreement is reached. Three phases are often distinguished:

1 each side makes long speeches, emphasizing the strength of its case, Ns taking the representative role;
2 the range of possible solutions is explored and information is

exchanged, Ns now assuming a more cooperative and problem-solving role;

3 there is harder bargaining, and decision-taking, over the actual settlement point.

The moves and strategies which are made in the course of negotiation indicate the complexity of this bargaining process – e.g. perceiving and exploiting power, standing firm but signalling flexibility (Morley, 1981). One famous strategy is Osgood's GRIT (1960) – Graduated Reciprocation in Tension Reduction – recommended for disarmament talks. N announces that he will make small concessions, and that if these are matched by the other side he will make more. Another approach is what Pruitt (1976) has described as 'integrative behaviour', focusing on possible concessions, new alternatives and the maximum joint profits involved.

Certain styles of negotiation have been found to be more successful than others in actual cases or in simulations:

1 N should make a strong case, make strong demands and give small concessions;

2 N should not be too tough, however, or there may be no agreement, and he should not attack or irritate the other side;

3 N should be open to a wide range of alternatives, and not plan a particular outcome in advance;

4 N should adopt a rational, problem-solving approach, in which he explores all the options, finds out a lot about the other side and their problems as well as giving information himself, and communicates clearly and without ambiguity;

5 N should create a reputation for honesty and firmness, and enhance the image of his party.

(Rackham and Carlisle, 1978, 1979)

FURTHER READING

Interviewing

The selection interview

McHenry, R., 'The selection interview', in Argyle, M. (ed.), *Social Skills and Work*, Methuen, 1981.

Urgerson, B., *Recruitment Handbook*, Gower Press, 1975.

The social survey interview

Brenner, M., 'Skills in the Research Interview', in Argyle, M. (ed.), *Social Skills and Work*, Methuen, 1981.

Kahn, R. L., and Katz, C. F., *The Dynamics of Interviewing*, Wiley, New York, 1957.

Selling

Poppleton, S. E., 'The social skills of selling', in Argyle, M. (ed.), *Social Skills and Work*, Methuen, 1981.

Woodward, J., *The Saleswoman*, Pitman, 1960.

Social Skills of Doctors and Nurses

Doctors

Maguire, P., 'Doctor–patient skills', in Argyle, M. (ed.), *Social Skills and Health*, Methuen, 1981.

Nurses

Davis, B., 'Social skills in nursing', in Argyle, M. (ed.), *Social Skills and Health*, Methuen, 1981.

Psychotherapy and Counselling

Bergin, A. E., and Garfield, S. L., *Handbook of Psychotherapy* 2nd edn, Wiley, New York, 1978.

Trower, P., and Dryden, W., 'Psychotherapy', in Argyle, M. (ed.), *Social Skills and Health*, Methuen, 1981.

Teaching

Dunkin, M. J., and Biddle, B. J., *The Study of Teaching*, Holt, Rinehart and Winston, New York, 1974.
Rosenshine, B., *Teaching Behaviour and Student Achievement*, N.F.E.R., 1971.

Public Speaking and Lecturing

Bligh, D. A., *What's the Use of Lectures?* Penguin Books, 1972.
Knapper, C. K., 'Presenting and public speaking', in Argyle, M. (ed.), *Social Skills and Work*, Methuen, 1981.

Supervision of Groups

Georgiades, N. J., and Orlaux, V., 'The supervision of working groups', in Argyle, M. (ed.), *Social Skills and Work*, Methuen, 1981.
Hollander, E. P., *Leadership Dynamics*, Collier Macmillan, New York, 1978.

Management Skills

Committee chairmanship

Hoffman, L. R., 'Group problem-solving', *Advances in Experimental Social Psychology*, vol. 2, 1965, pp. 99–132.

Negotiation

Morley, I., 'Negotiation and bargaining', in Argyle, M. (ed.), *Social Skills and Work*, Methuen, 1981.

CHAPTER 12

TRAINING IN SOCIAL SKILLS

MANY jobs consist mainly of dealing with people – teaching, interviewing and selling, for example. All jobs involve communication and cooperation, the giving and receiving of orders, maintaining relationships, and other basic social skills. Most of those in the first group get some training, though others have to pick it up on the job. However, some young teachers are not able to keep order, some interviewers get a lot of refusals, and some salesmen sell very little. For all of these people the training has failed. Perhaps a look at the possible methods of training may show how to improve the training of such people. In the modern world an increasing number of jobs consist more of dealing with people than of dealing with things; furthermore the speed of technological change means that many people have to be retrained for a new job once or even twice in the course of their working lives.

Social skills are also needed in everyday life, to deal with family, friends, neighbours, people in shops and offices, and so on. It is difficult to estimate the proportion of the population whose lives are seriously disrupted by the inability to make friends, or deal with other relationships, but our surveys suggest that it is at least seven per cent. Parents implicitly train their children in social skills; perhaps they could do it better. Schools train children in writing and speaking, and sometimes in other aspects of social behaviour; this too could be greatly extended. I believe that it would be possible to train people up to a higher level of sensitivity and competence than is common at present. This could have the effect of making social encounters and relationships far more enjoyable, effective and creative than they often are.

Social skills training has become widely used in recent years. Microteaching has been generally adopted for teacher training; similar kinds of role-playing are often used for social workers, interviewers, salesmen and others. T-groups and encounter groups have also been popular, though their effects are more dubious.

The definition of social competence, and the criteria of successful performance of social skills were discussed earlier (pp. 76f). How can it be decided whether or not a particular form of training works? Experience with various forms of training and therapy shows that while these are often enthusiastically praised by those who have been trained, more careful investigation sometimes shows that there is no real change in behaviour. It is necessary to take measures of performance before and after the training. These measures should not consist just of questionnaires – because people may merely learn what sort of answers to give – but of measures of performance or effectiveness on the job, or objective tests of what they can do. Often ratings by colleagues are used as the criteria; there is a danger that colleagues who believe in a training method will give higher ratings after than before in order to confirm their belief. This can be countered by the use of 'blind' ratings, where the raters do not know which of the individuals they are rating are being trained or belong to a control group. There should be a control group of similar people who are not being trained, in order to allow for improvement with the passage of time and the effects of practice in doing tests. There should be a greater improvement from before the training to after, for the trained group than for the control group, using some objective index of skill. Wherever possible, studies of this kind will be used below to assess the different methods of training.

LEARNING ON THE JOB

This is probably the commonest form of training. While manual workers are given carefully designed courses, those who have to deal with people often receive no training at all, because it is so difficult to tell them what they should do. In fact some manual operatives also learn by doing, and learning curves can be plotted which show their rate of progress.

Unfortunately this seems to be a very unreliable form of training. A person can do a job for years and never discover the right social skills; some experienced interviewers have great difficulty with candidates who will not talk, for example. Argyle *et al.* (1958) found that supervisors often learnt the *wrong* things by experience, e.g. to use close, punitive and authoritarian styles of supervision.

The author with Mary Lydall and Mansur Lalljee carried out several studies of the learning of social skills on the job. In one of them an attempt was made to plot the learning curve for selling, this task being chosen because there is an objective criterion of success. Annual fluctuations in trade were overcome by expressing the sales of a beginner as a percentage of the average sales of three experienced sellers in the same department. The average results from three shops are shown in Figure 24; it can be seen that there was an overall improvement, especially where there was an individual incentive scheme. However, individuals responded in a variety of ways, and while on average most improved, some did not, and others got steadily worse. Again it seems that simply doing the job doesn't always lead to improvement.

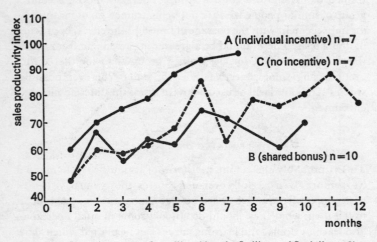

Figure 24. Learning curves for selling (Argyle, Lalljee and Lydall, 1958).

McPhail (1967) studied the process of acquiring social competence during adolescence. He gave problem situations to 100 males and 100 females aged 12–18. Alternative solutions were selected and these were found to change with age in an interesting way. The younger subjects gave a lot of rather crude, aggressive, dominating responses. McPhail classified these as 'experimental' attempts to acquire by trial and error social skills for dealing with the new situations that adolescents face. The older ones on the other hand used more skilful, sophisticated social techniques, similar to those employed by adults (Figure 25).

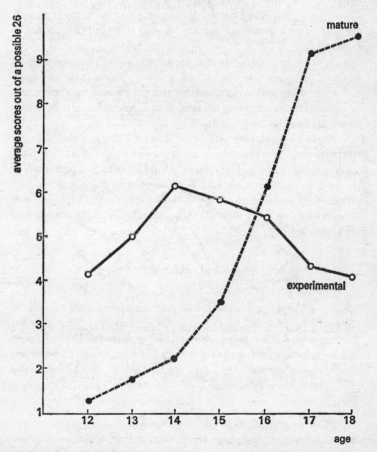

Figure 25. Acquisition of social skills in adolescence (McPhail, 1967).

Learning on the job has a great advantage over all other forms of training – there is no problem of transfer from the training situation to real life. A number of studies suggest the conditions under which training on the job can be successful.

1 Clear feedback must be given on what the trainee is doing wrong. Gage *et al.* (1960) asked 3,900 school children to fill in rating scales to describe their ideal teacher and how their actual teachers behaved; the results were shown to half of the teachers, who subsequently improved on ten of the twelve scales, compared with the no-feedback group. In most situations this kind of feedback is not available.

2 In order to improve performance new social techniques must be found. The best way of generating new responses is for an expert to suggest them and to demonstrate them. Learning on the job can be speeded up by imitating successful performers, but it may not be clear exactly what they are doing.

3 Learning on the job will occur if there is a trainer on the spot who frequently sees the trainee in action, and holds regular feedback and coaching sessions. The trainer should be an expert performer of the skill himself, and should be sensitized to the elements and processes of social interaction. The success of such coaching will depend on there being a good relationship between the trainee and the supervisor.

ROLE-PLAYING

Most forms of SST (social skills training) are varieties of role-playing. Role-playing consists of trying out a social skill away from the real situation, in the lab, clinic, or training centre, on other trainees or on role partners provided for the purpose. The training is usually a series of sessions which may last from one to three hours, depending on the size and stamina of the group. In each session a particular aspect of the skill or a particular range of problem situations is dealt with. There are three main phases to role-playing exercises.

1 There is a lecture, discussion, demonstration, tape-recording or film about a particular aspect of the skill. This is particularly

important when an unfamiliar skill is being taught or when rather subtle social techniques are involved. The demonstration is particularly important: this is known as 'modelling'.

2 A problem situation is defined, and stooges are produced for trainees to role-play with, for seven to fifteen minutes each. The background to the situation may be filled in with written materials, such as the application forms of candidates for interview or background information about personnel problems. The stooges may be carefully trained beforehand to provide various problems, such as talking too much or having elaborate and plausible excuses.

3 There is a feedback session, consisting of verbal comments by the trainer, discussion with the other trainees and playback of audio- or videotapes. Verbal feedback is used to draw attention, constructively and tactfully, to what the trainee was doing wrong, and to suggest alternative styles of behaviour. The tape-recordings provide clear evidence for the accuracy of what is being said.

There is often a fourth phase, in which the role-playing, phase 2, is repeated. In microteaching this is known as 're-teaching'.

There are two important preliminary steps to this form of training. Firstly it is necessary to draw up a list of the main problem situations to be faced by those being trained; this can be done by 'critical incident' surveys, or more informally by consulting a number of experienced practitioners – of selling, interviewing, teaching, or whatever is being taught. Secondly it is necessary to find out the best social techniques for dealing with the problem situations.

Follow-up studies show that role-playing is the most effective form of SST at present available. Experimental comparisons of different procedures show that the full package we described originally is the most effective. It is necessary to include:

1 modelling;
2 instructions;
3 role-play practice;
4 an instructor to give the feedback;
5 realistic stooges, e.g. children for microteaching.

However, there is some doubt as to whether the video is necessary, and some trainers have obtained good results without it.

Feedback is one of the crucial components. It can come from several sources:

1 It may come from the other members of the group, either in free discussion, discussion in smaller groups, questionnaires or behavioural check lists. These things must be done carefully, or they will be disturbing to the recipients of the feedback; on the other hand, they are probably a valuable part of the training process for those observing.

2 It may be given by the trainer, who should be in a position to give expert guidance on the social techniques which are effective, and who may be able to increase sensitivity to the subtler nuances of interaction. He may correct errors – such as interrupting, looking or sounding unfriendly. He can suggest alternative social techniques, such as ways of dealing with awkward clients or situations. This has to be done very carefully: the trainer's remarks should be gentle and kind enough not to upset, but firm and clear enough to have some effect.

3 Sound tape-recordings may be taken and played back to the trainee immediately after his performance. The author's experience is that the trainer's comments should precede the playback, so that trainees know what to look for.

4 Videotape recordings can be used in a similar way: a television film is played back to the trainee after his performance. This directs his attention to the behavioural (facial, bodily and gestural) aspects of his performance, as well as to the auditory. It may be useful to play back the sound tape separately to focus attention on sound.

Use of homework The main difficulty with role-playing is that trainees have to transfer what they have learnt in the training centre to the real world. Some of the best results have been obtained when traineees have been persuaded to try out what they have learnt a number of times between sessions. Gabrielle Maxwell (1976) in New Zealand refused to see her patients again until they had done so. Morton (1965) used role-playing with mental patients on such domestic problems as disciplining children, keeping a budget and keeping things peaceful. For the role-playing sessions nurses and others were used in the complementary roles. Patients returned home at weekends, after which they reported their progress. This was then discussed by the trainer and the group of trainees.

Modelling Modelling can consist of demonstrations by one of the therapists or the showing of films or videotapes. It is used when it is difficult to teach the patient by verbal descriptions alone. This applies to complex skills for neurotic or volunteer clients, and to simpler skills for more disturbed patients and children. It is generally used in conjunction with role-playing (between sessions) and is accompanied by verbal instructions, i.e. coaching.

Modelling has been found to be most effective under the following conditions:

when the model is similar to the trainee, e.g. in age;

when the model is not *too* expert;

when there is a verbal narrative labelling the model's behaviour;

with a live model and with multiple models;

when the model's behaviour is seen to lead to favourable consequences.

(Thelen *et al.*, 1979)

Video playback has been widely used, especially by trainers who focus on non-verbal communication. The results indicating whether or not SST is more effective when video is used are conflicting, but most studies show that it does make a difference (Bailey and Sowder, 1970). Some people find it mildly disturbing at first, but they soon get used to it. However, it should perhaps not be used with very anxious or self-conscious patients.

Equipment Role-playing can be conducted without the use of any specialized equipment, but it is greatly assisted if certain laboratory arrangements are available. An ideal set up for interviewer training is shown in Figure 26. The role-playing takes place on one side of a one-way screen, and is observed by the trainer and other trainees. A video-tape is taken of the role-playing. The trainer is able to communicate with the role-player through an ear-microphone; the trainer can give comments and suggestions to the trainee while the role-playing is proceeding. (The author once had to advise an interviewer trainee dealing with an over-amorous 'candidate' to move his seat back three feet.)

Interviewing training One of the first social skills to be taught by role-playing was selection interviewing.

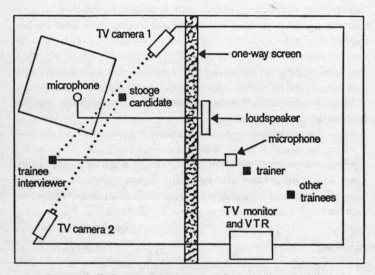

Figure 26. Laboratory arrangements for interviewer training.

In the course for selection interviewing devised by Elizabeth Sidney and the author some of the exercises are designed to teach participants how to deal with 'awkward' candidates (p. 237). Trainees interview special stooges who talk too much, too little, are nervous, bombastic, anxious, and so on. Each role-playing session on this course begins with a lecture and a film about the problems to be role-played. There is also training in how to assess stability, judgement, achievement, motivation, etc. in the interview, and how to avoid common errors of person perception.

Microteaching This is now widely used for teacher training. A trainee prepares a short lesson, and teaches five or six children for ten to fifteen minutes; this is followed by a videotape playback and comments by the trainer, after which the trainee takes the same lesson again. There are usually a number of sessions, each being devoted to one particular teaching skill – asking higher-order questions, encouraging pupil participation, explaining clearly with examples, etc. (pp. 256f). This form of training is found to be faster than alternative forms, and is probably the best way of eliminating bad teaching habits (Brown, 1975; Peck and Tucker, 1973).

Assertiveness training This was one of the earliest forms of SST; it came from the behaviour therapy tradition, and the rationale was that arousing incompatible (assertive) responses would remove anxious and submissive ones. By assertiveness is meant standing up for your rights, saying no, making requests, initiating conversation and so on. The method of training has consisted of standard role-playing procedures with modelling and VTR playback. It has been widely used with normal adults who think they need it, for example submissive males, and with mental patients. Follow-up studies show a considerable degree of success (Rich and Schroeder, 1976). It is a mistake, however, to regard assertiveness as the only goal of SST: control of others is important, but then so is the dimension of interpersonal warmth (pp. 143f), which is probably more important for people who complain that they haven't got any friends.

Heterosexual skills Many young people suffer from lack of contact with the opposite sex ('minimal dating'), or feel anxious in the presence of the opposite sex. This may be due to lack of social skills, which in turn is usually due to lack of experience or to anxiety caused by unsuccessful experiences in the past. Training courses have been devised to teach the necessary skills for making dates and for behaviour during dates. Follow-up studies have found these to be very successful; one, for example, increased the average number of dates per week from 0·8 to 1·9 (Curran, 1977).

Social skills training for mental patients This has been developed along similar lines. There is usually modelling and role-playing, with videotape playback, of the skills needed by individual patients or of skills needed by several patients if done in groups. The form of SST which we have developed at Oxford for neurotic mental patients is based on role-playing. It is different from other forms in that we recognize a large number of different kinds of social incompetence, each one corresponding to the breakdown of one of the basic processes of social behaviour. Some of these can be corrected by straight role-playing, but others require special techniques, which are described below.

Management skills Rackham and Morgan (1977) have developed a set of procedures for training in committee work, chairmanship, selling and related skills. They use a set of categories, which is modified for particular skills, containing items such as content proposals, procedural proposals, building, supporting, disagreeing, defending/attacking, testing understanding, summarizing, seeking information and giving information (the Chairman list). Good and bad performers at the skill are discovered and their rates of using the categories compared. Trainees learn the use of the categories and participate in role-play exercises while observers record how often they use the categories. The trainer then gives feedback, consisting of information about each trainee's score on the categories, which are compared with the rates for the good performers. Follow-up studies do show positive results, although these were not very carefully controlled.

SPECIAL TECHNIQUES FOR SOCIAL SKILLS TRAINING

We have shown that a number of quite different processes contribute to social competence; each can go wrong in a number of ways, and training can be focused on one process at a time rather than on social performance in general.

Expression of NV signals In training mental patients it is common to coach them in NV communication, since they are often very inexpressive in this sphere, or send NV messages which are hostile rather than friendly. Study of a patient's role-played performance in the clinic shows which NV signals require training, though the commonest ones are face and voice. Facial expression can be trained with the help of a mirror and later with a videotape-recorder. Trainees are asked to take part in short conversations, while expressing certain emotions in the face, such as sadness or happiness. If there is difficulty in producing the correct expression in all parts of the face, the photographs by Ekman and Friesen (1975) can be used as models. The voice can be trained with the help of an audiotape-recorder. Trainees are asked to read passages from the paper in, for example, friendly, dominant or surprised tones of voice, and these are then played back and discussed.

Situational analysis Some mental patients and many adults have difficulty in coping with specific social situations. In the case of a number of professional social skills the performer has to deal with a variety of situations; for example, social workers and supervisors. It would be possible to include in the training some analysis of the main situations involved, and especially of those which are found difficult, in terms of goals and goal structure, rules, roles, etc. Situational analysis has been used in the treatment of obesity, by discovering the situations in which over-eating occurs and the series of events leading up to it (Ferguson, 1975) A similar approach is commonly used in the treatment of alcoholics.

Taking the role of the other Chandler (1973) succeeded in improving the ability to see another's point of view (and reducing delinquency) by means of exercises in which groups of five young delinquents developed and made video-recordings of skits about relevant real-life situations, each member of the group playing a part.

Self-presentation In addition to the usual role-playing exercises, trainees can be given advice over clothes, hair and other aspects of appearance. Their voices can be trained to produce a more appropriate accent or tone of voice. There is a correlation between physical attractiveness and mental health, and some therapeutic success has been obtained by improving the appearance of patients. The recidivism of male criminals has been reduced by removing tattooing and scars.

Perceptual training It may also be necessary to train people in the perception of NV signals. Some convicts, for example, can't tell when people are becoming upset, so that fights start. For professional skills like social work and psychotherapy it is important to be able to judge the emotional states of others. The Ekman and Friesen photographs can be used to train people to decode facial expression. Trainees can be taught to appreciate tones of voice by listening to tape-recordings of neutral messages produced in different emotional states (Davitz, 1964). In each case it is easy to test the subject, for example by finding out the percentage of recordings which they can decode correctly.

Planning and the use of feedback The social skills model suggests some further points at which training can be useful. A common problem with mental patients is a failure to pursue persistent goals and a tendency to react passively to others. Assertiveness training is also directed at making the trainees take more initiative and pursue their goals. We have used special exercises for this problem; trainees are asked to carry out a simple skill, like interviewing, which requires that they take the initiative throughout. They can plan the encounter and take notes; the trainer communicates with an ear-microphone during the role-playing if the performer runs out of conversation.

Conversational sequences We have seen that socially inadequate people are often very bad conversationalists (pp. 72f); they may be incapable of sustaining a conversation, and manage to kill it in one of a number of ways. All social skills use conversation, i.e. a sequence of utterances, and the control of sequences is an important part of the skill. Teachers need to be able to control such cycles of interaction as teacher lectures → teacher asks question → pupil replies (p. 257), and other longer cycles. During repeated sequences of this sort there is also a build-up in the complexity of the topic being taught. The selection interview is similar: there is a certain structure of questions, answers, modified and follow-up questions, and a structure of episodes and sub-episodes, based on topics and sub-topics. Every social skill uses certain conversational sequences, which can be learned, and in every case there are a number of difficulties, for which the solution can be taught. Salesmen may have difficulty in controlling interaction with the client; doctors may find it is hard to terminate encounters; and survey interviewers may have to deal with respondents who wander off the point.

T-GROUPS AND ENCOUNTER GROUPS

T-groups T (training)-groups were first developed in the National Training Laboratories at Bethel, Maine, in 1947, and they became very popular in the 1960s and early 1970s as a form of management training. The members of a T-group spend their time studying the group and the processes of social interaction that take place in it. The trainer typically starts off by saying: 'My name is —, and I am the appointed staff trainer of this group and am here to help you in the study of this group as best I can.' T-groups consist of about twelve trainees who meet for a series of two-hour periods, weekly or during a residential course. The sessions are often combined with lectures, role-playing and other activities, but the T-group is regarded as central.

Behaviour in T-groups has a strange quality, the conversation being somewhat stilted and embarrassed, some members either not taking part at all or engaging in irrelevant conversation ('pairing'). A curious pattern of role differentiation has been reported in Harvard T-groups, including 'distressed females', who take little part in the conversation, 'paranoid' and 'moralistic' resisters, who oppose the official task, and 'sexual scapegoats', who present their masculinity problems for the group to study (Mann *et al.*, 1967).

One of the main things that the trainer does is to teach people to give and receive feedback, so that members may become aware of the impact of their behaviour on others and find out how others see them. The trainer shows how to make non-evaluative comments on the behaviour of others, and tries to reduce the defensiveness of those whose behaviour is being commented upon. Feedback is provided in other ways; members may take turns to act as observers who later report back to the group, tape-recordings of previous sessions are studied, and analyses by professional observers may be presented.

Encounter groups These use a number of exercises designed to give experience of intimacy and other social relationships. Here are some examples of the exercises used at Esalen (Schutz, 1967).

1 'Break in' – to help those who are withdrawn and have difficulty in making contact with other people. Some of the group form a tight circle with interlocking arms. The person left out tries to break through the circle in any way he can.

2 'The press' – to help those who are unable to express hostility or competition. Two people stand facing one another, place their hands on each other's shoulders and try to press the other to the ground.

3 'Give and take affection' – to help people who have difficulty in giving or receiving affection, who avoid emotional closeness. One person stands in the centre of a circle with his eyes shut. The others approach and express their feelings towards him non-verbally however they wish – usually by hugging, stroking, massaging, lifting, etc.

How successful are T-groups and encounter groups? Those who have been in them report that they have undergone a powerful experience. Many feel better, but some feel worse. A careful follow-up study was carried out of 206 Stanford students who attended encounter groups, T-groups, etc., using 69 control subjects. Success was estimated by a combination of criteria – self-ratings, ratings by friends, and so on. The results were as follows:

	Percentage group members	Percentage controls
dropouts	13	—
casualties	8	—
negative change	8	23
unchanged	38	60
moderate positive change	20 ⎫ 34	13 ⎫ 17
high positive change	14 ⎭	4 ⎭

About a third of the group members and seventeen per cent of the controls improved, while eight per cent of the group members were harmed by the experience (for example, needing psychiatric help afterwards) in addition to the dropouts and those who showed negative changes. There were no consistent differences between encounter and non-touching groups; variations between individual group leaders were more important (Lieberman, Yalom and Miles, 1973).

Similar results have been obtained in a number of other studies – while about a third of the subjects benefit, up to ten per cent become worse, this being the main focus of criticism of T-groups and encounter groups. A problem with encounter groups which use a lot of bodily contact is that some clients end up with a different spouse from the one they started with. Some people enjoy themselves so much that they lose interest in ordinary life and want to spend all their time having 'deep and meaningful experiences' in groups.

Encounter group techniques have been incorporated in a number of therapeutic packages and adopted by quasi-religious sects, along with meditation and other Indian practices. None of these packages has been subjected to follow-up study, and it is very likely that, as with encounter groups themselves, some people benefit, many are unchanged and some become worse.

READING, LECTURES, DISCUSSION, CASE-STUDIES AND FILMS

It may be possible to teach social skills by more traditional methods. It is important to explore these since they are much cheaper and more widely available than those described so far, which need specially qualified trainers or expensive equipment.

Early attempts to teach supervisory skills by lectures and discussion were not a success; social skills cannot be learned without having a go, just as you can't learn to swim by reading books about it. However, most skills require some new knowledge, and this is where educational methods come in.

Reading This is one of the most widely used methods of education. Many self-improvement books have been produced, particularly in the U.S.A., such as that by Carnegie (1936), which has been widely read. More recently there have been a number of books on do-it-yourself assertiveness training, e.g. Bower and Bower (1976), though no follow-up studies have been carried out. 'Bibliotherapy' produces short-term benefits at least in a number of areas, including weight reduction, study behaviour, fear reduction and exercise, though often some minimal therapist contact is needed (Glasgow and Rosen, 1978). One area of social skills where reading is regularly used is inter-cultural communication, which we have seen is quite successful (p. 190). However, in this field it is normal to combine learning by reading with more active forms of training, and self-help manuals usually include guidance on exercises to be carried out. It may be necessary in such cases to have someone who can take the role of trainer and give some feedback on performance.

Lectures can be given in which various aspects of skill are explained. They may focus on the basic principles of social behaviour or the details of recommended social techniques, and can be followed by discussion among the trainees. Experience with management training shows that lectures on 'human relations' are often very popular and are a good means of conveying knowledge, though not a good way of changing attitudes. Can social skills be taught by means of lectures? Follow-up studies show that lectures on human relations lead to improved scores on questionnaires, but it has not been shown whether any behavioural changes in skill are produced. There are certain difficulties with lectures. They are no good unless the audience is really interested in what the lecturer has to say, or unless he can make them interested by the forcefulness of his presentation, and unless he has a manner and status which make him personally acceptable.*

Case studies These can provide a good basis for discussion, and often do so in management training. They consist of problem situations to which the group has to find the best solution, and may be presented as film-strips or in written form. Case studies are used for general education in management problems, but can also be focused entirely on the human relations aspects. The main weakness is that trainees do not acquire any general principles of social behaviour. It

_____
* See Argyle, Smith and Kirton (1962) for a review of these studies.

might be possible to design case studies in such a way that they would illustrate and draw attention to basic principles; perhaps if a large enough number of cases were used trainees could be helped to make inductive generalizations from them.

This method has been used for teaching social skills to school children. A case is presented by the teacher, or from a text book, which illustrates problems such as dealing with authority, emotional problems at home or moral dilemmas. The case is then discussed by the class under the guidance of the teacher (McPhail *et al.*, 1972).

Films These are sometimes used for modelling in connection with role-playing. A number of suitable films are now available, mainly for management skills. Social skills trainers often make up their own video-tapes of modelling behaviour for trainees. However, no follow-up studies are yet available on the use of films for this purpose. Films have been used for training in *manual* skills for some time, and these are found to be successful under certain conditions – if the learner has to try out part of the skill after each piece of film; if there is discussion before or after the film; if the film is shot from his point of view, e.g. over his shoulder; and if appropriate use is made of slow motion, animation and sequences of stills, showing the successive steps in the skill. Again it looks as if films can play an important part in an overall training scheme, but are not much good alone and so far there are very few suitable ones available.

METHODS RECOMMENDED FOR DIFFERENT PURPOSES

Professional social skills These were traditionally learnt on the job, but role-playing is now widely used for teachers, interviewers, managers and others. Along the lines described above, it is the most effective form of training available. It can be supplemented by lectures and discussion, instructional films when available, and by reading when new knowledge is required, e.g. with inter-cultural communication.

A trainer is needed who is reasonably experienced and competent at the skill in question himself, and who is familiar with the use of these training methods.

Further problems arise with those people who suffer from particularly serious interpersonal difficulties at work. They need more specialized forms of treatment, as described in the next section.

Treatment of individuals with interpersonal difficulties This includes people who are quarrelsome and difficult at work, those who are anxious in social situations and those who are lonely and isolated, as well as a proportion of mental patients. Some of these come to psychiatrists and some are given SST; more get help from friends, family, doctors and clergy. They are difficult to help, however, without a little knowledge of interpersonal processes. The best treatment is role-playing supplemented by the special techniques which were described above. Such treatment is increasingly widely available for mental patients and prisoners, but not so easy to find for the general public. I would like to see it established in such non-medical settings as community centres or adult education centres.

In schools SST is being tried out in a number of schools, as part of English, Social Studies, Moral Education or Biology. Some textbooks and classroom materials are now available (e.g. McPhail, 1972), and many schools have videotape recorders at the disposal. It would be quite feasible to teach a new school subject – Social Behaviour – which could be of great practical use.

SOME PROBLEMS OF SOCIAL SKILLS TRAINING

Prerequisites for successful training To carry out role-playing or most other forms of training it is necessary to have a working vocabulary of the main elements in the repertoire for the skill being taught. This is needed to communicate with trainees, to label their behaviour, and for them to monitor their own performance. This book has attempted to provide such a vocabulary.

A second prerequisite is knowledge of the skills which are most successful. Without such knowledge the trainer has to fall back on common sense, which is very fallible in this field. A serious problem is that the most effective social skill may vary with situational factors, such as characteristics of the others being handled; this has been studied most in the case of supervisory skills. The best skills may also vary among classes, races or other subcultures. This is a particular problem with the training of mental patients, since the skills which they should be taught may differ considerably with their social class, etc. Very often this kind of knowledge is not available.

Transfer to real life Training on the job is the only form of training which does not have to face the problem of transferring the skills which have been learnt in training centre, lab or clinic to the real world. T-groups are very different from the outside world and it has been said that all they train for is other T-groups. Role-playing usually tries to deal with this problem by means of homework (pp. 278f); however, trainees are often reluctant to try the new skills out or may refuse to do so. Some role-playing uses quite realistic simulations of the real situations; examples are the model villages constructed in the Caribbean and Hawaii for preparing members of the Peace Corps for Latin America and the Far East (Guthrie, 1966). There are other ways of preparing trainees for varied and unexpected incidents in real life. More abstract principles of behaviour may be taught, as opposed to specific skills. An example is 'be rewarding', where this can take a variety of forms. It is also possible to acquire the habit of learning new social skills whenever these are needed, by imitation of successful performers and studying the behaviour which is effective and ineffective.

The search for more economical methods If most professional people, many mental patients and 7–10 per cent of the normal population need, or could profit by, SST, who is going to administer it? The use of group methods is common, because it saves trainer time and provides role partners. What of do-it-yourself procedures? We have seen that 'bibliotherapy' can be useful, if combined with more active means.

Some microteaching has been carried out without trainers: trainees simply record and play back videotapes of their own role-playing and compare them with films of model teachers.

However, microteaching is more successful when there is a trainer (Peck and Tucker, 1973).

Another method is simply to arrange for clients to have practice encounters with one another without a trainer. Arkowitz has found that this is successful in improving subjective feelings of confidence and reducing anxiety after six practice dates (Arkowitz, 1977).

The need for other aspects of personal growth For several skills it is not enough simply to learn the correct social moves, as it may be impossible to use these skills unless certain emotional problems have been dealt with. Some skill situations commonly arouse anxiety – for example, public speaking, dealing with hostile people or opposing others. Learning effective skills is certainly part of the answer and practising successfully helps but may not be sufficient. Performers may simply lack the self-confidence to take the responsibilities required, for example, by doctors and social workers. This entails a change in self-image, which is usually produced by simply doing the job. Training courses often include an element of guided group discussion, which can help trainees to talk about these matters and receive some social support. Newcomers to a social role often need a set of ideas or principles which will help them to deal with the moral, political or wider (even philosophical) issues at stake: for example, doctors may be concerned about how long to keep patients alive, social workers about conflicts between the demands of law and the interests of clients. Again, this goes beyond social skills and can be tackled by guided group discussion, together with reflecting on the experience of performing the skill.

FURTHER READING

Argyle, M. (ed.), *Social Skills and Work*, Methuen, 1981.
Bellack, A. S., and Hersen, M. (eds.), *Research and Practice in Social Skills Training*, Plenum, New York and London, 1979.
Trower, P., Bryant, B., and Argyle, M., *Social Skills and Mental Health*, Methuen, 1978.

CHAPTER 13

EPILOGUE

I have tried to outline what has been found out, mainly by experimental research, in an important area of human behaviour. Several hundred investigations have been described, and there are several thousand others which have been kept in the background.* The main variables have been introduced, and the main processes behind interpersonal behaviour have been described.

Interpersonal behaviour is a centrally important part of human life. Relationships with others are one of the main sources of happiness, but when they go wrong they produce very great distress and are one of the roots of mental disorder. Can our new knowledge of social behaviour help?

APPLICATIONS OF THE NEW KNOWLEDGE

There are several fields where this new knowledge has already been applied, and where it could be applied more extensively.

1 *Social skills training* It is no longer necessary for a sizeable proportion of the human race to be lonely, isolated, miserable or mentally ill through lack of social skills. Many thousands have already been trained by one technique or another, and training could easily become available to all. The most useful step would be to include social skills ('human relations') training in the school curriculum, and to make SST available to adults in community centres or elsewhere. Through this sort of training, it would be possible to raise the whole *quality* of normal social behaviour so that it is more efficient and more enjoyable, and results in help, cooperation and trust rather than rejection, misunderstanding and social barriers. This would also raise the number of really outstanding performers in the field of social behaviour, which would be of benefit to all.

* Some of these are reviewed in Argyle (1969, 1975) and Argyle, Furnham and Graham (1982).

2 *Re-design of groups and organizations* A lot is now understood about social interaction in various kinds of groups and organizations. It is known that with certain designs there is alienation, frustration, and failure of communication, while other designs work much better. It is recognized, for example, that there should be small, cooperative teams under democratic and employee-centred supervisors, and that there should be few levels in the hierarchy, with delegation and representation of junior members. These are not optional extras which slightly increase job satisfaction, but may be essential if an organization is to survive (Argyle, 1972).

3 *Resolving conflicts between groups* A number of the most important social problems are due to conflict between people of different race, class, age and even sex. Some are due to real differences in wealth or opportunities, but others, numbering among the worst, are between groups of very similar affluence. These conflicts are partly due to the difficulties of interacting with people from another culture, who follow different rules and conventions, use different non-verbal signals and have different ideas. We have seen that a quite short period of training can make people better at dealing with intercultural encounters (pp. 190f). Such training could be a normal part of the school curriculum.

Conflicts between management and unions (and other groups) can be resolved faster and more effectively if better negotiating skills are used (pp. 267f).

A NEW MODEL OF MAN

Our research in this area shows that previous psychological models of man were mistaken or incomplete through not taking account of the interpersonal nature of man. This aspect has, as a result, remained somewhat mysterious, a fitting domain for theologians, moralists and novelists (not to mention the authors of pop songs and *Mad* magazine). These writers have indeed recognized that relations with others are the most important part of human life, and that most of the essential human characteristics cannot be manifested by a person in isolation. They have rightly been unconvinced of the relevance to human affairs of experiments with people (or rats) studied while they perform laboratory tasks in isolation (Argyle, 1969, pp. 430–31).

Unfortunately, much work in social psychology has been little better – artificial experiments often on one person, sometimes preventing verbal or non-verbal communication, and often in a laboratory vacuum resembling no situation in the outside world (Israel and Tajfel, 1972). The formulations of social psychologists have often been highly inadequate – the importance of non-verbal communication and the roles of gaze are recent discoveries, and only very lately have social psychologists become aware of the effects of situations and their rules, the way social acts fit together in sequence, and the effect of ideas and language on behaviour.

The model of man we have arrived at is something like this: For the survival of individuals and their genes, for the satisfaction of biological needs and for the continuation of the species, cooperation in groups is necessary; there are innate tendencies to respond to others, which require experiences in the family to become fully realized; there is a system of non-verbal signals for communicating interpersonal intentions and attitudes; there is a means of communication unique to the species – language; social behaviour is produced as a stream of closely integrated responses, subject to continuous correction as a result of feedback, controlled by more or less conscious plans, and subject to partly verbalized rules derived from the culture; and social interaction takes place in a limited range of situations, each with its characteristic structure of rules, roles and purposes.

There is probably one more essential component – an innate concern for members of the immediate family and group, resulting in care for others and restraint of aggression. We have seen that sympathy appears in young children, and that taking account of the point of view of others is an essential ingredient in interaction. Concern with the views of another takes a second important form: the self-image is largely constructed out of the reactions of others, and this leads to self-presentation behaviour designed to elicit appropriate responses in later social situations.

This basic equipment, partly innate, partly acquired from the culture, leads to the formation of interpersonal bonds, small social groups and social structures. Different relationships are formed with spouses, children, friends, work-mates and others, in ways partly defined by the culture. Interaction patterns in small groups (families, circles of colleagues and friends) tend to be complex, involving norms of behaviour and differentiation of roles. In larger groups, the roles become formalized and the pattern of interaction follows a regular pattern, which is learnt by new members; this is called a social structure.

The views of social psychologists about the nature of man have also changed in a fundamental way. We no longer think that man's behaviour is controlled by causal laws, in a deterministic way, or that it is totally predictable. Experiments do, of course, discover regularities, in which one variable is found to affect another. However, when people are told about one of these regularities they are perfectly able to resist it, and thought processes can override reflex responses or similar processes. Linguists make no attempt to predict what anyone will say, and regard this as impossible since most utterances have never been produced before. Similarly, some social psychologists are trying to find the generative rules of social behaviour, which will give understanding but not necessarily prediction (Clarke, 1983).

Some recent developments in therapy have been directed towards increasing the individual's power of self-control, i.e. freeing him from lower-level causal processes (Meichenbaum, 1977). It is hoped that the knowledge of, and the language for describing, social behaviour contained in this book, in conjunction with the training techniques described, will increase understanding in the field. This in its turn can contribute to the process of self-growth, consisting of a build-up of skills, of control over emotions and of the elaboration of cognitive constructs.

POSSIBLE DANGERS OF THE NEW KNOWLEDGE

It has been suggested that the new knowledge of interpersonal behaviour might have some undesirable consequences, as well as desirable ones.

1 It is possible that when people become trained to interact better their behaviour may become more contrived and insincere,

become more like acting. This is a complex and controversial issue: while authenticity and sincerity are attractive, it may also be argued that civilization depends on the restraint of many interpersonal feelings – aggressive, sexual and disapproving in particular. The most effective and desirable kind of behaviour does not necessarily consist of the direct outward expression of inner feelings.

2 It is objected that people will become self-conscious, awkward and unspontaneous in their social behaviour. As we have seen, much social behaviour has the characteristics of a motor skill. When a person learns a new skill, such as handling the gears of a strange car, he goes through a period when the behaviour is awkward, requires full conscious attention and is accompanied by actual or silent speech. This phase rapidly comes to an end as the skill is learnt and becomes habitual.

3 It has been suggested that the discovery of better ways of performing in social situations creates a danger that people may be 'manipulated' by practitioners of the new skills. All scientific discoveries can be used for good or ill, and findings in the field of social interaction are no exception. It need not be assumed that the skilled performer will spend his time outwitting other people and controlling situations to his own advantage. On many occasions it is in the interests of all that people should be socially competent – for example, that a school teacher should be good at teaching. It is in situations of conflict that the more socially skilled person is at an advantage – though the same is true of whoever is most verbally or technically skilled.

RULES AND MORALS

In a previous book it was suggested that the social scientist may,

from time to time, step outside his role of hard-boiled investigator and play the part of the social reformer or critic. His qualification to do so is the insight he gains into new human goals, and new ways of reaching old ones . . . The social scientist is often the critic and guardian of our highest ideals. He may have a further role to play in sensitizing public opinion to new ideals and standards as yet unthought of [Argyle, 1964, p. 203].

What implication does the new knowledge have for how we should conduct our everyday life? The level of social competence could be raised if there were clear social or moral rules indicating which kinds of conduct are to be recommended. There are of course plenty of such rules already, but as was pointed out earlier, most moral prescriptions are so vague that it is hard to know precisely what to do in a particular situation. How exactly does one love one's neighbour, or treat people as ends in themselves? What precisely does one do about a naughty child, an incompetent employee or an uncooperative colleague? The research which has been discussed does suggest the social techniques and relationships which are most effective in some of these situations, and they do not in general consist merely of being nice to people or behaving in a yielding, unaggressive sort of way. The kinds of behaviour which may be regarded as morally most desirable have to be found out by means of detailed research for each situation. Some of these can be recommended because they enhance the welfare of others, or because they bring about a mutually satisfying relation, or simply because they lead to the efficient execution of cooperative tasks. Several examples have been reported earlier and will be mentioned briefly once more.

1 People are often in trouble and distress, and in need of help. It has been found that much can be done by those who are untrained and unskilled in psychotherapy, provided they can establish a helping relationship. This involves an acceptance of the other, a sympathetic appreciation of his problems, and the provision of a warm and supporting relationship (pp. 252f).

2 Those who are in charge of others can bring about the greatest satisfaction and productive effort by establishing a particular kind of relationship. This relationship is not obvious to common sense, and goes beyond traditional moral ideas in some ways. Subordinates should be consulted, and their ideas about the work used as far as possible. They should be helped to set their own goals and evaluate their own progress; when disciplinary action has to be taken it should be more a matter of discussing such goals and evaluations in a sympathetic, therapeutic, but firm manner. A leader should exercise influence and control, as he thinks right, in a persuasive way (pp. 262f).

3 Parents, teachers, and anyone else in charge of children will be faced by special problems. To exercise effectively the guidance and

help the children need requires a combination of warmth and firmness; without warmth the relationship collapses, without control there is no influence. Adults must maintain a certain distance or aloofness, in that they do not share the children's values or points of view and can only share their activities to a limited extent.

4 How can we love our enemies? The study of rules of relationships reported earlier (p. 162) suggests fairly specific ways of treating people at work whom we don't like.

5 Should we be sincere in our dealings with other people? Research on deception has suggested that there are situations in which most people conceal their true feelings and that this may have beneficial results; for example, where aggressive and sexual impulses are involved.

REFERENCES

Abercrombie, K. (1968), 'Paralanguage', *British Journal of Diseases of Communication*, vol. 3, pp. 55–9.

Adams, B. N. (1967), 'Interaction theory and the social network', *Sociometry*, vol. 30, pp. 64–78.

Adams, B. N. (1968), *Kinship in an Urban Setting*, Markham, Chicago.

Alexander, R. D. (1979), 'Beyond the dyad: approaches to explaining exchange in developing relationships', in Burgess, R. L., and Huston, T. L. (eds), *Social Exchange in Developing Relationships*, Academic Press, New York.

Allan, G. A. (1979), *A Sociology of Friendship and Kinship*, Allen and Unwin.

Altman, I. (1975), *The Environment and Social Behavior: Privacy, Personal Space, Territory and Crowding*, Brooks/Cole, Monterey, California.

Amir, Y. (1969), 'Contact hypothesis in ethnic relations', *Psychological Bulletin*, vol. 71, pp. 319–42.

Anderson, E. R. (1973), *The Role of the Nurse*, Royal College of Nursing.

Argyle, M. (1964), *Psychology and Social Problems*, Methuen.

Argyle, M. (1969), *Social Interaction*, Methuen.

Argyle, M. (1972), *The Social Psychology of Work*, Penguin Books.

Argyle, M. (1975), *Bodily Communication*, Methuen.

Argyle, M. (1976), 'Personality and social behaviour', in Harré, R. (ed.), *Personality*, Blackwell.

Argyle, M., and Beit-Hallahmi, B. (1975), *The Social Psychology of Religion*, Routledge & Kegan Paul.

Argyle, M., and Dean, J. (1965), 'Eye-contact, distance and affiliation', *Sociometry*, vol. 28, pp. 289–304.

Argyle, M., and Furnham, A. (in press), 'Sources of satisfaction and conflict in long-term relationships', *Journal of Marriage and the Family*.

Argyle, M., and Furnham, A. (1982), 'The ecology of relationships: choice of situation as a function of relationship', *British Journal of Social Psychology*, vol. 21, pp. 259–62.

Argyle, M., Furnham, A., and Graham, J. A. (1982), *Social Situations*, Cambridge University Press.

Argyle, M., Gardner, G., and Cioffi, F. (1958), 'Supervisory methods related to productivity, absenteeism and labour turnover', *Human Relations*, vol. 11, pp. 23–45.

Argyle, M., Ginsburg, G. P., Forgas, J. P., and Campbell, A. (1981), 'Personality constructs in relation to situations', in Argyle, M., Furnham, A., and Graham, J. A., *Social Situations*, Cambridge University Press.

Argyle, M., and Graham, J. A. (1977), 'The Central Europe experiment – looking at persons and looking at things', *Journal of Environmental Psychology and Nonverbal Behavior*, vol. 1, pp. 6–16.

Argyle, M., Graham, J. A., Campbell, A., and White, P. (1979), 'The rules of different situations', *New Zealand Psychologist*, vol. 8, pp. 13–22.

Argyle, M., Graham, J. A., and Kreckel, M. (1982), 'The structure of behavioral elements in social and work situations', in Key, M. R. (ed.), *Nonverbal Communication Today: Current Research*, Mouton, The Hague.

Argyle, M., and Ingham, R. (1972), 'Gaze, mutual gaze and distance', *Semiotica*, vol. 6, pp. 32–49.

Argyle, M., Ingham, R., Alkema, F., and McCallin, M. (1973), 'The different functions of gaze', *Semiotica*, vol. 7, pp. 19–32.

Argyle, M., Lalljee, M., and Cook, M. (1968), 'The effects of visibility on interaction in a dyad', *Human Relations*, vol. 21, pp. 3–17.

Argyle, M., Lefebvre, L., and Cook, M. (1974), 'The meaning of five patterns of gaze', *European Journal of Social Psychology*, vol. 4, pp. 125–36.

Argyle, M., and McHenry, R. (1970), 'Do spectacles really increase judgments of intelligence?', *British Journal of Social and Clinical Psychology*, vol. 10, pp. 27–9.

Argyle, M., Salter, V., Nicholson, H., Williams, M., and Burgess, P. (1970), 'The communication of inferior and superior attitudes by verbal and non-verbal signals', *British Journal of Social and Clinical Psychology*, vol. 9, pp. 221–31.

Argyle, M., Shimoda, K., and Little, B. (1978), 'Variance due to persons and situations in England and Japan', *British Journal of Social and Clinical Psychology*, vol. 15, pp. 335–7.

Argyle, M., Smith, T., and Kirton, M. (1962), *Training Managers*, Acton Society Trust.

Argyle, M., and Williams, M. (1969), 'Observer or observed? A reversible perspective in person perception', *Sociometry*, vol. 32, pp. 396–412.

Arkowitz, H. (1977), 'Measurement and modification of minimal dating behavior', in Hersen, M. (ed.), *Progress in Behavior Modification*, Academic Press, New York, vol. 5.

Atkinson, J. M. (1970), *Social Isolation and Communication in Old Age*, unpublished report to the G.P.O., Essex University.

Bailey, K. G., and Sowder, W. T. (1970), 'Audiotape and videotape self-confrontation in psychotherapy', *Psychological Bulletin*, vol. 74, pp. 127–37.

Bakan, P. (1971), 'The eyes have it', *Psychology Today*, vol. 4, pp. 64–7.

Bales, R. F. (1950), *Interaction Process Analysis*, Addison-Wesley, Reading, Massachusetts.

Bales, R. F. (1953), 'The equilibrium problem in small groups', in Parsons, T., Bales, R. F., and Shils, E. A. (eds), *Working papers in the Theory of Action*, Free Press, Glencoe, Illinois.

Bannister, D., and Salmon, P. (1966), 'Schizophrenic thought disorder: specific or diffuse?', *British Journal of Medical Psychology*, vol. 39, pp. 215–19.

Baron, R. A., and Byrne, D. (1981), *Social Psychology: Understanding Human Interaction*, Allyn and Bacon, Boston.

Beattie, G. W. (1980), 'The skilled art of conversational interaction', in Singleton, W. T., *et al.* (eds), *The Analysis of Social Skill*, Plenum Press, New York.

Beattie, G. W. (1981), 'A further investigation of the cognitive interference hypothesis of gaze patterns in interaction', *British Journal of Social Psychology*, vol. 20, pp. 243–8.

Bell, C. R. (1968), *Middle-Class Families*, Routledge & Kegan Paul.

Bem, D., and Allan, A. (1974), 'On predicting some of the people some of the time: the search for cross-situational consistency in behavior', *Psychological Review*, vol. 81, pp. 506–20.

Bennis, W. G., *et al.* (1964), *Interpersonal Dynamics*, Dorsey Press, Homewood, Illinois.

Berger, A. (1965), 'A test of the double-bind hypothesis of schizophrenia', *Family Process*, vol. 4, pp. 198–205.

Berne, E. (1966), *Games People Play*, Deutsch.

Bernstein, B. (1959), 'A public language: some sociological implications of a linguistic form', *British Journal of Sociology*, vol. 10, pp. 311–26.

Berscheid, E., *et al.* (1971), 'Physical attractiveness and dating choice: a test of the matching hypothesis', *Journal of Experimental Social Psychology*, vol. 7, pp. 173–89.

Berscheid, E., and Walster, E. (1974a), 'Physical attractiveness', *Advances in Experimental Social Psychology*, vol. 7, pp. 158–215.

Berscheid, E., and Walster, E. (1974b), 'Romantic love', in Huston, T. L. (ed.), *Foundations of Interpersonal Attraction*, Academic Press, New York.

Bills, R. E., Vance, E. L., and McLean, O. S. (1951), 'An index of adjustment and values', *Journal of Consulting Psychology*, vol. 15, pp. 257–61.

Blanck, P. D., *et al.* (1981), 'Sex differences in eavesdropping on nonverbal cues: developmental changes', *Journal of Personality and Social Psychology*, vol. 41, pp. 391–6.

Bochner, S., McLeod, B. M., and Lin, A. (1977), 'Friendship patterns of overseas students: a functional model', *International Journal of Psychology*, vol. 12, pp. 277–94.

Borgatta, E. F., and Bales, R. F. (1953), 'Interaction of individuals in reconstituted groups', *Sociometry*, vol. 16, pp. 302-20.

Bourne, E. (1978), 'The state of research on ego identity – a review', *Journal of Youth and Adolescence*, vol. 7, pp. 223-51 and 371-91.

Bower, S. A., and Bower, G. H. (1976), *Asserting Yourself*, Addison-Wesley, Reading, Massachusetts.

Bowers, K. S. (1973), 'Situationism in psychology: an analysis and a critique', *Psychological Review*, vol. 30, pp. 307-36.

Brackman, J. (1967), 'The put-on', *New Yorker*, 24 June, pp. 34-73.

Braginsky, B. M., Braginsky, D. D., and Ring, K. (1969), *Methods of Madness, The Mental Hospital as a Last Resort*, Holt, Rinehart and Winston, New York.

Breer, P. E. (1960), 'Predicting interpersonal behavior from personality and role' (unpublished), Harvard University Ph.D.

Brenner, M. (1981), 'Skills in the research interview', in Argyle, M. (ed.), *Social Skills and Work*, Methuen.

Brislin, R. W., and Pedersen, P. (1976), *Cross-Cultural Orientation Programs*, Gardner Press, New York.

Brown, G. A. (1975), 'Microteaching: research and developments', in Chanan, G., and Delamont, S. (eds), *Frontiers of Classroom Research*, N.F.E.R.

Brown, G. W., and Harris, T. (1978), *Social Origins of Depression*, Tavistock.

Brown, G. W., Harris, T. O., and Peto, J. (1973), 'Life events and psychiatric disorders, Part 2: nature of causal link', *Psychological Medicine*, vol. 3, pp. 159-76.

Brown, R., and Lenneberg, E. H. (1954), 'A study of language and cognition', *Journal of Abnormal and Social Psychology*, vol. 49, pp. 454-62.

Brown, R. (1965), *Social Psychology*, Collier-Macmillan, New York.

Brun, T. (1969), *The International Dictionary of Sign Language*, Wolfe Publications.

Bruner, J. (1975), 'The ontogenesis of speech acts', *Journal of Child Language*, vol. 2, pp. 1-19.

Bryan, J. H., and Walbek, N. H. (1970), 'Preaching and practising generosity: children's actions and reactions', *Child Development*, vol. 41, pp. 329-53.

Bryant, B., *et al.* (1976), 'A survey of social inadequacy among psychiatric outpatients', *Psychological Medicine*, vol. 6, pp. 101-12.

Buck, R. (1979), 'Individual differences in nonverbal sending accuracy and electrodermal responding: the externalizing–internalizing dimension', in Rosenthal, R. (ed.), *Skill in Nonverbal Communication: Individual Differences*, Oelgeschlager, Gunn & Hain, Cambridge, Massachusetts.

Bugenthal, D., Kaswan, J. W., and Love, L. R. (1970), 'Perception of contradictory meanings conveyed by verbal and non-verbal channels', *Journal of Personality and Social Psychology*, vol. 16, pp. 647–55.

Burger, J. M. (1981), 'Motivational biases in the attribution of responsibility for an accident: a meta-analysis of the defensive attribution hypothesis', *Psychological Bulletin*, vol. 90, pp. 496–512.

Burgess, R. L. (1981), 'Relationships in marriage and the family', in Duck, S., and Gilmour, R. (eds.), *Personal Relationships I. Studying Personal Relationships*, Academic Press.

Byrne, P. S., and Long, B. E. (1976), *Doctors Talking to Patients*, H.M.S.O.

Campbell, D. T. (1975), 'On the conflicts between biological and social evolution and between psychology and moral tradition', *American Psychologist*, vol. 30, pp. 1103–26.

Canter, D. (in press), *The Social Psychology of Building*, Pergamon.

Cantor, N., and Mischel, W. (1979), 'Prototypes in person perception', *Advances in Experimental Social Psychology*, vol. 12, pp. 3–52.

Carnegie, D. (1936), *How to Win Friends and Influence People*, Simon and Schuster, New York.

Carpenter, W. A., and Hollander, E. P. (in press), 'Overcoming hurdles to independence in groups', *Journal of Social Psychology*.

Cartwright, A. (1964), *Human Relations and Hospital Care*, Routledge & Kegan Paul.

Carver, C. S. (1979), 'A cybernetic model of self-attribution processes', *Journal of Personality and Social Psychology*, vol. 37, pp. 1251–81.

Chaikin, A. L., and Derlega, V. J. (1976), 'Self disclosure', in Thibaut, J. W., Spence, J. T., and Carson, R. C. (eds), *Contemporary Topics in Social Psychology*, General Learning Press, Morristown, New Jersey.

Chandler, M. J. (1973), 'Egocentrism and anti-social behavior: the assessment and training of social perspective-training skills', *Developmental Psychology*, vol. 9, pp. 326–32.

Chapple, E. D. (1956), *The Interaction Chronograph Manual*, E. D. Chapple Inc., Moroton, Connecticut.

Chapple, E. D., and Donald, G. (1947), 'An evaluation of department store salespeople by the interaction chronograph', *Journal of Marketing*, vol. 13, pp. 173–85.

Cialdini, R. B., Caciapopo, J. T., Bassett, R., and Miller, J. A. (1978), 'Low-ball procedure for producing compliance commitment then cost', *Journal of Personality and Social Psychology*, vol. 36, pp. 463–76.

Clancy, H., and McBride, G. (1969), 'The autistic process and its treatment', *Journal of Child Psychology and Psychiatry*, vol. 10, pp. 233–44.

Clark, M. S. (1981), 'Noncomparability of benefits given and received: a cue to the existence of friendship', *Social Psychology Quarterly*, vol. 44, pp. 375–81.

Clarke, D. D. (1975), 'The use and recognition of sequential structure in dialogue', *British Journal of Social and Clinical Psychology*, vol. 14, pp. 333–9.

Clarke, D. D. (1983), *Future-Grammar: A Generative Account of Interaction Sequences*, Pergamon.

Clarke, R. V. G., and Mayhew, P. (eds) (1980), *Designing Out Crime*, H.M.S.O.

Cline, V. B., and Richards, J. M. (1960), 'Accuracy of interpersonal perception – a general trait?', *Journal of Abnormal and Social Psychology*, vol. 60, pp. 1–7.

Cochrane, R. (1980), 'Life stresses and psychological consequences', in Feldman, P., and Orford, J. (eds), *Psychological Problems: The Social Context*, Wiley.

Cohen, S., and McKay, G. (1981), 'Social support, stress and the buffering hypothesis: a review of naturalistic studies' (unpublished), University of Oregon MS.

Collett, P. (1971), 'On training Englishmen in the non-verbal behaviour of Arabs: an experiment in intercultural communication', *International Journal of Psychology*, vol. 6, pp. 209–15.

Collett, P. (ed.) (1977), *Social Rules and Social Behaviour*, Blackwell.

Condon, W. S., and Ogston, W. D. (1966), 'Sound film analysis of normal and pathological behavior patterns', *Journal of Nervous and Mental Diseases*, vol. 143, pp. 338–47.

Cooper, J. E., *et al.* (1972), *Psychiatric Diagnosis in New York and London*, Oxford University Press.

Cotton, J. L. (1981), 'A review of research on Schachter's theory of emotion and the misattribution of arousal', *European Journal of Social Psychology*, vol. 11, pp. 365–97.

Cottrell, N. B., *et al.* (1968), 'Social facilitation of dominant responses by the presence of an audience and the mere presence of others', *Journal of Personality and Social Psychology*, vol. 9, pp. 245–50.

Crawford, D. G., and Signori, E. I. (1962), 'An application of the critical incident technique to university teaching', *Canadian Psychologist*, vol. 3a, no. 4.

Crook, J. H. (1970), 'The socio-ecology of primates', in Crook, J. H. (ed.), *Social Behaviour in Birds and Mammals*, Academic Press.

Curran, J. P. (1977), 'Skills training as an approach to the treatment of heterosexual–social anxiety', *Psychological Bulletin*, vol. 84, pp. 140–57.

Davis, B. (1981), 'Social skills in nursing', in Argyle, M. (ed.), *Social Skills and Health*, Methuen.

Davitz, J. R. (1964), *The Communication of Emotional Meaning*, McGraw-Hill, New York.

Dawkins, R. (1976a), *The Selfish Gene*, Oxford University Press.

Dawkins, R. (1976b), 'Hierarchical organization: a candidate principle for zoology', in Bateson, P. P. G., and Hinde, R. A. (eds.), *Growing Points in Ethology*, Cambridge University Press.

Dawson, J., Whitney, R. E., and Lan, R. T. S. (1971), 'Scaling Chinese traditional–modern attitudes and the GSR measurement of "Important" versus "Unimportant" Chinese concepts', *Journal of Cross-Cultural Psychology*, vol. 2, pp. 1–27.

Dickens, W. J., and Perlman, D. (1981), 'Friendship over the life cycle', in Duck, S., and Gilmour, R. (eds), *Personal Relationships 2, Developing Individual Relationships*, Academic Press.

Dickman, H. R. (1963), 'The perception of behavioral units', in Barker, R. G. (ed.), *The Stream of Behavior*, Appleton-Century-Crofts, New York.

Dion, K., Berscheid, E., and Walster, E. (1972), 'What is beautiful is good', *Journal of Personality and Social Psychology*, vol. 24, pp. 285–90.

Dion, K. K., and Dion, K. L. (1975), 'Self-esteem and romantic love', in *Journal of Personality*, vol. 43, pp. 39–57.

Dominian, J. (1980), *Marital Pathology*, Darton Longman and Todd, and B.M.A.

Duck, S. W. (1973), *Personal Relationships and Personal Constructs*, Wiley.

Duncan, S., and Fiske, D. W. (1977), *Face-to-Face Interaction*, Erlbaum, Hillsdale, New York.

Dutton, D. G., and Aron, A. P. (1974), 'Some evidence for heightened sexual attraction under conditions of high anxiety', *Journal of Personality and Social Psychology*, vol. 30, pp. 510–17.

Duval, S., and Wicklund, R. A. (1972), *A Theory of Objective Self Awareness*, Academic Press, New York.

Edelmann, R. J., and Hampson, S. E. (1979), 'Changes in non-verbal behaviour during embarrassment', *British Journal of Social and Clinical Psychology*, vol. 18, pp. 385–90.

Eibl-Eibesfeldt, I. (1972), 'Similarities and differences between cultures in expressive movements', in Hinde, R. A. (ed.), *Nonverbal Communication*, Royal Society and Cambridge University Press.

Ekman, P. (1972), 'Universals and cultural differences in facial expressions of emotion', *Nebraska Symposium on Motivation*, University of Nebraska Press, Lincoln, Nebraska.

Ekman, P., and Friesen, W. V. (1975), *Unmasking the Face*, Prentice-Hall, Englewood Cliffs, New Jersey.

Ekman, P., Friesen, W. V., and Ancoli, S. (1980), 'Facial signs of emotional experience', *Journal of Personality and Social Psychology*, vol. 39, pp. 1125–34.

Ekman, P., Friesen, W. V., and Ellsworth, P. (1972), *Emotions in the Human Face*, Pergamon, Elmsford, New York.

Ellsworth, P. (1975), 'Direct gaze as a social stimulus: the example of aggression', in Pliner, P., Kramer, L., and Alloway, T. (eds), *Nonverbal Communication and Aggression*, Plenum, New York.

Ellyson, S. L., Dovidio, J. F., and Fehr, B. J. (1981), 'Visual behavior and dominance in women and men', in Mayo, C., and Henley, N. M. (eds), *Gender and Nonverbal Behavior*, Springer-Verlag, New York.

Endler, N. S. (1965), 'The effects of verbal reinforcement on conformity and deviant behavior', *Journal of Social Psychology*, vol. 66, pp. 147–54.

Endler, N. S., and Magnusson, D. (eds) (1976), *Interactional Psychology and Personality*, Hemisphere, Washington.

Endler, N. S., and Okada, M. (1975), 'A multidimensional measure of trait anxiety: the S-R inventory of general trait anxiousness', *Journal of Consulting and Clinical Psychology*, vol. 43, pp. 319–29.

Erikson, E. H. (1956), 'The problem of ego identity', *American Journal of Psychoanalysis*, vol. 4, pp. 56–121.

Etzioni, A. (1961), *A Comparative Analysis of Complex Organizations*, Free Press, Glencoe, Illinois.

Exline, R. V. (1963), 'Explorations in the process of person perception: visual interaction in relation to competition, sex and need for affiliation', *Journal of Personality*, vol. 31, pp. 1–20.

Exline, R. V. (1971), 'Visual interaction: the glances of power and preference', *Nebraska Symposium on Motivation*, University of Nebraska Press, Lincoln, Nebraska.

Exline, R. V., and Fehr, B J. (1970), 'Applications of semiosis to the study of visual interaction', in Siegman, A. W., and Feldstein, S. (eds), *Nonverbal Behavior and Communication*, Erlbaum, Hillsdale, New Jersey.

Exline, R. V., and Winters, L. C. (1965), 'Affective relations and mutual glances in dyads', in Tomkins, S., and Izard, C. (eds), *Affect, Cognition and Personality*, Springer, New York.

Exline, R. V., and Yellin, A. (1969), 'Eye contact as a sign between man and monkey', paper to International Congress of Psychology, London, cited in Exline (1971).

Exline, R. V., *et al.* (1970), 'Visual interaction in relation to Machievellianism and an unethical act', in Christie, R., and Geis, F. L. (eds), *Studies in Machiavellianism*, Academic Press, New York.

Eysenck, H. J. (1957), *The Dynamics of Anxiety and Hysteria*, Routledge & Kegan Paul.

Eysenck, H. J., and Eysenck, S. B. G. (1969), *Personality Structure and Measurement*, Routledge & Kegan Paul.

Fairweather, G. W., *et al.* (1969), *Community Life for the Mentally Ill*, Aldine, Chicago.

Felson, R. B. (1978), 'Aggression as impression management', *Social Psychology*, vol. 41, pp. 205–13.

Ferguson, J. M. (1975), *Learning to Eat: Behavior Modification for Weight Control*, Hawthorn Books, New York.

Fiedler, F. E. (1978), 'Recent developments in research on the contingency model', in Berkowitz, L. (ed.), *Group Processes*, Academic Press, New York.

Fiedler, F. E., Mitchell, R., and Triandis, H. C. (1971), 'The culture assimilator: an approach to cross-cultural training', *Journal of Applied Psychology*, vol. 55, pp. 95–102.

Firth, R., Hubert, J., and Forge, A. (1969), *Families and their Relatives*, Routledge & Kegan Paul.

Flanders, N. A. (1970), *Analyzing Teaching Behavior*, Addison-Wesley, Reading, Massachusetts.

Fleishman, E. A., and Harris, E. F. (1962), 'Patterns of leadership behavior related to employee grievances and turnover', *Personnel Psychology*, vol. 15, pp. 43–56.

Forbes, R. J., and Jackson, P. R. (1980), 'Non-verbal behaviour and the outcome of selection interviews', *Journal of Occupational Psychology*, vol. 53, pp. 65–72.

Forgas, J., Argyle, M., and Ginsburg, G. J. (1979), 'Person perception as a function of the interaction episode: the fluctuating structure of an academic group', *Journal of Social Psychology*, vol. 109, pp. 207–22.

Freedman, B., Rosenthal, L., Donahoe, C., Schlundt, D., and McFall, R. (1978), 'A social-behavioral analysis of skill deficits in delinquent and nondelinquent adolescent boys', *Journal of Consulting and Clinical Psychology*, vol. 46, 1448–62.

Freedman, J. L. (1978), *Happy People*, Harcourt Brace Jovanovich, New York and London.

Freedman, J. L., and Fraser, S. C. (1966), 'Compliance without pressure: the foot-in-the-door technique', *Journal of Personality and Social Psychology*, vol. 4, pp. 195–202.

Friedman, H. S., Prince, L. M., Riggio, R. E., and DiMatteo, M. R. (1980), 'Understanding and assessing nonverbal expressiveness: the affective communication test', *Journal of Personality and Social Psychology*, vol. 39, pp. 333–51.

Furnham, A. (1981), 'Personality and activity preference', *British Journal of Social Psychology*, vol. 20, pp. 57–68.

Gage, N. L., Runkel, P. J., and Chatterjee, B. B. (1960), *Equilibrium Theory and Behavior Change: an experiment in feedback from pupils to teachers*, Bureau of Educational Research, Urbana, Illinois.

Gergen, K. J., and Morse, S. J. (1967), 'Self-consistency: measurement and validation', *Proceedings of the American Psychological Association*, pp. 207–8.

Gibbins, K. (1969), 'Communication aspects of women's clothes and their relation to fashionability', *British Journal of Social and Clinical Psychology*, vol. 8, pp. 301–12.

Giles, H., and Powesland, P. F. (1975), *Speech Style and Social Evaluation*, Academic Press.

Glasgow, R. E., and Rosen, G. M. (1978), 'Behavioral bibliotherapy: a review of self-help behavior therapy manuals', *Psychological Bulletin*, vol. 5, pp. 1–23.

Goffman, E. (1956a), *The Presentation of Self in Everyday Life*, Edinburgh University Press.

Goffman, E. (1956b), 'Embarrassment and social organization', *American Journal of Sociology*, vol. 62, pp. 264–74.

Goffman, E. (1961), *Encounters*, Bobbs-Merrill, Indianapolis.

Goffman, E. (1963), *Behavior in Public Places*, Free Press, Glencoe, Illinois.

Goffman, E. (1971), *Relations in Public*, Allen Lane.

Goffman, E. (1981), *Forms of Talk*, Blackwell.

Goldthorpe, J., et al. (1969), *The Affluent Worker in the Class Structure*, Cambridge University Press.

Gorer, G. (1965), *Death, Grief and Mourning*, Doubleday, New York.

Gottman, J. M. (1979), *Marital Interaction*, Academic Press, New York.

Gough, H. G. (1957), *Manual for the California Psychological Inventory*, Consulting Psychologists Press, Palo Alto.

Gough, H. G., and Heilbrun, A. B. (1965), *The Adjective Check List Manual*, Consulting Psychologists Press, Palo Alto.

Gove, W. R., et al. (1980), 'Playing dumb: a form of impression management with undesirable side effects', *Social Psychology Quarterly*, vol. 43, pp. 89–102.

Graham, J. A., and Argyle, M. (1975), 'A cross-cultural study of the communication of extra-verbal meaning by gesture', *International Journal of Psychology*, vol. 10, pp. 57–67.

Graham, J. A., Argyle, M., and Furnham, A. (1980), 'The goals and goal structure of social situations', *European Journal of Social Psychology*, vol. 10, pp. 345–66.

Graham, J. A., Ricci Bitti, P., and Argyle, M. (1975), 'A cross-cultural study of the communication of emotion by facial and gestural cues', *Journal of Human Movement Studies*, vol. 1, pp. 68–77.

Grice, H. P. (1975), 'Logic and conversation', in Cole, P., and Morgan, J. L. (eds), *Syntax and Semantics. Vol. 3. Speech Acts*, Academic Press, New York and London.

Griffitt, W., and Veitch, R. (1971), 'Hot and crowded: influence of population density and temperature on interpersonal affective behavior', *Journal of Personality and Social Psychology*, vol. 17, pp. 92–8.

Griffitt, W., and Veitch, R. (1974), 'Ten days in a fall-out shelter', *Sociometry*, vol. 37, pp. 164–73.

Gross, E., and Stone, G. P. (1964), 'Embarrassment and the analysis of role requirements', *American Journal of Sociology*, vol. 70, pp. 1–15.

Guthrie, G. M. (1966), 'Cultural preparation for the Philippines', in Textor, R. B. (ed.), *Cultural Frontiers of the Peace Corps*, M.I.T. Press, Cambridge, Massachusetts.

Hall, E. T. (1955), 'The anthropology of manners', *Scientific American*, vol. 192, pp. 84–90.

Hall, E. T. (1966), *The Hidden Dimension*, Doubleday, New York.

Halliday, M. A. K. (1978), *Language as Social Semiotic*, Arnold.

Harré, R. (1976), 'Living up to a name', in Harré, R. (ed.), *Personality*, Blackwell.

Harré, R., and Secord, P. (1972), *The Explanation of Social Behaviour*, Blackwell.

Hastorf, A. H., and Cantril, H. (1954), 'They saw a game: a case study', *Journal of Abnormal and Social Psychology*, vol. 49, pp. 129–34.

Hatfield, E., Utre, M., and Traupman, J. (1979), 'Equity theory and intimate relationships', in Burgess, R. L., and Huston, T. (eds), *Social Exchange in Developing Relationships*, Academic Press, New York.

Haythorn, W. (1956), 'The effects of varying combinations of authoritarian and equalitarian leaders and followers', *Journal of Abnormal and Social Psychology*, vol. 52, pp. 210–19.

Henderson, S., Duncan-Jones, P., McAuley, H., and Ritchie, K. (1978), 'The patient's primary group', *British Journal of Psychiatry*, vol. 132, pp. 74–86.

Hersen, M. (1979), 'Modification of skill deficits in psychiatric patients', in Bellack, A. S., and Hersen, M. (eds), *Research and Practice in Social Skills Training*, Plenum, New York and London.

Hewstone, M., Argyle, M., and Furnham, A. (in press), 'Favouritism, fairness and joint profit in long-term relationships', *European Journal of Social Psychology*.

Hill, C. T., Rubin, Z., and Peplau, L. A. (1976), 'Breakups before marriage: the end of 103 affairs', *Journal of Social Issues*, vol. 32, pp. 147–68.

Hochschild, A. R. (1979), 'Emotion work, feeling rules and social structure', *American Journal of Sociology*, vol. 85, pp. 551–75.

Hoffman, L. R. (1965), 'Group problem-solving', *Advances in Experimental Social Psychology*, vol. 2, pp. 99–132.

Hollander, E. P. (1958), 'Conformity, status and idiosyncracy credit', *Psychological Review*, vol. 65, pp. 117–27.

Howes, M. J., and Hokanson, J. E. (1979), 'Conversational and social responses to depressive interpersonal behavior', *Journal of Abnormal Psychology*, vol. 88, pp. 625–34.

Hunt, J. G., and Larson, L. L. (1977), *Leadership: the Cutting Edge*, South Illinois University Press, Carbondale.

Hurlock, E. B. (1929), 'Motivation in fashion', *Archives of Psychology*, vol. 3, pp. 1–72.

Hyman, H. H., *et al.* (1955), *Interviewing in Social Research*, University of Chicago Press.

Israel, J., and Tajfel, H. (eds) (1972), *The Context of Social Psychology: A Critical Assessment*, Academic Press.

Izard, C. E. (1971), *The Face of Emotion*, Appleton-Century-Crofts, New York.

Izard, C. E. (1975), 'Patterns of emotions and emotion communication in "hostility" and aggression', in Pliner, P., Kramer, L., and Alloway, T. (eds), *Nonverbal Communication of Aggression*, Plenum, New York.

Jackson, J. M., and Latané, B. (1981), 'All alone in front of all those people: stage fright as a function of number and type of co-performers and audience', *Journal of Personality and Social Psychology*, vol. 40, pp. 73–85.

Jacob, T. (1975), 'Family interaction in disturbed and normal families: a methodological and substantive review', *Psychological Bulletin*, vol. 82, pp. 33–65.

Jacobson, N. S. (1979), 'Behavioral treatments for marital discord: a critical appraisal', *Progress in Behavior Modification*, vol. 8, pp. 169–205.

Jacobson, N. S., and Margolin, G. (1979), *Marital Therapy*, Brunner/Mazel, New York.

Janis, I. L., and Mann, L. (1977), *Decision Making*, Free Press, New York.

Jennings, H. H. (1950), *Leadership and Isolation*, Longmans Green, New York.

Jones, E. E. (1964), *Ingratiation: a Social Psychological Analysis*, Appleton-Century-Crofts, New York.

Jones, E. E., and Davis, K. E. (1966), 'From acts to dispositions', *Advances in Experimental Social Psychology*, vol. 2, pp. 220–67.

Jones, E. E., and Gerard, H. B. (1967), *Foundations of Social Psychology*, Wiley, New York.

Jones, E. E., and Nisbett, R. E. (1972), 'The actor and the observer: divergent perceptions of the causes of behavior', in Jones, E. E., *et al.* (eds), *Attribution: Perceiving the Causes of Behavior*, General Learning Press, Morristown, New Jersey.

Jourard, S. M. (1964), *The Transparent Self*, Van Nostrand, Princeton, New Jersey.

Jourard, S. M. (1966), 'An exploratory study of body-accessibility', *British Journal of Social and Clinical Psychology*, vol. 5, pp. 221–31.

Jourard, S. M. (1971), *Self-Disclosure*, Wiley-Interscience, New York.

Jourard, S. M., and Secord, P. F. (1955), 'Body-cathexis and personality', *British Journal of Psychology*, vol. 46, pp. 130–38.

Kahn, R. I., and Cannell, C. F. (1957), *The Dynamics of Interviewing*, Wiley, New York.

Kahn, R. L., Wolfe, D. M., Quinn, R. P., and Snoek, H. D. (1964), *Organizational Stress*, Wiley, New York.

Kalven, H. G., and Zeisel, H. (1966), *The American Jury*, Little, Brown and Co., Boston.

Katz, D., and Braly, K. W. (1933), 'Racial prejudice and racial stereotypes', *Journal of Abnormal and Social Psychology*, vol. 30, pp. 175–93.

Kazdin, A. E., and Wilcoxon, L. A. (1976), 'Systematic desensitization and non-specific treatment effects: a methodological evaluation', *Psychological Bulletin*, vol. 83, pp. 729–58.

Kelley, H. H. (1950), 'The warm–cold variable in first impressions of persons', *Journal of Personality*, vol. 18, pp. 431–9.

Kelley, H. H. (1967), 'Attribution theory in social psychology', *Nebraska Symposium on Motivation*, University of Nebraska Press, vol. 15.

Kelly, G. A. (1955), *The Psychology of Personal Constructs*, W. W. Norton, New York.

Kendon, A. (1967), 'Some functions of gaze direction in social interaction', *Acta Psychologica*, vol. 28, no. 1, pp. 1–47.

Kendon, A. (1972), 'Some relationships between body motion and speech: an analysis of an example', in Siegman, A., and Pope, B. (eds), *Studies in Dyadic Communication*, Pergamon, Elmsford, New York.

Kendon, A. (1977), *Studies in the Behavior of Social Interaction*, Indiana University Press, Bloomington, Indiana.

Kendon, A., and Cook, M. (1969), 'The consistency of gaze patterns in social interaction', *British Journal of Psychology*, vol. 60, pp. 481–94.

Kendon, A., and Ferber, A. (1973), 'A description of some human greetings', in Michael, R. P., and Crook, J. H. (eds), *Comparative Ecology and Behaviour of Primates*, Academic Press.

Kenrick, D. T., and Stringfield, D. C. (1980), 'Personality traits and the eye of the beholder: crossing some traditional philosophical boundaries in the search for consistency in all of the people', *Psychological Review*, vol. 87, pp. 88–104.

Kraut, R. E., and Johnston, R. E. (1979), 'Social and emotional messages of smiling: an ethological approach', *Journal of Personality and Social Psychology*, vol. 37, pp. 1539–53.

Kraut, R. E., and Poe, D. (1980), 'Behavioral roots of person perception: the deceptive judgments of customs inspectors and laymen', *Journal of Personality and Social Psychology*, vol. 39, pp. 784–98.

Krech, D., Crutchfield, R. S., and Ballachey, E. L. (1962), *Individual in Society*, McGraw-Hill, New York.

Kuhn, M. H., and McPartland, T. S. (1954), 'An empirical investigation of self-attitudes', *American Sociological Review*, vol. 19, pp. 68–76.

Kurtz, J. (1975), 'Nonverbal norm-sending and territorial defense' (unpublished), University of Delaware Ph.D., cited by Exline and Fehr (1978).

Laing, R. D., Phillipson, H., and Lee, A. R. (1966), *Interpersonal Perception*, Tavistock.

Laird, J. D. (1974), 'Self-attribution of emotion: the effects of expressive behavior on the quality of emotional experience', *Journal of Personality and Social Psychology*, vol. 29, pp. 475–86.

Lanzetta, J. T., Cartwright-Smith, J., and Kleck, R. E. (1976), 'Effects of nonverbal dissimilation on emotional experience and autonomic arousal', *Journal of Personality and Social Psychology*, vol. 33, pp. 354–70.

Latané, B. (ed.) (1966), 'Studies in social comparison', *Journal of Experimental Social Psychology*, Supplement 1.

Latané, B. (1981), 'The psychology of social impact', *American Psychologist*, vol. 36, pp. 343–6.

Latané, B., and Wolf, S. (1981), 'The social impact of majorities and minorities', *Psychological Review*, vol. 88, pp. 438–53.

Lefebvre, L. (1975), 'Encoding and decoding of ingratiation in modes of smiling and gaze', *British Journal of Social and Clinical Psychology*, vol. 14, pp. 33–42.

Lemmert, E. M. (1962), 'Paranoia and the dynamics of exclusion', *Sociometry*, vol. 25, pp. 2–20.

Lennard, H. L., and Bernstein, A. (1960), *The Anatomy of Psychotherapy*, Columbia University Press, New York.

Lenrow, P. D. (1965), 'Studies of Sympathy', in Tomkins, S. S., and Izard C. E. (eds), *Affect, Cognition and Personality*, Tavistock.

Lett, R. E., Clark, W., and Altman, I. (1969), *A Propositional Inventory of Research on Interpersonal Space*, Naval Medical Research Institute, Washington.

Leventhal, H. (1974), 'Emotions: a basic problem for social psychology', in C. Nemeth (ed.), *Social Psychology: Classic and Contemporary Integrations*, Rand McNally, Chicago, Illinois.

Leventhal, H. (1980), 'Toward a comprehensive theory of emotion', *Advances in Experimental Social Psychology*, vol. 13, pp. 140–207.

Levine, M. H., and Sutton-Smith, B. (1973), 'Effects of age, sex, and task on visual behavior during dyadic interaction', *Developmental Psychology*, vol. 9, pp. 400–405.

Lewinsohn, P. M. (1975), 'The behavioral study and treatment of depression', in Hersen, M., Eisler, R. M., and Miller, P. M. (eds), *Progress in Behavior Modification*, vol. 1, pp. 19–64.

Ley, P. (1977), 'Psychological studies of doctor–patient communication', in Rachman, S. (ed.), *Contributions to Medical Psychology*, Pergamon Press.

Leyens, J. P., Carmino, L., Parke, R. D., and Berkowitz, L. (1975), 'Effects of movie violence on aggression in a field setting as a function of group dominance and cohesion', *Journal of Personality and Social Psychology*, vol. 32, pp. 346–60.

Libet, J. M., and Lewinsohn, P. M. (1973), 'Concept of social skills with special reference to the behavior of depressed persons', *Journal of Consulting and Clinical Psychology*, vol. 40, pp. 304–312.

Lieberman, M. A., Yalóm, I. D., and Miles, M. B. (1973), *Encounter Groups: First Facts*, Basic Books, New York.

Likert, R. (1961), *New Patterns of Management*, McGraw-Hill, New York.

Lippa, R. (1978), 'Expressive control, expression consistency, and the correspondence between expressive behavior and personality', *Journal of Personality*, vol. 46, pp. 438–61.

Livesley, W. J., and Bromley, D. B. (1973), *Person Perception in Childhood and Adolescence*, Wiley.

Lombard, G. G. F. (1955), *Behavior in a Selling Group*, Harvard University Press.

Lott, A. J., and Lott, B. E. (1960), 'The formation of positive attitudes towards group members', *Journal of Abnormal and Social Psychology*, vol. 61, pp. 297–300.

Lott, A. J., and Lott, B. E. (1965), 'Group cohesiveness as interpersonal attraction: a review of relationships with antecedent and consequent variables', *Psychological Bulletin*, vol. 64, pp. 259–309.

Luborsky, L., *et al.* (1971), 'Factors influencing the outcome of psychotherapy: a review of quantitative research', *Psychological Bulletin*, vol. 75, pp. 145–85.

Lynch, J. J. (1977), *The Broken Heart*, Basic Books, New York.

McClelland, D. C., and Winter, D. G. (1969), *Motivating Economic Achievement*, Free Press, New York.

McDavid, J., and Schroder, H. M. (1957), 'The interpretation of approval and disapproval by delinquent and non-delinquent adolescents', *Journal of Personality*, vol. 25, pp. 539–49.

McDowall, J. J. (1978), 'Interactional synchrony: a reappraisal', *Journal of Personality and Social Psychology*, vol. 36, pp. 963–75.

McGrath, J. E. (1966), 'A social psychological approach to the study of negotiation', in Bowers, R. (ed.), *Studies on Behavior in Organizations: A Research Symposium*, University of Georgia Press, Athens, Georgia.

McPhail, P. (1967), 'The development of social skills in adolescents' (unpublished), Oxford Department of Education, paper to B.P.S.

McPhail, P. (1972), *Moral Education in Secondary Schools*, Longmans.

Maguire, P. (1981), 'Doctor–patient skills', in Argyle, M. (ed.), *Social Skills and Health*, Methuen.

Maier, N. R. F., and Solem, A. R. (1952), 'The contribution of a discussion leader to the quality of group thinking: the effective use of minority opinion', *Human Relations*, vol. 5, pp. 277–88.

Mann, J. W. (1963), 'Rivals of different rank', *Journal of Social Psychology*, vol. 61, pp. 11–28.

Mann, R. D. *et al.* (1967), *Interpersonal Styles and Group Development*. Wiley, New York.

Manosevitz, M., Prentice, N. M., and Wilson, F. (1973), 'Individual and family correlates of imaginary companions', *Developmental Psychology*, vol. 8, pp. 72–79.

Marcia, J. E. (1966), 'Development and validation of ego-identity status', *Journal of Personality and Social Psychology*, vol. 3, pp. 551–8.

Marsh, P., Harré, R., and Rosser, E. (1978), *The Rules of Disorder*, Routledge & Kegan Paul.

Maxwell, G. M. (1976), 'An evaluation of social skills training' (unpublished), University of Otago

May, P. R. A. (ed.) (1968), *Treatment of Schizophrenia*. Science House, New York.

Megargee, E. I. (1966), 'Undercontrolled and overcontrolled personality types in extreme antisocial aggression', *Psychological Monographs*, vol. 80.

Mehrabian, A. (1969), *Tactics in Social Influence*, Prentice-Hall, Englewood Cliffs, New Jersey.

Mehrabian, A. (1970), 'The development and validation of measures of affiliative tendency and sensitivity to rejection', *Educational and Psychological Measurement*, vol. 30, pp. 417–28.

Meichenbaum, S. (1977), *Cognitive-Behavior Modification*, Plenum Press, New York.

Meldman, M. J. (1967), 'Verbal behavior analysis of self-hyperattentionism', *Disorders of the Nervous System*, vol. 28, pp. 469–73.

Melly, G. (1965), 'Gesture goes classless', *New Society*, 17 June, pp. 26–7.

Merton, R., *et al.* (1957), *The Student-Physician*, Harvard University Press.

Milgram, S. (1974), *Obedience to Authority*, Harper & Row, New York.

Miller, N. E. (1944), 'Experimental studies of conflict', in Hunt, J. McV. (ed.), *Personality and the Behavior Disorders*, Ronald, New York.

Minsky, M. (1975), 'A framework for representing knowledge', in Winston, P. H. (ed.), *The Psychology of Computer Vision*, McGraw-Hill, New York.

Modigliani, A. (1971), 'Embarrassment, facework and eye contact: testing a theory of embarrassment', *Journal of Personality and Social Psychology*, vol. 17, pp. 15–24.

Moos, R. H. (1968), 'Situational analysis of a therapeutic community milieu', *Journal of Abnormal Psychology*, vol. 73, pp. 49–61.

Moos, R. H. (1969), 'Sources of variance in responses to questionnaires and in behavior', *Journal of Abnormal Psychology*, vol. 74, pp. 405–12.

Morley, I. E., and Stephenson, G. M. (1977), *The Social Psychology of Bargaining*, Allen and Unwin.

Morris, D., Collett, P., Marsh, P., and O'Shaughnessy, M. (1979), *Gestures: their Origins and Distribution*, Cape.

Morris, L. W. (1979), *Extraversion and Introversion*, Wiley, New York.

Morton, R. B. (1965), 'The uses of the laboratory method in a psychiatric hospital', in Schein, E. H., and Bennis, W. G. (eds), *Personal and Organizational Change through Group Methods*, Wiley, New York.

Moscovici, S. (1967), 'Communication processes and the properties of language', *Advances in Experimental Social Psychology*, vol. 3, pp. 226–70.

Moscovici, S. (1980), 'Toward a theory of conversion behaviour', *Advances in Experimental Social Psychology*, vol. 13, pp. 209–39.

Mosher, D. L. (1979), 'Sex guilt and sex myths in college men and women', *Journal of Sex Research*, vol. 15, pp. 224–34.

Mussen, P., and Distler, L. (1964), 'Child-rearing antecedents of masculine identification in kindergarten boys', *Child Development*, vol. 31, pp. 89–100.

Muuss, R. E. (1962), *Theories of Adolescence*, Random House, New York.

Naegele, K. D. (1958), 'Friendship and acquaintance: an exploration of some social distinctions', *Harvard Educational Review*, vol. 28, no. 3, pp. 232–52.

Newtson, D. (1977), 'The objective basis of behavior units', *Journal of Personality and Social Psychology*, vol. 35, pp. 847–62.

Nicholson, J. (1980), *Seven Ages*, Fontana.

Noesjirwan, J. (1978), 'A rule-based analysis of cultural differences in social behaviour: Indonesia and Australia', *International Journal of Psychology*, vol. 13, pp. 305–16.

Noller, P. (1980), 'Misunderstandings in marital communication: a study of couples' nonverbal communication', *Journal of Personality and Social Psychology*, vol. 39, pp. 1135–48.

Oeser, O. A. (1955), *Teacher, Pupil and Task*, Tavistock.

Osgood, C. E. (1960), *Graduated Reciprocation in Tension Reduction: A Key to Initiative in Foreign Policy*, Institute of Communications Research, University of Illinois, Urbana, Illinois.

Osgood, C. E., Suci, G. J., and Tannenbaum, P. H. (1957), *The Measurement of Meaning*, University of Illinois Press.

Paivio, A. (1965), 'Personality and audience influence', *Progress in Experimental Personality Research*, vol. 2, pp. 127–73.

Parkes, K. R. (1980), 'Occupational stress among student nurses', *Nursing Times*, vol. 76, pp. 113–16 and 117–20.

Parnell, R. W. (1958), *Behavior and Physique*, Arnold.

Patterson, M. (1973), 'Compensation in nonverbal immediacy behaviors: a review', *Sociometry*, vol. 36, pp. 237–352.

Patterson, M. L. (1976), 'An arousal model of interpersonal intimacy', *Psychological Review*, vol. 83, pp. 235–45.

Paul, G. L. (1966), *Insight vs. Desensitization in Psychotherapy*, Stanford University Press.

Paykel, E. S., McGuiness, B., and Gomez, J. (1976), 'An Anglo-American comparison of the scaling of life-events', *British Journal of Medical Psychology*, vol. 49, pp. 237–47.

Payne, R. (1980), 'Organizational stress and social support'; in Cooper, C. L., and Payne, R. (eds.), *Current Concerns in Organizational Stress*, Wiley.

Peck, R. F., and Tucker, J. A. (1973), 'Research on teacher education', in Travers, R. M. W. (ed.), *Second Handbook of Research on Teaching*, Rand McNally, Chicago.

Pendleton, D. A. (1981), 'Doctor–patient communication', D.Phil. thesis, Oxford Department of Experimental Psychology.

Pervin, L. (in press), 'The stasis and flow of behavior: toward a theory of goals', *Nebraska Symposium on Motivation*, University of Nebraska Press, Lincoln, Nebraska.

Phares, E. (1976), *Locus of Control in Personality*, General Learning Press, Morristown, New Jersey.

Piliavin, I. M., Rodin, J., and Piliavin, J. A. (1969), 'Good Samaritanism: an underground phenomenon', *Journal of Personality and Social Psychology*, vol. 13, pp. 289–99.

Poppleton, S. F. (1981), 'The social skills of selling', in Argyle, M. (ed.), *Social Skills and Work*, Methuen.

Potter, S. (1952), *One-Upmanship*, Hart-Davis.

Pruitt, D. G. (1976), 'Power and bargaining', in Seidenberg, B., and Snadowsky, A. (eds), *Social Psychology: an Introduction*, Free Press, New York.

Rackham, N., and Carlisle, J. (1978, 1979), 'The effective negotiator', *Journal of European Industrial Training*, vol. 2, no. 6 pp. 6–11, no. 7 pp. 2–5.

Rackham, N., and Morgan, T. (1977), *Behaviour Analysis and Training*, McGraw–Hill.

Rathus, S. A. (1973), 'A 30-item schedule for assessing assertive behavior', *Behavior Therapy*, vol. 4, pp. 398–406.

Regan, D. T. (1971), 'Effects of a favor and liking on compliance', *Journal of Experimental Social Psychology*, vol. 7, pp. 627–39.

Revelle, W., Humphreys, M. S., Simon, L., and Gilliland, K. (1980), 'The interactive effect of personality, time of day, and caffeine: a test of the arousal model', *Journal of Experimental Psychology: General*, vol. 109, pp. 1–31.

Rich, A. R., and Schroeder, H. E. (1976), 'Research issues in assertiveness training', *Psychological Bulletin*, vol. 83, pp. 1081–96.

Richardson, D. C., Berstein, S., and Taylor, S. P. (1979), 'The effect of situational contingencies on female retaliative behavior', *Journal of Personality and Social Psychology*, vol. 37, pp. 2044–8.

Robinson, P. (1978), *Language Management in Education*, Allen and Unwin, Sydney.

Robson, R. A. H. (1966), 'Group structure in mixed sex triads' (unpublished), University of British Columbia MS.

Rogers, C. R. (1942), *Counselling and Psychotherapy*, Houghton Mifflin, Boston.

Rommetveit, R. (1974), *On Message Structure: A Conceptual Framework for the Study of Language and Communication*, Wiley.

Rosenberg, M. (1965), *Society and the Adolescent Self-image*, Princeton University Press.

Rosenberg, M. (1981), 'The self-concept: social product and social force', in Rosenberg, M. and Turner, R. H. (eds), *Social Psychology: Sociological Perspectives*, Basic Books, New York.

Rosenfeld, H. M. (1967), 'Non-verbal reciprocation of approval: an experimental analysis', *Journal of Personality and Social Psychology*, vol. 3, pp. 102–11.

Rosenfeld, H. M. (1981), 'Whither interactional sychrony?', in Bloom, K. (ed.), *Prospective Issues in Infancy Research*, Erlbaum, New York.

Rosenfeld, H. M., and Hancks, M. (1980), 'The nonverbal context of verbal listener responses', in Key, M. R. (ed.), *The Relationship of Verbal and Nonverbal Communication*, Mouton, The Hague.

Rosenshine, B. (1971), *Teaching Behaviours and Student Achievement*, N.F.E.R.

Rosenthal, R. (ed.) (1979), *Skill in Nonverbal Communication: Individual Differences*, Oelgeschlager, Gunn and Hain, Cambridge, Massachusetts.

Rubin, Z. (1973), *Liking and Loving*, Holt, Rinehart and Winston, New York.

Runyan, W. (1978), 'The life course as a theoretical orientation: sequences of person-situation interaction', *Journal of Personality*, vol. 46, pp. 569–93.

Rutter, D. (1976), 'Visual interaction in recently admitted and chronic long-stay schizophrenic patients', *British Journal of Social and Clinical Psychology*, vol. 15, pp. 295–303.

Rutter, D. R., and Stephenson, G. M. (1979), 'The functions of looking: effects of friendship on gaze', *British Journal of Social and Clinical Psychology*, vol. 18, pp. 203–5.

Sanders, G. S. (1981), 'Driven by distraction: an integrative review of social facilitation theory and research', *Journal of Experimental Social Psychology*, vol. 17, pp. 227–51.

Sarason, I. G., and Ganzer, V. J. (1971), *Modeling: an approach to the rehabilitation of juvenile offenders*, U.S. Department of Health, Education and Welfare.

Sarbin, T. R., and Hardyk, C. (1953), 'Contributions to role-taking theory: role-perception on the basis of postural cues', unpublished, cited by Sarbin, T. R. (1954), 'Role theory', in Lindzey, G. (ed.), *Handbook of Social Psychology*, Addison-Wesley, Cambridge, Massachusetts.

Sarbin, T. R., and Jones, D. S. (1956), 'An experimental analysis of role behavior', *Journal of Abnormal and Social Psychology*, vol. 51, pp. 236–41.

Sargant, W. (1957), *Battle for the Mind*, Heinemann.

Scaife, M., and Bruner, J. S. (1975), 'The capacity for joint visual attention in the infant', *Nature*, vol. 253, pp. 265–6.

Schachter, S. (1959), *The Psychology of Affiliation*, Stanford University Press.

Schachter, S., and Singer, J. (1962), 'Cognitive, social and physiological determinants of emotional state', *Psychological Review*, vol. 69, pp. 379–99.

Schaffer, H. R., and Emerson, P. E. (1964), 'The development of social attachments in infancy', *Monographs of Social Research on Child Development*, vol. 29, no. 3.

Scherer, K. R. (1974), 'Acoustic concomitants of emotional dimensions: judging affect from synthesized tone sequences', in Weitz, S. (ed.), *Nonverbal Communication*, Oxford University Press, New York.

Scherer, K. R. (1979), 'Non-linguistic vocal indicators of emotion and psychopathology', in Izard, C. E. (ed.), *Emotions in Personality and Psychotherapy*, Plenum Press, New York.

Schneider, D. (1972), 'Patterns of social interaction', in Szalai, A. (ed.), *The Use of Time*, Mouton, The Hague.

Schneider, D. (1968), *American Kinship: a Cultural Account*, Prentice-Hall, Englewood Cliffs, New Jersey.

Schneider, D. J., Hastorf, A. H., and Ellsworth, P. C. (1979), *Person Perception*, Addison-Wesley, Reading, Massachusetts.

Schofield, W. (1964), *Psychotherapy, the Purchase of Friendship*, Prentice-Hall, Englewood Cliffs, New Jersey.

Schutz, W. C. (1958), *FIRO: A three-dimensional theory of interpersonal behaviour*, Holt, Rinehart and Winston, New York.

Schutz, W. C. (1967), *Joy*, Grove Press, New York.

Secord, P. F., and Backman, C. W. (1974), *Social Psychology*, McGraw-Hill, New York.

Seligman, M. E. P. (1975), *Helplessness*, Freeman, San Francisco.

Semin, G. R., and Manstead, A. S. R. (1981), 'The beholder beheld: a study of social emotionality', *European Journal of Social Psychology*, vol. 11, pp. 253–65.

Shanas, E., Townsend, P., et al. (1968), *Old People in Three Industrial Societies*, Atherton, New York.

Sheehan, D. V. et al. (1981), 'Psychosocial predictors of accident/error rates in nursing students: a prospective study', in *International Journal of Psychiatry in Medicine*, vol. 11, pp. 125–36.

Sherif, M., et al. (1961), *Intergroup Conflict and Cooperation: The Robbers Cave Experiment*, University of Oklahoma Book Exchange, Norman.

Shimoda, K., Argyle, M., and Ricci Bitti, P. (1978), 'The intercultural recognition of emotional expressions by three national groups – English, Italian and Japanese', *European Journal of Social Psychology*, vol. 8, pp. 169–79.

Short, J., Williams, E., and Christie, B. (1976), *The Social Psychology of Telecommunications*, Wiley.

Shouby, E. (1951), 'The influence of the Arabic language on the psychology of the Arabs', *Middle East Journal*, vol. 5, pp. 284–302.

Shrauger, J. S. (1975), 'Responses to evaluation as a function of initial self-perceptions', *Psychological Bulletin*, vol. 82, pp. 581–96.

Simon, A., and Boyer, E. G. (eds) (1974), 'Mirrors for Behavior', 3rd edn, *Classroom Interaction Newsletter*, Communication Materials Center, Wyncote, Pennsylvania.

Singer, J. E. (1964), 'The use of manipulation strategies: Machiavellianism and attractiveness', *Sociometry*, vol. 27, pp. 138–50.

Sissons, M. (1971), 'The psychology of social class', in *Money, Wealth and Class*, The Open University Press.

Slater, P. E. (1955), 'Role differentiation in small groups', in Hare, A. P., et al. (eds), *Small Groups*, Knopf, New York.

Smith, M. L., and Glass, G. V. (1977), 'Meta-analysis of psychotherapy outcome studies', *American Psychologist*, vol. 32, pp. 752–60.

Snyder, M. (1979), 'Self-monitoring processes', *Advances in Experimental Social Psychology*, vol. 12, pp. 85–128.

Sommer, R. (1965), 'Further studies of small group ecology', *Sociometry*, vol. 28, pp. 337–48.

Spielberger, C. A. (ed.) (1972), *Anxiety: Current Trends in Theory and Research*, Academic Press, New York, vol. 2.

Staples, L. M., and Robinson, W. P. (1974), 'Address forms used by members of a department store', *British Journal of Social and Clinical Psychology*, vol. 13, pp. 131–42.

Stein, R. T., Hoffman, L. R., Cooley, S. J., and Pearse, R. W. (1980), 'Leadership valence: Modeling and measuring the process of emergent leadership', in Hunt, J. G., and Larson, L. L. (eds), *Crosscurrents in Leadership*, Southern Illinois University Press, Carbondale.

Stone, G. C., Gage, N. L., and Leavitt, G. S. (1957), 'Two kinds of accuracy in predicting another's responses', *Journal of Social Psychology*, vol. 45, pp. 245–54.

Straus, M. A., Gelles, R. J., and Steinmetz, S. K. (1980), *Behind Closed Doors: Violence in the American Family*, Doubleday, New York.

Subotnik, L. (1972), 'Spontaneous remission: fact or artifact?', *Psychological Bulletin*, vol. 77, pp. 32–48.

Sundberg, N. D., and Tyler, L. E. (1962), *Clinical Psychology*, Appleton-Century-Crofts, New York.

Sydiaha, D. (1961), '"Bales" interaction process analysis of personnel selection interviews', *Journal of Applied Psychology*, vol. 45, pp. 393–401.

Sykes, G. M., and Matza, D. (1957), 'Techniques of neutralization: a theory of delinquency', *American Sociological Review*, vol. 22, pp. 667–89.

Szasz, T. S. (1961), *The Myth of Mental Illness*, Secker and Warburg.

Tagiuri, R. (1958), 'Social preference and its perception', in Tagiuri, R., and Petrullo, L. (eds), *Person Perception and Interpersonal Behavior*, Stanford University Press.

Tajfel, H. (1970), 'Experiments in intergroup discrimination', *Scientific American*, vol. 223, no. 5, pp. 96–102.

Thayer, S., and Schiff, W. (1969), 'Stimulus factors in observer judgment of social interaction: facial expression and motion pattern', *American Journal of Psychology*, vol. 82, pp. 73–85.

Thelen, H., Fry, R. A., Fehrenbach, P. A., and Frautschl, N. M. (1979), 'Therapeutic videotape and film modeling: a review', *Psychological Bulletin*, vol. 86, pp. 701–20.

Thibaut, J., and Riecken, H. W. (1955), 'Some determinants and consequences of the perception of social causality', *Journal of Personality*, vol. 24, pp. 113–33.

Thomas, E. J., and Fink, C. F. (1963), 'Effects of group size', *Psychological Bulletin*, vol. 60, pp. 371–84.

Townsend, P. (1968), 'The structure of the family', in Shanas, E., Townsend, P., *et al.* (eds) *Old People in Three Industrial Societies* Atherton, New York.

Triandis, H. (1972), *The Analysis of Subjective Culture*, Wiley, New York.

Trist, E. L., *et al.* (1963), *Organizational Choice*, Tavistock.

Trower, P. (1980), 'Situational analysis of the components and processes of socially skilled and unskilled patients', *Journal of Consulting and Clinical Psychology*, vol. 48, pp. 327–39.

Trower, P., Bryant, B., and Argyle, M. (1978), *Social Skills and Mental Health*, Methuen.

Trower, P., and Dryden, W. (1981), 'Psychotherapy', in Argyle, M. (ed.), *Social Skills and Health*, Methuen.

Trower, P., Yardley, K., Bryant, B., and Shaw, P. H. (1978), 'The treatment of social failure: a comparison of anxiety reduction and skill-acquisition on two social problems', *Behavior Modification*, vol. 2, pp. 41–60.

Tuckman, B. W. (1965), 'Developmental sequences in small groups', *Psychological Bulletin*, vol. 63, pp. 384–99.

Turner, J., and Giles, H. (eds) (1981), *Intergroup Behaviour*, Blackwell.

Turner, R. H. (1956), 'Role-taking, role standpoint, and reference group behavior', *American Journal of Sociology*, vol. 61, pp. 316–28.

Twentyman, C. T., and Zimering, R. T. (1979), 'Behavioral treatment of social skills: a critical review', *Progress in Behavior Modification*, vol. 7, pp. 321–400.

Ulrich, L., and Trumbo, D. (1965), 'The selection interview since 1949', *Psychological Bulletin*, vol. 63, pp. 100–116.

Valins, S. (1966), 'Cognitive effects of false heart-rate feedback', *Journal of Personality and Social Psychology*, vol. 4, pp. 400–408.

Van Gennep, A. (1908), *The Rites of Passage*, University of Chicago Press.

Van Hooff, J. A. R. A. M. (1972), 'A comparative approach to the phylogeny of laughter and smiling', in Hinde, R. A. (ed.), *Non-verbal Communication*, Royal Society and Cambridge University Press.

Videbeck, R. (1960), 'Self-conception and the reactions of others', *Sociometry*, vol. 23, pp. 351–9.

Von Cranach, M., and Ellgring, J. H. (1973), 'Problems in the recognition of gaze direction', in von Cranach, M., and Vine, I. (eds), *Social Communication and Movement*, Academic Press.

Wachtel, P. (1973), 'Psychodynamic behavior therapy, and the implacable experimenter: an inquiry into the consistency of personality', *Journal of Abnormal Psychology*, vol. 82, pp. 324–34.

Walster, E., *et al.* (1966), 'Importance of physical attractiveness in dating behavior', *Journal of Personality and Social Psychology*, vol 4, pp. 508–16.

Walters, R. H., and Parke, R. D. (1964), 'Social motivation, dependency, and susceptibility to social influence', in Berkowitz, L. (ed.), *Advances in Experimental Social Psychology*, vol. 1, pp. 232–76.

Warr, P. B., and Knapper, C. (1968), *The Perception of People and Events*, Wiley, New York.

Watson, O. M. (1972), *Proxemic Behavior: A Cross Cultural Study*, Mouton, The Hague.

Watzlawick, P., Beavin, J. H., and Jackson, D. D. (1967), *Pragmatics of Human Communication*, W. W. Norton, New York.

Weiner, B. (1974), *Achievement Motivation and Attribution Theory*, General Learning Press, Morristown, New Jersey.

Weiner, B. (1980), *Human Motivation*, Holt, Rinehart and Winston, New York.

Weitz, S. (1972), 'Attitude, voice and behavior', *Journal of Personality and Social Psychology*, vol. 24, pp. 14–24.

Wellman, B. (1979), 'The community question: the intimate networks of East Yorkers', *American Journal of Sociology*, vol. 84, pp. 1201–31.

Whitcher, S. J., and Fisher, J. D. (1979), 'Multidimensional reaction to therapeutic touch in a hospital setting', *Journal of Personality and Social Psychology*, vol. 37, pp. 87–96.

Wicklund, R. A. (1975), 'Objective self-awareness', *Advances in Experimental Social Psychology*, vol. 8, pp. 233–75.

Williams, E. (1974), 'An analysis of gaze in schizophrenia', *British Journal of Social and Clinical Psychology*, vol. 13, pp. 1–8.

Wilson, E. O. (1975), *Sociobiology: The New Synthesis*, Harvard University Press, Cambridge, Massachusetts.

Wilson, G., and Nias, D. (1976), *Love's Mysteries: the Psychology of Sexual Attraction*, Open Books.

Wing, J. K. (1967), 'Institutionalism in mental hospitals', in Scheff, T. (ed.), *Mental Illness and Social Processes*, Harper & Row, New York.

Winter, D. G. (1973), *The Power Motive*, Free Press, New York.

Wish, M., Deutsch, M., and Kaplan, S. J. (1976), 'Perceived dimensions of interpersonal relations', *Sociometry*, vol. 40, pp. 234–46.

Wish, M., and Kaplan, S. J. (1977), 'Toward an implicit theory of interpersonal communication', *Sociometry*, vol. 40, pp. 234–46.

Woodward, J. (1960), *The Saleswoman*, Pitman.

Wortman, C. B., and Brehm, J. (1975), 'Responses to uncontrollable outcomes: an integration of reactance theory and the learned helplessness model', *Advances in Experimental Social Psychology*, vol. 8, pp. 278–336.

Wylie, R. C. (1974), *The Self-Concept: Vol. I. A Review of Methodological*

Considerations and Measuring Instruments, University of Nebraska Press, Lincoln, Nebraska.

Wylie, R. (1979), *The Self-Concept: Vol. 2. Theory and Research on Selected Topics*, University of Nebraska Press, Lincoln, Nebraska.

Zajonc, R. B. (1965), 'Social facilitation', *Science*, vol. 149, pp. 269–74.

Zeiss, A. M., Lewinsohn, P. M., and Munoz, R. F. (1979), 'Nonspecific improvement effects in depression using interpersonal skills training, pleasant activity schedules, or cognitive training', *Journal of Consulting and Clinical Psychology*, vol. 47, pp. 423–39.

Zigler, E., and Child, I. L. (1969), 'Socialization', in Lindzey, G., and Aronson, E. (eds), *Handbook of Social Psychology*, vol. 3, Addison-Wesley, Reading, Massachusetts.

Zimbardo, P. G. (1969), 'The human choice: individuation and order versus deindividuation, impulse and chaos', *Nebraska Symposium on Motivation*, University of Nebraska Press, vol. 17.

Zimbardo, P. G. (1973), 'A Pirandellian prison', *New York Times Sunday Magazine*, 8 April, pp. 38–60.

INDEX OF NAMES

SUBJECT INDEX